The Conspicuous Corporation

The Conspicuous Corporation

Business, Public Policy, and Representative Democracy

NEIL J. MITCHELL

Ann Arbor

THE UNIVERSITY OF MICHIGAN PRESS

Copyright © by the University of Michigan 1997
All rights reserved
Published in the United States of America by
The University of Michigan Press
Manufactured in the United States of America
⊗ Printed on acid-free paper

2000   1999   1998   1997   4   3   2   1

A CIP catalog record for this book is available from the British Library

Library of Congress Cataloging-in-Publication Data

Mitchell, Neil J. (Neil James), 1953–
    The conspicuous corporation : business, public policy, and
representative democracy / Neil J. Mitchell.
        p.   cm.
    Includes bibliographical references and index.
    ISBN 0-472-10818-2 (acid-free paper)
    1. Business and politics—United States.   2. Business and
politics—Great Britain.   3. Business and politics.   I. Title.
JK467.M57   1997
322'.3'0973—dc21   97-4704
                                                    CIP

To Susan and our children, Colin and Kate.

Acknowledgments

I have accumulated various debts in writing this book. In particular, I owe the reviewers for the University of Michigan Press for their extensive comments. Having been both the giver and the receiver of reviews for a number of years, I know how fortunate I am to have had such thoughtful and careful commentary to guide my revisions. I owe colleagues at the University of New Mexico, notably Allan Parkman and Karen Remmer, for suffering earlier versions of the manuscript. The final result may not address all their comments and suggestions, but it is a better book for trying to do so. Parts of the analysis presented in chapters 5, 6, and 7 appeared in articles in the *British Journal of Political Science, Comparative Political Studies, Journal of Politics,* and *Polity.*

Contents

PART 1

Business and Politics

CHAPTER 1

The Conspicuous Corporation

Resources, connections, attentiveness, and preferences load the political system in favor of business. Against the odds, when the conspicuous corporation meets the virtuous politician, business loses in the policy struggle.

"We want parliament and the country to practice a notable piece of self-denial, and to do a magnificent act of justice—to pass a kind of self-denying ordinance," wrote a member of the House of Commons in August 1806, "and we can only hope that a parliament will do this heroic deed in some fit of heroism" (Anstey 1975, 388). In May 1807, the British unilaterally ended British participation in the slave trade. Social scientists, incurably suspicious, are reluctant to entertain even the idea of "heroic public policy." Yet cases like this one are remarkable because they appear to be policy decisions in which humanity triumphs over business interests. Although in the twentieth century not just humanity but other members of the animal kingdom—California gnat catchers, spotted owls, as well as the occasional fish—triumph over business interests. With these interests' dominance of formal democratic procedures and their use of informal channels of political influence, it remains surprising when they lose in the policy struggle. In this book I investigate the political resources and activity of business, and politicians' particular incentives to align themselves with business, and why, despite these advantages, business can still end up on the losing side.

Combining the claim that the political system is loaded to favor business with the claim that business still can lose differentiates this analysis from other approaches. It challenges pluralists, policy community, issue network, and multi-actor theorists who are generally uncomfortable with "monolithic" categories like business and are conscious of the complexities of the policy process, the shifting nature of coalitions, and the difficulties in identifying any interest as routinely advantaged in the policy process. It challenges business dominance theorists, on the other hand, by conceding that business interests do sometimes lose. It is a defensible, if somewhat isolated position, grounded in the political constraints on translating economic power into political power, notably policymakers' agendas and the perceived legitimacy of business practices.

In investigating the place of business in representative democracy and the struggle over public policy, the traditional path of inquiry is to identify the circumstances and attributes of business and democracy that contribute, positively or negatively, to the political position of business. Although this path is well trodden, there are some inconsistencies in the observations and assessments of earlier travelers. Some discovered that business occupies a "privileged position," others found it more precariously placed in the policy struggle. This first path of inquiry, then, remains interesting.

It is some years since Charles Lindblom, in *Politics and Markets,* traveled this path (1977). The argument of his book is well-known and provides a useful benchmark to measure our progress in understanding how business can influence governments and a useful organizational device for the second part of the book.[1] Lindblom's argument was part of a larger comparison of planned and market systems, but his discussion of business power in representative democracies became the focus of critical attention. One can identify three major pillars supporting what Lindblom referred to as the "privileged position of business." The first pillar is business's power to shape public preferences, its ideological power. The second pillar is the claim that because business's economic decisions affect voters' assessments of government performance, government officials prefer policies that maintain business confidence, sometimes referred to as the structural power of business. The third pillar is business's advantages in the system of political interest representation.

The argument that business generally enjoys popular legitimacy and indoctrinates citizens to hold views in support of the business position and ignore political issues that are awkward for business incensed Lindblom's critics. The debate over this first pillar of business power is a methodological and conceptual debate as well as an empirical debate. All can more or less agree on the state of public opinion at a given point in time and on the position of such and such a business on the environment. The dispute, as Nelson Polsby (1980) suggests, is over what sorts of inferences you can legitimately draw to connect the two. To illustrate with an example familiar to political scientists, pollution may not be a political problem in Gary, Indiana, but that is not the result of the local U.S. Steel factory influencing the preferences of citizens, as they expressed them between labored breaths. Matthew Crenson's analysis of the development of the pollution issue, business activities, and pollution policies compared

---

1. In 1995 this book won the American Political Science Association prize for the best work by a living political theorist that is still considered significant at least fifteen years after its original publication.

the political processes of East Chicago with Gary, concluding that U.S. Steel's influence on preferences was subtle but critical (1971; see also Polsby 1980; Wilson 1985). Some argue that there is no means of distinguishing between expressed preferences and interests, and they are disinterested in the determinants of public preferences. The research priority is to accept preferences as they are and treat them as exogenous causes of actions. Others seem to subscribe to the view that if there are no manifest efforts to control information and preferences, as in authoritarian systems, then the only alternative is the free competition of ideas, as in Gary, Indiana, presumably.

Assuming politicians have an interest in retaining power, then irrespective of their ideological views or party affiliations they will be attentive to the demands of business, as personal and collective economic experiences color voters' views of government, or so the structural power argument goes. Since the late 1970s political scientists have gathered some convincing evidence on the importance of "economic voting" and in this way have provided some indirect evidence for the structural power argument. That is, if government officials are interested in continuing in office, and given the importance of the economy to voters, they ought to include in their decision-making calculations the anticipated impact of their choices on business decision making, sometimes referred to as the business confidence factor. On the other hand, we have not gotten much further in accumulating direct evidence on the importance of structural power or the mediating influence of political parties on the exercise of this power. While we can plausibly argue that it ought to exist, that elected governments are instinctively fearful of upsetting business interests, it is much more difficult to find direct evidence of structural power than is the case with the more readily observable instruments of political power like contributions to election campaigns, the formation of associations with explicit political goals, and lobbying. One of the themes I pursue in this book is that we may have been looking in the wrong place. The connotation of structural power is that it has an impersonal and constant quality that operates independently of the other dimensions of business power. However, accepting governments' general predisposition to improving or maintaining business confidence, the measures that governments need to take, or the actions they should avoid to achieve these goals, are not self-evident. They must be communicated to government officials, and officials must make choices in the context of their own economic-theoretical assessment of the policy problem. Business lobbyists and economists represent the "structural power" of business in the arguments that they make to policymakers, and in this way governments gather information relevant to anticipating the impact of their decisions on business decisions. For analysis it makes sense to separate the pillars of business power, yet this separation is artificial.

While arousing less hostility, it is true that the claim that business dominates the interest representation system has not been without its critics. Typically these critics will argue that business is not so different from other groups interested in shaping public policy, and that business interests are often divided. If they concede that business has superior political resources, such as money, organization, and status, these critics will argue that it does not mean that those resources make much difference or are effectively deployed (Wilson 1981). The effective use of resources is an empirical question. For example, some research on the consequences of political action committee (PAC) spending and lobbying activities speaks to this criticism. While the earlier results (early to mid-1980s) were mixed, recent analyses, working with wider measures of political behavior than congressional voting, are suggesting the importance of these activities in the policy process (Snyder 1992). What is noticeable is that theories of the policy process are lagging behind the empirical work in this area; generally, they have not adequately recognized the advantages business has in the process.

I examine the status of Lindblom's largely theoretical argument with the empirical evidence. On the basis of new data as well as the work of other scholars, I argue that Lindblom's claims stand up quite well. The evidence at least does not knock down the first pillar, partially supports the second, and strengthens the third. It is plausible to claim that business exercises disproportionate ideological influence, that maintaining business confidence concerns government officials, and that business political resources, supplemented by the improved mobility of capital, are formidable. In sustaining this last part of the argument for business's advantages in the policy process of course we cannot consider business political resources on their own. It is true that there are many worthwhile books that focus exclusively on business or on trade unions, for example, but to appreciate either as a political force requires looking at both. As David Marsh and Gareth Locksley pointed out with respect to unions: "the other major weakness in the literature of both disciplines lies in the failure to analyse the power of the unions in relation to that of other groups, particularly capital" (1981, 35). Neither can we understand business without antibusiness, so to speak, although we shall find that to consider the opposition to business is not as straightforward a task as it seems, for there are shifting alliances of opponents, and business interests are not homogeneous and at least at times oppose each other.

With business's raw power, the political system is loaded in its favor, although we have no measure of business interests' overall success rate in this system. In part, there is the problem of treating "non-issues" and "non-decisions," and how interests are served by keeping topics off as well as on the agenda: "The dominant business interests resist appeals to the government" (Schattschneider 1960, 40; see also Bachrach and Baratz 1963, 632; Lindblom 1977, 205). The idea is that success in a policy area may lie in preventing an issue from becoming defined as a policy problem in the first place. For those issues on the agenda, the survey data I present suggests that business interests themselves consider their position in the policy process as privileged in terms of access and benefits. Nevertheless, business interests do, at times, fail, and the political process is sticky. The failures are not easy to undo, as illustrated, for example, by the length of time it has taken even committed Conservative governments to roll back trade union rights in the United Kingdom. These failures generally result in a ratcheting of regulation that defines acceptable standards for behavior in the community. In this sense there has been a *civilization* of business, at least within national communities.

In pointing to business failures in the policy struggle, Lindblom's critics suggest an alternative approach to the analysis of the political power of business, although in a sense they overlook the theoretical importance of their suggestion. For critics of the privileged position of business argument, the fact of business defeats means that they can consign business to the same category as other interests seeking to affect public policy. In doing so they miss the opportunity to explore cases of business interests losing in the policy struggle as a way of coming to a more precise understanding of the limits of business's special advantages. They miss the diagnostic moment. Instead of thinking about political power as an all-or-nothing, now-and-forever proposition, we need to think of it more contingently. The question of why does business fail in the policy struggle is complementary to the question of why does business have so much influence over public policy. Indeed, the question of why business fails only becomes interesting once the considerable political resources of business interests, and how they translate these resources into political influence, are explicitly recognized. While Lindblom pays scant attention to business losses in the policy process, these cases that contradict the theoretical argument of business dominance provide the analytical opportunity to identify the conditions under which business political power breaks down and to refine theory (see Eckstein 1975; Rogowski 1995). Exploring these different paths of inquiry promises a more complete appreciation of how business and governments interact, and on what terms, in representative democracy.

I use the term *business* to refer to large, privately owned companies and to the trade and business organizations to which they belong. I draw primarily on the experience of business interests in the United Kingdom and the United States and to a much lesser extent on other advanced industrial countries. Earlier research on business and government has tended to concentrate either on the United States or the United Kingdom (Grant 1993; Vogel 1989; Useem 1984 is an exception). As far as the aim is to move toward a more general understanding of the exercise of power in industrial societies, it is worth trying to go beyond single country analyses. These countries provide an appropriate context for this effort at theory building, permitting some interesting institutional contrasts within a larger, stable structure of private ownership, markets, relative prosperity, and representative democracy. Further, the focus on these countries allows the consideration of the evidence and arguments presented in the light of a large literature. But a comparative approach is not without its difficulties.

The multidimensional nature of business power and the paths of inquiry to be followed defy any easy resolution of the theoretically interesting questions in a single data set. Perhaps in part because of the available theories that tend to define away the problem by either claiming the general dominance of business or alternatively that it occupies no special place, there has been little in the way of disaggregating the dimensions of business power and the development of comparative measures, nothing comparable to the measures developed on union power that are discussed in chapter 7. Disaggregation is the methodological touchstone of this analysis of the power of business, making explicit the dimensions (the three pillars) that Lindblom discusses. The aim is to present the evidence and arguments in an accessible way, with appropriate references made to more detailed and elaborate presentations of the evidence. The book is not wedded to a particular form of data and a particular method but, depending on the question, synthesizes both quantitative data created through survey techniques or developed from published sources, and qualitative evidence based on case analysis to substantiate the theoretical argument. While there are some very useful studies presenting survey data on interest groups' interaction with public policymakers in the United States (Schlozman and Tierney 1986; Heinz et al. 1993), there are few comparable studies for other countries. I present data gathered from surveys focused on the political activities of economic organizations in the United Kingdom within this comparative framework and use it in conjunction with qualitative data to address a variety of theoretically interesting questions. The term *triangulation* is sometimes used to refer to this technique of bringing a variety of types of data and methods to bear on a research problem.

In that the argument and evidence show business as overrepresented in the political process it raises the issue of democratic reform. I do not

pursue this issue in a systematic way. However, the cases of business political failure are suggestive in the sense of identifying the conditions under
which the political power of specific business interests was successfully
countered without any fundamental rearrangement of the business system.
What is taken for granted is that the democratic norm of political equality
is an independently appropriate measure to evaluate political performance, within the context of an economic system that takes as given
inequalities in wealth and income. In this sense the reform issue becomes
one of "democratic insulation" for the political system (Tobin 1988, 165).
Thus the argument that there are other compensating benefits for overrepresentation is not investigated. No attempt, systematic or unsystematic, is
made to evaluate the overall economic impact of the political overrepresentation of business and to address the question of whether the political
price is a worthwhile exchange for the comparative economic prosperity
enjoyed. That would be a different book. Nor will I look in any detail at
the argument that because the ownership of large corporations is often
quite dispersed that in this sense what is overrepresented are the financial,
perhaps even retirement interests of the multitude of ordinary citizens who
invest individually or collectively in these corporations. The implication of
this argument would be that business overrepresentation was only something to worry about in the era of robber barons, "family capitalism" as
some call it. Even if most citizens were investors, this argument underesti-
mates the difficulties for these investors in communicating their interests to
management. Further, the argument depends on the assumption that these
investors' financial interests take priority over their other interests as citizens. Fundamentally this book is about the structures and processes of citizenship, rather than consumption or investment.

The analysis concentrates on the revealed and likely motivations of
people acting in the relevant institutional contexts, the resources they can
bring to bear, and the political exchanges that take place largely through
conventional political channels. This statement might serve to presage the
lean, tight arguments of an economist's treatment of political phenomena.
While willing to start with the assumption of narrowly construed utility
maximization in some institutional circumstances, as much for the questions raised as the solutions offered, and to recognize the intellectual pen-
etration achieved by this sort of treatment, in this book I am too tolerant
of additional motivations—commitments as well as careers—too concerned with the development of beliefs and legitimacy, and probably too
empirical to satisfy an economist, who will look in vain for the Spartan
mathematical beauty of her theoretical world.

An alternative is to approach an account of business influence
through the manners and mores that senior corporate officials share with

leading politicians. Sociologists interested in business political activity began, in the 1980s, looking at capitalists as a "class" once again. Corporate interlocks and business association and club memberships give business women and men a collective consciousness directed toward the long-term interests of business and promote expanded political and social activity by corporations. The captains of industry share common social and sometimes professional, educational, and recreational experiences with politicians and leading civil servants (Useem 1984). In this book, I explore how far we can go without resort to this more complicated, more informal, and less visible account of power relationships. The book intersects with this sociological approach at the empirical point that business is more unified than in conflict in its political relationships, and in its "socioeconomic" interest in the institutional and social origins of beliefs and preferences.

Particular attention is paid to the conditions under which business loses in the policy struggle, where nonbusiness groups put the issue on the agenda and the policy carries despite business political opposition. Given the political advantages of business described in the first part of the book, the motivation of the policymaker is identified as the weak link in the chain of interests connecting business organizations and beneficial policy outcomes. At the end of the day the policymaker chooses positions on policies and is liable to fits of heroism. Admittedly heroism is too rich and poetic a concept to hold the interest of social scientists for long (particularly those with a "structural perspective"; for example, see Skocpol 1994, 9), and in any case policy-making seems too sedentary an occupation to produce many heroes. But if heroism is something to do with following one's principles or doing the right thing with indifference to the personal risks, then the political world too will present its share of opportunities for heroism.

Thomas Carlyle could find heroic poets and "men of letters," so why not a politician willing, against the odds, to pursue an idea wherever it may lead? It is not far-fetched to describe defiance of the powers exercised by business interests as heroic, as did that early nineteenth century member of Parliament. One ought to note, too, the emphasis on other-regarding action in the call to end the slave trade. In contrast, Homeric heroism contained "no social conscience . . . no responsibility other than familial, no obligation to anyone or anything but one's own prowess and one's own drive to victory and power" (Finley 1977, 28). The modern usage, with its emphasis on self-denial and social obligation fits better with the argument of this book. So in defense of the concept it is one that suggests the relative power of business interests in the policy struggle, the infrequency of business losses, risk taking, and acting on principle, all part of the explanation of business success and failure that I advance in this book.

Nevertheless, a social scientist would not want to end an account of a policy by attributing it to heroism, and so political heroism is reduced to both the narrower and broader set of incentives within which the policy-maker is operating. This approach is not restricted to political heroism. Even Napoleon, after all, generally found courage to be a result of calculation—"I have rarely met with two o'clock in the morning courage: I mean instantaneous courage." Whether any deed is heroic is likely to become more ambiguous the more closely it is examined. Was it cavalry-men fearing their own officers more than Russian gunnery, drunken folly (there is a report that Russian gunners smelled the breath of the cavalry-men [Fraser 1986, 112]), foolishly choosing the wrong valley, or heroism that is really immortalized in the Charge of the Light Brigade? In the political arena, the likelihood of instantaneous heroism decreases as decision-making responsibilities broaden. If the heroic deed requires a collective decision, it is more likely to be a result of calculated courage where the business position is conspicuously vulnerable to appeals to social obligation, and politicians can afford to be virtuous.

To return to the words of the member of Parliament, note that he said that heroism comes in fits, not streams, nor, as recent analyses of business power suggest, cycles. Students of business-government relations observe regular changes in the political climate for business interests. Some interesting analyses of business political success and failure support cyclical policy theories and suggest mechanisms to account for the cyclical pattern identified (Vogel 1989). For my argument, "fits" is a more useful metaphor than "cycles." The idea to be conveyed is of interruptions in the flow of favorable policies delivered to business interests by a loaded system. The house, of course, does not always win, or no one else would play.

Thinking about the influence that business exercises over government leads to the other major question that interests political scientists and sociologists, as well as some economists, in business. How to account for corporate political activity? The principal goal of business is economic success, not to participate in politics. While political scientists have no general political theory of the firm, we have come some way in testing a set of propositions to explain this activity derived from the general assumption of the firm as profit maximizing. A variety of industry and market characteristics are used to operationalize self-interest. Scholars also investigate the political strategy of a firm to test its conformity with the behavior expected if the firm is pursuing its self-interest. Alternatively, sociologists have argued that an awareness of cross-firm collective interests, generated by social and bureaucratic changes in corporate relations, encourages firms to participate in politics and society. So far this argument enjoys only weak empirical support. Although, to be fair, it is true that even the best results of the political science approach only explain a relatively small proportion of corporate political activity. In the controversy over "micropolitical theory," which I enter into in this book insofar as it is important to the question of business influence in the policy process, it fits somewhere between these approaches with the position that the motivations of corporate officials are wider than the notion of self-interest construed in narrow economic terms and defined by a varied array of economic data concerning the firm.

For both the question of how much influence does business have over policy, and how to account for corporate political activity, explicit attention should be given to the different levels of public decision making that affect business interests. While much of the discussion of the business-government relationship is set in the context of national policy arenas, the impact of other arenas is of increasing interest. In the United States federalism means that corporations are affected by and interested in state-level decision making. At the same time these corporations may have to be attentive to political developments in other nations and international organizations. So far as they are participants in a global economy, they are also "citizens" of a global polity. Strangely, the impact of the variety of extra-national and international political arenas on the relationship between business and government, raising as it does significant questions of both normative and empirical theory, has not yet attracted the attention it deserves. Without examining the international dimension, the general effort to understand business political activity will become increasingly incomplete. Both the longer term trend to a more internationally "interlinked" economy, and the widespread public interest and policymaker concern about foreign economic and political intervention in the domestic system, underline the importance of systematic description and analysis in this research area.

Beyond the effort to develop the particular theoretical argument, my goal in this book is to communicate some of the interest and excitement that the relationship between business and government holds for me as a social scientist. It is a core topic in the social sciences and gives access to all sorts of issues of social and political significance. It takes us from grand theories of the state to low-level explanations of election financing, from heroic struggles to quite sordid episodes of political corruption. To begin to do the topic justice requires more than an examination of business interests in their interactions with public policymakers. In this way an interest in business-government relations can quickly develop into an interest in union-government relations, environmental group–government relations, and even social movement–government relations, as well as in the institutional structures that channel these relations.

Chapter 2 provides a critical discussion of existing theories of the policy process in representative democracies and sketches an alternative theoretical argument for understanding that process and the specific place of business interests. Part 2 discusses the contested claim that the system is loaded in favor of business. It is supported with an examination of the resources and mechanisms through which business exerts political influence, organized around the three pillars of business power. From detailed knowledge of the channels of communication used by business interests to contact government, their relative effectiveness, the relative strengths of business interests organized for politics in comparison to their opponents in the policy struggle, and the motivations of both the representatives of business and policy-makers, it should be possible to speak with some authority on the relationship between business and government. At the same time the attention to detail must be balanced by an effort to conceive the relationship in sufficient generality to be interesting beyond a specific industry or policy, country or period. From this examination of business advantages and successes we move, in part 3, to a discussion of its opposition and then, in part 4, to its failures—not to argue that business's political influence is after all much like all other interests, but to probe for the conditions under which the special advantages of business break down. This discussion begins with a fuller description of the causal relationships that extract the most useful insights from existing theory, fit with the empirical evidence, and allow for business policy failure.

Empirically, the book reassesses the dimensions of business power and contributes new information on business political activities and the strength of its opposition. Parts 2 and 3 synthesize findings from earlier research with data derived from a survey of economic organizations in the United Kingdom, with data on business political finance in the United States and the United Kingdom, and with data on union power in advanced industrial countries. In addition, the book gathers evidence on and redirects our attention to some well-known and some less well-known policy decisions affecting business interests. Theoretically, and unlike other arguments for the special political advantages of business, the last part of the book explicitly recognize business policy losses as problematical and of primary theoretical interest. (One defensive tactic of business dominance theorists confronted with business political defeats is to distinguish between the short and long term—almost anything can be reconciled with the long-term interest of business.)

So I have four interrelated tasks. The first is to critically review existing theories of the policy process. The second is to disaggregate and examine the special resources and influence that business interests command in the policy process. The third is to assess the position of business opposition. And the fourth task is to seek to improve theories of the policy process by identifying, from the evidence presented, the conditions under which business interests will not dominate.

CHAPTER 2

Three Views of Business and Politics: Group, State, and Policy Theories

When American political leaders met Japanese leaders in Tokyo in January 1992, an infirm President George Bush was a supplicant for an aging and apparently equally under-the-weather American industry. Lee Iaccoca and fellow captains of the big car companies were the president's entourage. With their economic power threatened in their own market place, these business people withdrew to the political arena in search of the leverage necessary to improve their competitive position.

On an individual level business people enjoy considerable attention from politicians. Business leaders are a special category in representative democracies. The formal and individualized equality of voting, and other procedures founded on the democratic premise of equal treatment, dress corporate officials in the common uniform of citizenship, yet disguise their real political weight. Their membership of this special category, the traveling companions of presidents, rests on their institutional affiliations, not on the characteristics of the individuals involved. How, then, do we go about understanding the relationship between business and government in institutional rather than individual terms?

A variety of theories describe the relationship of organized interests to government. We can consider these theories in three broad categories: group theory, state theory, and policy theory. These are theories of how choices are made and implemented, of how power is exercised, and they entail directly or indirectly many of the same elements. Group theories contain or imply statements concerning the government, state theories contain or imply statements concerning groups, and policy theories contain or imply statements about groups and government. Consequently, it is sometimes difficult to assign theories to these categories. Distinguishing theories in this way is of value insofar as it draws attention to the principal vantage point of the analyst as he or she tries to identify the forces important to a decision. Different types of group theorists may come to different conclusions about which group is most important, but they share the assumption that looking in at government from the perspective of the groups involved is the best vantage point. State theorists see government as a more or less independent generator of policy and look outward at the consequences for groups and society. Policy theorists look backward, as it were, from the characteristics of a policy and assess group political prospects by these characteristics and as driven by differential incentives to participate. A general problem, whichever vantage point is adopted, is the place given business in its relationship to other organizations and government, either by underestimating the political advantages of business or by not conceptualizing business failure. My theoretical aim is to provide an account that better fits a political world in which business interests have distinct political advantages, yet can still lose in the policy struggle.

A group theory, pluralism, is the dominant theoretical tradition in twentieth century political science, stretching from first decade to fin de siècle. Its dominance is not unchallenged. Within group theory, dissenting theoretical positions have, from time to time, developed around the proposition that business is not a group like other groups. Outside America, in other advanced industrial countries, neocorporatism has represented the major theoretical alternative to pluralism, generally signifying the stronger position of working-class organizations.

For pluralist theorists, politics is group politics. Government policies are responses to pressure from competing organized, or even unorganized, interests. As David Truman pointed out, the threat of the unorganized organizing gives even these interests some influence (1951, 511). There are numerous influential interests, and all "legitimate" ones enjoy access to government. Policy victories represent a temporary competitive advantage of one interest or coalition over others. Policy is predictable insofar as the political scientist can accurately identify the influential interests and gauge the disposition of strengths. This task is difficult for "the work of one political interest group, whether a business association or a group representing some other interest in the society—labor unions for instance—results in a wave like development of interest group activity; other groups are created to present different claims and to push opposing policies . . ." (1951, 79). The idea of elected or appointed public officials independently developing and sustaining a policy "agenda" is anathema to pluralism. Policy agendas will founder in the midst of shifting pressures, and the obvious source of such agendas, political parties, are generally neglected in pluralist theory.

Group strength is a result of the size and type of membership, financial resources, monopolistic control of expertise and information, status and access to government and the media, the capacity to influence public preferences, the organizational structure of the group, and the organization of government. Size of membership is an important component of a group's political credibility. At the same time larger membership groups reduce the significance of any individual member and are consequently more likely to meet the problem of free riders, those who will not join but would enjoy the benefits. Not all members are equal. Some groups can improve their visibility with celebrity members and increase their impact with members known to be politically active, otherwise inactive or retired people for example. Expertise and information are valuable to policymakers, and they will tend to be more responsive to groups with such resources. Groups that can supply expertise relieve policymakers of the inconvenience and expense of gathering information for themselves and offer "truth" as a defense for a policy decision. Some of these factors are interrelated. Access to the media and the capacity to influence public preferences will depend, in part, on financial resources. Access to government may result from the government's preference for meeting with certain groups rather than others (insider versus outsider status) and the institutional structures in place (Maloney, Jordan, and McLaughlin 1994). The structures of interest groups vary and carry certain advantages and disadvantages in the policy process. As Robert Salisbury (1984) points out, "institutional groups," like business corporations, for whom politics is a secondary activity, tend to be able to sustain a more permanent presence in the policy-making process and are unconstrained by the need to seek membership approval. Associational or membership groups are, in comparison, relatively disadvantaged.

There has been some confusion about how pluralism depicts the role of government structures. It is clear from the work of pluralist theorists that the organization of government can have a differential impact on group political opportunities. Critics of pluralism, particularly those adopting a state theory vantage point, have oversimplified the pluralist position in criticizing a theory that depicts the government (state) as neutral: "Pure interest group versions of pluralism virtually ignore public actors and institutions. The government is seen as a cash register that totals up and then averages the preferences and political power of societal actors" (Krasner 1984, 227). On the other hand, Gabriel Almond has argued vigorously that state theorists have entirely misread pluralism. It is a theory "in which the explanatory logic goes in both directions, from society to the state and from the state to the society" (1988, 868). While sometimes the issue is finessed by defining parts of governments as "groups," Almond overstates the place of the state in pluralist theory. As far as one can frame a general understanding it is that this theory locates the identification and definition of policy problems, the goals of policy, and the formulation of policy in the interaction of organized and unorganized interests.

The idea of government officials coming up with and sustaining independent policy agendas is not part of the theory. Which is not the same as claiming that pluralists view the structure and the officials of government as neutral. Truman again: "in consequence of the structural peculiarities of our government some groups have better and more varied opportunities to influence key points of a decision than do others" (1951, 322). For example, the equality of the states in the U.S. Senate favors agricultural interests, he argues. In recounting the political history of New Haven, Robert Dahl recalls the last century as one in which domination of the political system shifted from a cohesive set of leaders to competition between many different leaders representing different combinations of political resources. The mayor led one effective group, whose success depended on knowing what voters and interest groups would "tolerate or support" (Dahl 1961, 86, 140). But acknowledging that the structure of government might favor some interests over others, by accident or design, or that elected officials in some circumstances may take a leading role in policy formulation, is not the same as arguing, as state theorists do, that officials have their own policy preferences and that they may sustain these preferences at times even without support from society.

It is not the case that for pluralists all groups are equal, although at times they come close to this position: "As Herring points out in his study of Congress, a large number of non-economic, non-occupational groups 'have their spokesmen who often equal and sometimes exceed in power the agents of vocations and industries'" (quoted in Truman 1951, 98). At least it is fair to say that business, in pluralist theory, occupies no special place. It is divided, often on opposite sides of a policy issue. If business wins in the policy struggle, it is the result of a temporary advantage, and it is effectively counterbalanced by other interests. It is on this issue of the place of business that an undercurrent of research periodically threatens to undermine pluralist theory.

In the United States, analysis of the distorting effects of economic power on democratic political arrangements has a venerable intellectual tradition. In 1908, the same year that Arthur Bentley launched pluralist theory, James Bryce remarked, as he looked back over the previous decade, that, in terms of power exercised, the president was followed by the Speaker of the House, who was followed by railroad owners. The latter, "the railroad monarch," had the advantage of serving for life, Bryce noted (1908, 648–53). Four years earlier, in *The Shame of the Cities,* Lincoln Steffens deplored business's corruption of American politics (1904). And Charles Beard uncovered, even at the bright dawn of American democracy, the old anxiety to "safeguard the rights of private property against any leveling tendencies on the part of the propertyless masses" (1957, 141). In postwar

America, the sociologist C. Wright Mills discovered the military, industrial, and political "power elite," and the political scientist E. E. Schattschneider wrote: "Pressure politics is a selective process ill designed to serve diffuse interests. The system is skewed, loaded, and unbalanced in favor of a fraction of a minority" (1960, 35; see also McConnell 1966, 349). Schattschneider's "realism," as he called it, involved an empirical assessment of the "dominance of business groups in the pressure system," presciently noting the greater difficulties of nonbusiness interests to organize for collective action and the importance of whether the benefit sought by the organization was exclusive or nonexclusive.

The work of Robert Dahl (1982) on the issue of corporate power and particularly Charles Lindblom (1977) on the "privileged position of business" represent the most recent, and perhaps the most telling, wave of criticism of pluralist theory. It is telling not just because of the quality of argument, but because it appears to be a departure from earlier work, almost self-critical.

Lindblom, a pluralist, argues that business is privileged because of its ideological influence, because of its structural influence deriving from control over the economy, and because of the superior resources it commits to the normal channels of interest group politics. Business enjoys a friendly climate of opinion that is partly of its own making. Second, good economic performance matters to government officials, and consequently government acts more deferentially to business than to any other interests. Third, business interests devote more resources to the party and interest group competition than do rival organizations. Democratic pluralism becomes an ideal, the best we can do in the modern nation state, not an empirical theory that usefully simplifies the practice of group and government interaction.

In response to this undercurrent of research, there have been some modifications to the pluralist position. Says Andrew McFarland: "Vogel, Graham Wilson, and I do give greater weight to business power than did the 1960s pluralists, who tended to assume a greater frequency of countervailing power to business." In this revision, McFarland explains, business becomes "the most important power group," but not the "dominant power group," as the "neo-Schattschneiders, such as Kay Schlozman and John Tierney, argue" (1991, 271). These pluralists focus on countervailing "cycles," instead of countervailing interests. McFarland argues that there is a thirty-year cycle in American policy-making, from a period of business political control to political reform. The cycle turns on business interests engaging in "excess" as they "eventually violate widely shared standards" (McFarland 1991, 263), which then gives reform groups the incentive to participate in politics.

David Vogel also sees a cyclical pattern in business policy influence but driven by a different mechanism that can explain more precisely the timing of shifts in business power: "There is no need to choose between the depictions of business power offered by the pluralists and their critics. The accuracy of each perspective depends on the period in which one is interested" (1989, 7; see also Mucciaroni 1995). He describes in some detail the legislative record of American business in the areas of environmental, health and safety, energy, and tax policy since the 1960s. In accounting for the variation, Vogel argues that the performance of the economy and the amount of unified business political activity determines the political effectiveness of American business. Good economic performance decreases business political power, as the public raise their expectations about what business can afford. Conversely, poor economic performance, through its affect on public perceptions, increases business political power. Here we have a specific explanation for the timing of reform. As Vogel implies, further strengthening of this theoretical position requires more attention to the anomalies: the New Deal—a time when the economy performed poorly and business suffered legislative defeats—or the 1920s and late 1940s and 1950s when relative prosperity and political influence appear to have coincided. It will require further analysis to know whether the 1960s to the 1980s was an exceptional period in the history of the business and government relationship.

To claim that the influence of economic institutions on public policy is linked to how well the economy performs is surely reasonable. But there are other important political effects of economic performance than the one Vogel emphasizes. There is evidence to suggest that poor economic performance decreases public confidence in business leaders (Lipset and Schneider 1987, 64), not just public expectations of business. Other things equal, falling public confidence in business would put business interests in a weaker political position. Additionally, business cycles effect business's opposition as well as business. In economic downturns not only will public expectations of business drop, but also the organization and arguments of business's opposition may suffer. High unemployment is the worst of economic environments for trade union organization and activity. It is also a hostile political context for an environmentalist's policy agenda, as jobs tend to come before environmental issues in citizens' preference hierarchies.

To anticipate an important theme of this book, beyond the impact of the business cycle on the interests involved, whether or not policymakers will listen to business in a depression—that is, the likelihood of business failure—will not depend only on the depths of the depression. It will depend on public policymakers' goals and their assessment of the reasons for poor economic performance, which will in turn depend on the historical and intellectual context. For policymakers faced with the depression in the 1930s, it was difficult to make the policy argument that the reason for economic decline was that unions were too powerful, that business was overregulated, or that Herbert Hoover's Washington had been too tough on the private sector, and that what was needed were fewer restrictions on business. Historically, a period where business enjoyed great political and social influence preceded the depression. Intellectually, the discussion of economic policy alternatives in the 1930s had moved beyond classical economics and the idea of minimal government interference with business. Similarly, Reaganism, or Thatcherism for that matter, are impossible to conceive without the postwar expansion of public-sector welfare provision, health and safety regulation, the experimentation with Keynesian approaches to managing the economy, and the gradual development, from Hayek on, of the economic counterarguments.

David Vogel concludes his analysis of the last three decades by describing the high level and sophistication of business political activity and speculating that "business is unlikely to be caught off guard again." He argues that union political influence has declined, and the environmental groups are "not powerful enough to bring about any major changes in federal regulatory policy that business strongly opposes. In this sense business has won" (Vogel 1989, 296–99). Thus a probusiness equilibrium may have actually replaced fluctuation. With unions in industrial and political decline, American business interests' remaining opponents are Japanese corporations—the most "privileged" business group—and themselves. Although offered as a defense of pluralism, at this point it becomes difficult to differentiate these cyclical depictions of business power from the "neo-Schattschneiders," difficult to discern much pluralistic competition of interests, and difficult to know what to make of the distinction between business as the "dominant" group and business as the "most important" group.

Similarly, John Heinz, Edward Laumann, Robert Nelson, and Robert Salisbury have argued that "the predominant pattern of policy-making is still pluralist" (1993, 404). Yet in the detail of their findings on which groups report high success rates for the various policy areas investigated, business interests seem to do comparatively well. In health policy it is trade associations and professional associations that report most success; in agriculture it is law firms and business organizations (346). These authors state that "there are no significant differences in the success rates of the various types of organizations in the other two domains" (347), but then go on to say that in the energy policy area "business groups are the dominant players" (348). The labor policy area, the other policy area investigated, was not characterized in these terms, although particularly given that their interviews were conducted in 1982 and 1983, one would not expect unions to be reporting higher success than business interests. These authors do, however, present evidence that economic ideology, what they call "economic liberalism," is significantly associated with success, in a negative direction, and they do characterize the groups ideologically. In group terms, "business and trade association representatives are significantly more conservative than the sample as a whole, while citizen-government and especially union representatives are at the liberal end of the scale" (350, 167). So the question for these theorists, embedded in these details, is the age-old one of how long it is useful to persevere with existing general theories, in this case pluralism, even as they contribute to the progressive filling out of an empirical record that is at odds with existing theory.

Pluralism has usually found a friendlier reception in the United States than in Europe. Since the 1970s, scholars have viewed neocorporatism, stripped by the prefix of its historical association with fascism, as a major theoretical alternative to describe the relationship of groups to government in European politics. Neocorporatist theory has renewed conceptual and empirical interest in this relationship and has itself launched numerous studies on interest group activities in advanced industrial countries. Even where corporatism is absent, the United States is the usual example, the question becomes explaining its absence. Yet from the perspective of this book it shares the pluralist deficiency of inadequately situating business interests in the struggle over public policy in representative democracies.

The differences between corporatist and pluralist theory lie in the descriptions of groups, of policy-making styles, and of policy outcomes. Under corporatism, groups are hierarchically organized and possess representational monopolies, in the sense of one group being the sole or at least dominant representative of an interest, as opposed to competition between groups to represent an interest (see Crouch 1979; Lehmbruch and Schmitter 1982; Schmitter and Lehmbruch 1979; Wilson 1983). Economic groups representing business, labor, and agriculture are the types of groups of principal interest to corporatist theorists. The term *mediate* sometimes replaces *represent* and conveys a two-way process of communication and influence between group members and government. Group leadership shapes and responds to both the demands of the membership and the demands of government. To make the group leaders a worthwhile negotiating partner for other groups and government requires centralized control and group discipline. The government plays an active role in conferring benefits on chosen groups, including preferred access to policymakers for some groups over others, positions on advisory or administrative committees for group representatives, and perhaps providing financial subsidies or tax advantages.

Access to the executive branch of government is the usual route to political influence associated with corporatism. Contacts with civil servants and ministers are preferred over lobbying members of the legislature. These contacts are routine and carried on in a collaborative spirit. Conflict, strikes, demonstrations, and public relations campaigns are not the political methods employed by groups in a corporatist setting. Policy consensus is a goal for the partners to negotiation, and they will define their interests broadly with an eye to the longer term, not to maximizing immediate group benefits. Policies coming out of this process will reflect the participation of all parties, not "winners" and "losers." Groups are involved in both the policy formulation stage and the implementation stage, and public policymakers are viewed as active participants in the policy process.

The earlier writings of corporatist theorists suggested a "trend toward corporatist intermediation," in advanced industrial countries. Not much attention was paid to the details of how corporatist institutions and styles would diffuse. It seemed that the low-conflict industrial relations associated with corporatism carried economic benefits that would become increasingly recognized, and that such a rationalization of group structure makes representative democracies easier to govern. In a parallel argument, Mancur Olson claims that nations with more "encompassing" groups are at an advantage with respect to economic growth as these sorts of groups are more likely to accommodate the broader interests of society (1983, 24; see also Olson 1982). Olson's argument is that as democracies age, groups proliferate and their self-interested activities impair overall economic performance. He explains the good economic performance of some exceptional older democracies in terms of exceptionally encompassing group structures.

The 1980s and 1990s sobered expectations of a trend toward corporatism. Thatcher was elected and reelected with an explicitly anticorporatist bias, single-minded on the priority of removing labor groups from policy-making and dedicated to the abolition of their institutionalized access to government. She reversed the trend of the mid- to late 1970s where the establishment of various tripartite organizations like the Health and Safety Commission and the Manpower Services Commission and the Social Contract wage negotiations between the Labour government and the Trades Union Congress (TUC) prompted analysts to categorize Britain as corporatist. By the early 1990s, even in Sweden, the cradle of neocorporatism, with its consultative process of decision making (the remiss system, Royal Commissions) and its autonomous state agencies such as the Labor Market Board that includes both representatives of business and labor, this policy-making model was in a more ambiguous status. Sweden had applied to join the European Community, had elected a bourgeois prime minister, and had doubled unemployment within a year of this election. When economic growth slows it is more difficult for the negotiating parties to compromise, leading some to wonder whether corporatism depended on economic prosperity, rather than the other way around.

Careful scholars of group-government interaction have found it difficult to reach agreement on the empirical applications of corporatist theory. The basic step of classifying political systems as corporatist or pluralist turns out to be very complicated. Arend Lijphart and Markus Crepaz try to fashion a usable comparative measure of corporatism by combining the differing assessments of twelve researchers (1991). Beyond Sweden and Austria, widely regarded as corporatist, and the United States, generally referred to as pluralist (but see Harris 1989), uncertainty surrounds the process of classification. Attempts to classify political systems become qualified by the policy sector: French politics cannot be described as corporatist, just agriculture and perhaps the business sector (Wilson 1983; Keeler 1985). Scholars qualify the attribution of corporatism with terms such as strong, moderate, or weak, and different levels of interaction within a political system are sometimes distinguished with referents like macrocorporatism, microcorporatism, and mesocorporatism (Cawson 1986).

These disputes are symptomatic of deeper theoretical problems that rob this approach of the capability of clearly delineating the key actors in the policy struggle. It is not that corporatism represents an "ideal type" to which reality only roughly approximates. It is more that under the corporatist umbrella a variety of attributes collect, without any clear identification of which are core and which are more theoretically peripheral, and without a clear specification of the relationships among these attributes. Tripartism for some is critical (Wilson 1985). Others regard it as less important (Cawson 1986; Crouch 1979, 131). For some the inclusion of labor is critical: "corporatist tendencies can be understood as a response in which governments attempt to cope with intensifying problems of inflation and stagflation by bringing the major economic actors, and most crucially organized labour, into the processes of policy formation and implementation" (Goldthorpe 1984, 12; see Schott 1984, 19). Yet others argue that corporatism can exist without labor included in policy-making. Such is the case with Japan. Its corporatism relied on the very close association of business with the Liberal Democrat government of Japan (Pempel 1979). In the twenty years since Philippe Schmitter resuscitated the concept, we still struggle for agreement on a conceptual and theoretical level and therefore have difficulty with empirical applications.

In spite of these difficulties, corporatist theory led us to think about how power will be exercised, how government influences groups as well as the other way around, and what political arrangement is consonant with good economic performance—but over a relatively narrow range of groups, without clear indication of who has power (are the partners to negotiation in rough equality?), and without clear discussion of the role of political parties. While the imprecision about the relative advantages of business in the policy struggle is of particular concern, the neglect of political parties is also a problem, to the degree that policymakers' ideas are an important factor in policy-making. Apart from the observation that corporatism often coincides with social democratic parties in government, the role of the political party in the policy-making process, its ideology and manifesto, is not of key theoretical interest. This neglect of political parties stems from the theoretical emphasis on "functional" over popular and territorial representation. Unfortunately, as the independent activity of policymakers is a more explicit aspect of corporatism than pluralism, the agendas policymakers themselves bring to the negotiations become important. Beyond a distaste for confrontation, the policy preferences of policymakers are generally poorly specified under corporatism. The political party, neglected by these theorists, is the most obvious source of such preferences. This inattention to policymakers' preferences in part accounts for these theorists being taken by surprise by the quite abrupt reversals in corporatist institution building in the 1980s.

Corporatism leads us to think about the costs to democracy in the sense of the displacement of parliaments by functional representation, the limited number of groups included in the policy process, and the hierarchical internal structure of groups. At the same time, when defined as including labor, and where it has developed under social democratic governments and on the basis of comparatively strong labor movements, the institutional pattern that at least some scholars associate with corporatism illustrates ways of designing institutionalized compensation for labors' political disadvantages with respect to business—an institutionalized system of countervailing power. Len Murray, former general secretary of the TUC understood the stakes quite clearly: "Tripartism—forget the jargon. What it means . . . is our right and our duty to represent the views of our members at every level. . . . We wanted permanent bodies, meeting regularly and with their own independent staffs. We were not satisfied with ad hoc arrangements where the Government could fob us off or even avoid meeting us altogether . . ." (TUC 1982, 537). The officials of the TUC know the difference that a "corporatist" style of policy-making can make, hence their tenacious attachment to the principle of tripartism.

In contrast to pluralist and corporatist theory, the theory of state autonomy, as the name implies, diminishes the significance of all groups, labor as well as business, in the policy-making process. Originally, state autonomy was associated with the work of Marxist scholars attempting to adjust the Marxist theory of the state to the realities of political power in the twentieth century. Both the rise of fascism and the development of the welfare state indicated the inadequacy of instrumentalist conceptions of the state. More recently other scholars, reacting as much to Marxist as to pluralist instrumentalism, have found value in giving the state itself pride of analytical place. States have their own preferences, in part derived from their situation in an international system of states, and they possess differing capacities. These factors are of central importance in accounting for political phenomena. According to these theorists, we should not conceive states as simply the place where social groups fight it out. States should be conceived as autonomous actors in the policy process. The explanatory reach of this theory extends from selected episodes in the reform of welfare policies to the great revolutions in human history (Evans, Rueschemeyer, and Skocpol 1985; Krasner 1978; Nordlinger 1981; Orloff and Skocpol 1984; Skocpol 1979).

These theorists argue that the state can generate policy preferences of its own, independently of groups, and can, at least at times, act on these preferences. Eric Nordlinger distinguishes three types of state autonomy by the relationship of public officials' preferences to society's preferences. The first type of state autonomy is where public officials act contrary to the positions of private actors (society). The second type is where preferences are opposed, but public officials successfully persuade private actors to adopt their position and then they take policy action. The third type of state autonomy is where public officials and private actors have convergent preferences, though arrive at them independently, and when the state acts on these preferences. Nordlinger sees state autonomy and what he refers to as the "society-centered models" (group theories) as complementary, rather than rival theories of the "authoritative actions of the democratic state" (1981, 197).

Theda Skocpol, objecting to approaches that "reduce" state actions to socioeconomic factors, "properly conceives" the state as "a set of administrative, policing, and military organizations headed, and more or less coordinated by, an executive authority" and which is "potentially autonomous" 1979, 29). In order to substantiate this claim of autonomy she argues that the state has an interest in maintaining political order and, in its interaction with other states, develops further interests independent of domestic groups or classes. Nordlinger argues that public officials belong to "state units" and develop institutional interests and possess "professional knowledge" that differentiates their preferences from others

(1981, 32–34). State officials also act on the basis of public interests such as social order, state legitimacy, duty to future generations, and "the concerns of the politically disadvantaged groups" (Nordlinger 1988, 882). The definition of public interest for public officials becomes a key issue with this approach.

The excitement and sense of novelty greeting the theory of state autonomy diminishes as the theory is applied to particular policy cases. When one examines how a state autonomy analysis is carried out, Gabriel Almond's (1988) exasperated claim to have heard it all before is understandable. For example, when examining the development of American welfare policies we are given an explanation centered on the importance of crises such as wars and depression, and the role of political parties, with a bit part for the labor movement. State factors are modestly credited with just a "mediating effect," which turns out to mean the impact of familiar constitutional features like the separation of powers, the extent of suffrage, or a single-member district election system (see Amenta and Skocpol 1989). It seems a rather ordinary piece of political analysis after the high hopes for a new and distinctive approach.

The way in which some state theorists characterized the inadequacies of group theories, and the use of the concept "the autonomy of the state" raised expectations, but as critics of the approach have pointed out, the meaning of the concept is elusive, and the boundary between state and its theoretical antonym "society" is indeterminate. The imprecision obscures the fact that the explanation usually ends up referring to the motivations of civil servants or elected officials. We are indebted to this theoretical enterprise for the notion of autonomy, not for the state. Its value lies in encouraging us to estimate the degree of independence that public officials exercise in the policy process and the sources of this independence. Its value diminishes as these officials are wrapped in the loose-fitting concept of the state. There is more to be gained from disaggregating the state, and society, too, for that matter. Heads of state and heads of government, cabinets, legislatures, political parties, civil servants, and interest groups have more precise referents. It is likely to be far more rewarding to assess the policy significance of these more readily recognizable actors than to try to come to some determination that the "state" acted autonomously or that "society" did it.

Ironically, only in splitting the state into its parts can we give the concept of autonomy its due. After all it is quite possible that these different parts, far from working in concert, may actually be at cross-purposes. The political control of the bureaucracy is a familiar research problem for mainstream political scientists. If the motivations of public officials are the source of autonomy, the focus must be on the ideology and resource constraints, money and careers, and most centrally on political parties. Political parties organize elected policymakers in all representative democracies and translate ideologies into domestic and foreign policy agendas. Their rules and structures are central to political careers. To the extent that it makes sense to see parties, institutions that link groups and individuals with elected officials, as autonomous from society, the autonomy of political parties is constrained by such factors as the influence of core constituencies, the positions of other political parties, and the type of election system. Depending on the relative importance of various influences such as professional training, civil service traditions, political control, and external incentive structures, the motivations of civil servants will be more or less autonomous. Finally, because of the effort to shift attention away from society, this approach is less useful in assessing the relative political advantages of social actors—business and labor for example. We need to disaggregate society, too, to its components.

Conversely, at least some analysts working from the third vantage point, policy theory, are acutely sensitive to an aspect of the political advantages of business interests: the political disinterest of everyone else. For policy theorists the purpose and type of policy is of critical importance in understanding the politics and outcomes of policy struggles. There are a variety of theoretical positions to consider, but there is no better place to start than with the work of George J. Stigler, the economist whose strikingly simple formulation provides a fixed point from which the position of the other theories can be established.

He wished to explain the regulatory policies of government. Regulation, he argues, "is acquired by the industry and is designed and operated primarily for its benefit" (Stigler 1975, 114). The regulator desires to maximize political support. The regulated industries are politically effective and have a great deal at stake in regulation policies. The political system, Stigler claims, generally favors those with strongly held preferences, whether they are in the majority or the minority. "The theory would be contradicted," he says," if, for a given regulatory policy, we found the group with larger benefits and lower costs of political action being dominated by another group with lesser benefits and higher costs of political action. Temporary accidents aside, such cases simply will not arise. . . . there is no alternative hypothesis" (140). According to Stigler, business interests generally seek subsidies, control over market entry, substitutes and complements, and price fixing arrangements from governments. (One could add to his list; for example, business interests may seek to sell goods or services to government, or they may seek limitations on union organization and activities and protection from other nonbusiness threats). The high stakes and their readiness for political action mean that business interests will generally prevail in a political system characterized by citizens' infrequent and ill-informed participation.

Stigler contrasts his explanation with the welfare economists view of public policies arising from market failures. For welfare economists, government intervenes when markets cannot supply goods or services efficiently. Some goods or services belong to a category referred to as public or collective goods, a characteristic of which is that it is very difficult to exclude those who did not pay from benefiting from the good or service. The community desires these goods or services, yet no incentive exists for anyone to provide them. We cannot limit the benefits of a climate of law and order, public cleanliness, or street lighting to those who would be able to pay, so provision of these things could not be supported privately. Lighthouses are sometimes used as an example. However, at least in some parts of the world government provision was avoided: "in those days the lighthouses in the Caribbean were private property, and their owners charged ships according to their size for the right to enter the port" (Garcia Marquez 1989, 95). Generally, to sustain the supply of these sorts of goods requires compulsory payment through taxation.

A second kind of market failure is sometimes referred to as information asymmetry, where individuals are not well enough informed to allow the market to function properly. To compensate for the difficulties of individuals obtaining the necessary information, the government may intervene in the service market, perhaps by licensing professions or, in manufacturing, by providing a quality seal—Adam Smith's "sterling mark upon plate." In this way the government can compensate for the consumers' ignorance by setting standards. Market failure can also occur through the wider ramifications of markets. The concept of externalities is used to refer to the effects of a market transaction on those who are not party to the transaction. Pollution of air, land, or water is a common kind of externality. The government may intervene to represent those experiencing the externalities but who would otherwise not be represented in the transaction.

Monopolies represent a market failure that may develop in the supply of some goods and services. These monopolies may have to be broken up (antitrust policies) or, where economic conditions make the existence of just one supplier more efficient (water companies), then regulation of the services and prices of the supplier is required. Finally, there are some goods or resources to which there is relatively open access, but which may be overexploited if self-seeking individuals are left to operate without interference. People, if left to their own devices, will deplete these common pool or common property resources, like grazing land or fishing banks, ultimately to every one's disadvantage. Assigning property rights is a way out of this policy problem for some types of resource. For others, particu-

larly mobile resources like fish, property rights may not represent a solution. At least where the use of the resource can be fairly narrowly contained to a small community there may be a nongovernmental cooperative
solution to the problem,[1] otherwise government intervention and management of the resource may be necessary.

Stigler, like Adam Smith before him, is unwilling to accept the public
interest justifications of public policy at face value. The market failure
argument for public policies assumes a public interest driven government.
Stigler claims the primacy of private interests in accounting for public policies, as did Smith: "It is to prevent this reduction of price . . . by restrain-
ing that free competition that would most certainly occasion it, that all
corporations, and the greater part of corporation laws, have been established" (Smith 1776, 227). Regulations on apprenticeship interested Adam
Smith. They had little to do with learning a trade and providing good
products to the public and much to do with restricting entry to the market.
Obviously, the market-failure view of public policy is only in contradiction
with Smith and Stigler's approach as an account of actual policies. It is
quite consistent to accept market failure as a normative argument for the
appropriate circumstances for government intervention in the economy, as
well as Stigler and Smith's empirical theory of regulatory policy.

Other economists have modified Stigler's bald theoretical statements
that describe the dominance of business interests and refined the economic
theory of the exercise of political power derived from differential incentives to political participation. Sam Peltzman observes that the size of the
interests affected by policies is central to the economic conception of the
policy process: "producer protection represents the dominance of a small
group with a large per capita stake over the large group (consumers) with
more diffused interests" (Peltzman 1976, 212). Peltzman formalizes and
modifies the theory by segmenting the opposition to producers into groups
with differing incentives to participate and hypothesizes that the regulator
also "desires the minimization of opposition (0) from consumers by
exploiting differences among them in per capita demand" (219). With the
regulator desiring to maximize net political support (Viscusi, Vernon, and
Harrington 1992, 315) and while regulation remains likely to benefit the
producer, particularly when industry growth slows, the winners in the policy struggle, according to Peltzman, are not necessarily limited to one economic interest. Neglected in the refined model are the "regulators" own
commitments and ideas and the political resources and ease of political

---

1. For discussions of these market failures see Downs 1967; Stokey and Zeckhauser
1978; Weimer and Vining 1989. On the particular problem of common property resources
and the possibilities of cooperative nongovernmental solutions see Ostrom 1990.

access of the different interests. Irrespective of incentive differences, interests may differ considerably in the effort they have to go to, to articulate their interest to the regulator and in the marginal cost that their contribution (say campaign contributions) represents.

Gary Becker borrows the "compensation principle" of welfare economics (1985). Unless the winner in a policy struggle could compensate the loser, then the loser's incentive to participate will exceed the winner's incentive to participate, and the policy will not survive. Becker's achievement is to show how this principle translated into incentives to participate might underlie real policy-making and therefore how socially harmful policies will not be implemented, contra Stigler as well as Olson's argument in *The Rise and Decline of Nations.* The trick lies in a political parallel of perfect competition. Becker assumes competing interest groups with a rough equality of resources and acknowledges a disregard for the independent influence of government officials.

Political scientists, naturally disposed to dwell on the greater complexities of public policy, have a wary regard for the economists' theoretical achievements. One of the more critical treatments is Kenneth Meier's empirical analysis of regulation (1988). Meier points to the thin empirical evidence that Stigler presents to support his theory. With evidence from the regulation of the insurance industry in the United States, he finds that "the insurance industry may have been the most powerful actor in this policy arena, but it clearly did not dominate the arena at all times" (87) and argues that Stigler's theory should be abandoned.[2] Meier's work provides grounds for arguing that Stigler's theory at least requires important additional complicating conditions—notably that business divisions over policy goals make its control over regulation less likely and that regulation has both a bureaucratic and political component. But before abandoning this approach it is worth noting that an influential type of policy analysis within political science questions the dominance of the regulated industries yet adopts a similar view to Stigler's of the critical elements of the political system, viewing the system as primarily responding to the incentives created by the actual or implied costs and benefits of a public policy.

James Q. Wilson's (1980) starting point in understanding policy and politics is to assess whether the costs and benefits of a policy are widely distributed or narrowly concentrated. Like Stigler, he assumes that citizens have a generally low level of natural political interest and considers as the

---

2. Meier's conclusion "that the time has long passed to abandon George Stigler's simplistic supply and demand regulatory theory" (1988, 170) was perhaps a reaction to Stigler's triumphalist conclusion that "economists should quickly establish the license to practice on the rational theory of political behavior" (1975, 133–34).

critical factor the variation in incentives to participate in the political decision process. Wilson also shares the weaknesses of Stigler's approach in focusing only on incentives to participate, on who is likely to pay attention to the policy issue, and not on differences in resources to participate, not on the possibility that perceptions of costs and benefits are subject to influence, and not on the perceptions that policymakers themselves bring to the policy struggle.

Wilson identifies four types of politics. Majoritarian politics characterizes a policy where the outcome is settled by the support of popular majorities—that is, where both the costs and benefits are distributed across large numbers of people (e.g., social security). Benefits concentrated on a particular group, and costs distributed across society are associated with client politics (e.g., agricultural price supports and some industry regulation). Policy cases where benefits and costs are concentrated on particular groups stimulate interest group politics (e.g., trade union policy). Finally, where costs are concentrated and benefits distributed, entrepreneurial politics results. Because of this distribution of costs and benefits and the incentive advantage for the cost bearers, successful examples of entrepreneurial policies are relatively rare. They would include some environmental policies.

For Wilson, the relationship between business and government is not confined to any one of these categories of politics. Wilson finds examples of policies toward business in all of them. Although the tenor of Wilson's argument is the diversity of politics and outcomes that business experiences, he provides no means of appreciating the volume of business political experience that falls in each of the categories. Perhaps Stigler is right and the rule in business-government relations is some form of what Wilson would call client politics. Further, of the other distributions of costs and benefits and categories of politics, the only one in which business is the clear loser is the entrepreneurial, and here Wilson himself says that "a regulatory agency created as a result of a scandal or some other form of entrepreneurial politics is obviously more vulnerable to being captured by the industry it is supposed to regulate than one created by a process of interest group conflict in which each organized party keeps a watchful eye on its rival" (Wilson 1980, 436). He illustrates interest group politics with policies toward trade unions and workplace safety. Apart from the exceptional Wagner Act, offset in twelve years by the Taft-Hartley Act, business's superior political resources have dominated policy on labor relations in the United States. Congress passed the Occupational Safety and Health Act in 1970, when public confidence in American business was arguably at its lowest point since the Progressive era: "the period from 1965 to 1975 . . . was one of enormous growth in anti-business sentiment"

(Lipset and Schneider 1987, 31). Even so, as Terry Moe has argued, the important struggle was not over the policy but over how to set up the organization to implement the policy: "Interest groups representing business actually did participate in the design of OSHA [Occupational Safety and Health Administration], they did use their portion of public authority to impose structures intended to cripple OSHA's performance—and these structures had the intended effect" (Moe 1990, 126; see also Moe 1989). Business interests did not capture OSHA, but they left it incapacitated.

Wilson uses antitrust policy to illustrate majoritarian politics. Historically, the capricious enforcement of the policy by the courts has meant that at times unions were in greater danger of being considered in restraint of trade or commerce than corporations. Only at the height of the Progressive era, say from the Northern Securities case in 1904 to the Standard Oil and American Tobacco cases of 1911, did antitrust policy create fear and uncertainty in the American business community. Otherwise it has been for the most part, with the notable exception of the AT&T case, an example of the "drama of state" (Edelman 1964, 162), signifying not very much to the business world. The policy problem was resolved in the second and third decades of the twentieth century not by reversing the trend toward concentration but by accepting corporate officials' arguments that there was a valid distinction between "good"—that is, socially responsible—and "bad" corporations (Mitchell 1989). Although corporations might have market power, corporate officials were able to use that power responsibly.

Accepting the insights on the importance of incentives in politics as well as economics and of the importance of public support to politicians — these insights are integrated in my theoretical argument in this book—one must also accept that the capture theory of regulation is too simple. We still need some way of knowing which of Wilson's categories typifies the relationship between business and government, and better evidence on how particular distributions of costs and benefits have advantaged business opponents. We need to consider explicitly the political resources of affected interests in addition to their incentives to use those resources. We need to recognize the different resources that those with a stake in the policy start off with in the policy struggle and their relative capacity to shape the perception of costs and benefits and to deliver the message on whether the community can afford the economic price of regulation. We also need to know something about the government officials with responsibility for making policy, most importantly their policy agendas. Neither Wilson nor Stigler have much to say about political parties in their discussions of policies affecting business. Their disinterest comes from an economic approach to the relationship between business and government in the empirical setting of American politics. Stigler treats political parties as substitutes: "If one party becomes extortionate . . . it is possible to elect another party which will provide the governmental services at a price more closely proportioned to costs of the party" (1975, 127). If the members of political parties were *only* interested in public support and election and reelection, this view might be adequate. To the extent that political parties develop common commitments among their members and core constituencies tied to distinguishable policy agendas it becomes less so.

Finally, an alternative theoretical approach to assessing the distribution of the costs and benefits of a policy and the incentives to political participation, and that is also critical of Stigler's theory of regulation, is to examine the ways in which policy issues are associated with particular constellations of groups and organizations. *Issue networks, policy networks, policy subsystems,* and *policy communities* are terms now used by many students of public policy to signal a new analytical turn away from the argument that policy is captured by particular groups.

Issue networks are defined in opposition to subgovernments or iron triangles to suggest that policy-making is not confined to a dominant interest, Congress, and the bureaucracy. Rather, the process of policy-making is open to many other actors and influences. It is suggested, in American politics at least, that whereas iron triangles or subgovernments may have once, say two decades ago, more accurately characterized policy-making, we live in an expanding political universe, characterized by an explosion of new interest groups, resulting in a more open and adversarial process. With this increasing complexity, knowing who belongs to the network is the first analytical challenge. Where scholars explicitly address this subject, the exchange of information and the sharing of substantive expertise determines inclusion within a network (Berry 1989, 242).[3] The network might include interest groups, government officials, academic experts, and representatives of the media.

A recent empirical analysis of interest representation in the United States finds that the sharing of information among interest groups is, contrary to the network depiction, quite constrained: "our data on collegial networks indicate that most exchange does not cross boundaries of group interest, social characteristics, or political ideology. Instead, policy discussions primarily take place with persons who can be trusted: employees of the same organization or persons with similar social and political characteristics" (Heinz et al. 1993, 375). Further, it is premature to refer to the issue network "model," for it amounts to identifying those interested in a

---

3. For discussion of policy networks in the context of European politics and a different conceptual emphasis see Jordan and Schubert 1992 and Rhodes and Marsh 1992.

policy issue, obviously a necessary first step, but not to specifying the nature of the more important relationships. There are, as yet, no general rules for distinguishing between those groups orbiting an issue inconsequentially and those that will have an impact. This approach avoids the issue of power. This avoidance is important because despite the use of words like *exchange, sharing,* and *community,* which might imply a consensual process, scholars seem to suggest that policy-making, at least in America, is more or less characterized by openness, conflict, and countervailing forces—so, still, the century of pluralism.

The available theories, all of which remain vital in the period since Lindblom identified business's political privileges, largely understate the role of business. Only Stigler's version of policy theory explicitly recognizes some of the advantages business interests bring to the policy process, almost too much so and consequently we are left with wanting a better understanding of how business fails in the policy struggle. Corporatism, it is true, narrows our attention to the relationship between producer groups and the executive, and points to the variation in strength of countervailing forces from political system to political system. Where systems or sectors are identified as corporatist is generally where labor is strong, even a 'social partner.' Unfortunately there has been little effort to sort out senior from junior partners, so to speak. Oddly, corporatist theorists have commonly referred to non-corporatist systems as pluralist, even though labor is weakest in these systems, and business faces less competition in the struggle over policy.

Thinking about the position of business interests in the policy struggle compels consideration of the general relationship between interests and policymakers in the policy struggle. Building on this critical review of the available theories, this book couches its explanation of business interests' position within a theory of the political forces that act on policymakers as they "design" policy. As Charles W. Anderson argues, policy is not just a response to environmental factors, to levels of industrialization or fluctuations in the rate of exchange. There are alternatives and the strategies and intentions of policymakers are critical (see Anderson 1975; Anderson 1978). But without consideration of political support, Stigler's focus, these strategies and intentions come to nothing. The focus is on elected officials and on policy at the stage of formulation rather than implementation. This statement describes the applicability of the theoretical argument and is not meant to suggest that the implementation stage is unimportant or not itself a field of struggle, and though the primary focus is on elected officials, some effort will be made to consider the role of bureaucrats "as actors with goals, strategies, and resources" operating in "agencies structured, staffed, and overseen by their creators, interest groups and politicians" (Moe 1990,

131). Bureaucratic agencies and implementation procedures can be designed to perform their tasks more or less efficiently and with more or less insulation built in against capture.

The general theoretical argument runs as follows: elected officials seek to turn their ideas and beliefs into policy, for which they seek political support.[4] They choose among the policy positions of rival interests on the basis of the congruence of those positions with their own ideas and on the basis of the capability of the interest to contribute to or detract from their public support. The capability of the interests is assessed not just by differing incentives to participate, but by resources such as money, information and expertise, time, numbers of members, and the other factors, specifically including the substance of the policy position they must justify, and that contribute to an interest's leverage on public opinion.

What does this argument imply for business interests? Generally, and as I attempt to demonstrate in the next two parts of the book, business interests' resources are superior in their ability to contribute to the political support of policymakers and, other things equal, can expect success rather than failure in the policy struggle. Most obviously, failures for at least some business interests can occur when business interests are significantly (something of a weasel word) divided.[5] More interestingly, and to anticipate the argument in the final part of the book, in the absence of significant business divisions failures can occur because (1) a policymaker is indifferent to superior resources and the consequences of the decision for his or her political support, or, more likely, because (2) the mobilization of resources by business opponents outweighs the business interest's contribution to a policymaker's public support, specifically by countering the business interest's leverage on public support, which is likely to occur over issues that raise questions concerning the legitimacy of the business position.

To develop the argument on an empirical level first requires showing, despite the recent criticism of this view, that business interests possess particular political advantages. What is the status of the three pillars of business power, the ideological power of business interests, the business confidence factor, and the conventional political resources of business relative to other interests, particularly unions? If as much of the available the-

---

4. This assumption combining the economists' (Stigler) focus on political support with political scientists' (Anderson) focus on intentions and values is consistent with Budge and Keman's theoretical approach to party government in parliamentary democracies that assumes that "parties seek to form that government capable of surviving legislative votes of confidence which will most effectively carry through their declared policy preferences under existing conditions" (1990, 34).

5. For an example of "significant" divisions see Martin 1991.

ory claims, at least when pitching statements at the general level, business possesses no great advantages, there is no need for a separate effort to account for business policy failures. Analytical interest in business policy failures increases to the degree we find the pillars of business power intact. In part 2, I examine these resources in some detail, and in part 3, I provide a comparison with the resources of the opponents of business interests. In part 4, I examine the circumstances under which the opponents of business interests can expect to successfully counter the resources that business mobilizes.

PART 2

Business Power

CHAPTER 3

The First Pillar of Business Power: Public Preferences, the Media, and Business

> . . . the corporation has always been up to its hips—and sometimes in over its head—in politics. It has seen the policy process, not as a source of trouble to be avoided or alien values to be neutralized, but as a mother lode of business advantage to be mined and refined. . . . over the years it has won a dazzling array of benefits—tariffs, subsidies, official monopolies, tax breaks, immunity from certain tort actions, government-supported research and development, free manpower training programs, countercyclical economic management, defense spending, wage controls, and so on . . .
>
> From the outset, the corporation has sought support for the probusiness welfare state by means of public relations—that is, communications that infuse business enterprise with a public interest and conceal the private interests involved.
>
> —Paul H. Weaver 1988

Government captures the attention of business people with its capacity to foster or to threaten their business interests. Optimally, for business people, it will be unnecessary to exert independent political pressure on public policymakers, for policymakers and the public to whom they are accountable will already want what they want. In thinking about the relationship between policy preferences and business interests, we can usefully organize the discussion around three questions. How much support from public opinion can business interests generally expect? Do business interests have advantages in the shaping of public preferences? If the public wants what business interests want, how do business interests pose a problem for democracy? Evidence and argument suggest an ideological pillar of business power. Yet, and to anticipate my more general argument, it is also this pillar that is likely to fail as business interests engage in a policy struggle.

Critics of the "privileged position of business" noted the political reversals business experienced, the power of other interests, and attacked, with vitriol, the argument about the ideological power of business (see

Hessen 1981). Lindblom argues that business influences political as well as consumer preferences and what is on, as well as what is not on, the public agenda. According to his critics, American society is intellectually diverse because there are left-wing magazines and books like *Politics and Markets* (de Sola Pool 1981, 28). Yet an apologist for the Soviet system in the 1960s could point to the publication of *One Day in the Life of Ivan Denisovich* as evidence of the Soviet Union's lively intellectual climate. A better approach to this issue is to examine systematically collected evidence on the level of support for business interests among the public. Since Lindblom wrote there has been considerable progress in understanding the content and formation of public preferences. In this chapter I draw on that research and some new data to examine where business interests fit. Comparatively, one would expect both historical and national differences corresponding to differences in political institutions and traditions and to differences in economic performance. One would expect that levels of public support for business would be higher in the United States than in the United Kingdom for example, with the absence of alternative, labor-oriented, political traditions, and in combination with the relative prosperity delivered. If we cannot find public support for business in the United States, we will not find it anywhere.

In their examination of American public opinion, Herbert McClosky and John Zaller (1984) disentangle two dominant themes: support for democratic values and support for capitalist values. In the event of a conflict between these themes, democratic values will prevail over capitalist values. In fact, conflicts of this sort may account for the general trend toward the regulation of business interests, according to McClosky and Zaller. Nonetheless, support for capitalist values remains generally high and although they discuss the potential conflict between capitalist and democratic values, these authors provide evidence that in the public mind capitalism is actually a necessary condition for democracy. When asked, "in your opinion, is the free enterprise system necessary for free government to survive," 80 percent of the public agreed. Over 60 percent thought that "the private enterprise system is generally a fair and efficient system" (133). The data are from the mid-1970s, and support for the economic system seems high in the context of Watergate, Vietnam, and the "sixties" shocks to the legitimacy of American institutions, coupled with the rise of issue advocacy groups at that time.

Corroboration for these findings comes from Seymour Martin Lipset and William Schneider's study *The Confidence Gap* (1987). They found similar levels of support for the business system: "fully 67 percent of the same respondents rated our political system as basically sound, while 64 percent felt the same way about our system of business and industry. Only

45 percent thought our system of organized labor was basically sound, but this was still considerably higher than the percentage who voiced high confidence in labor leaders" (385).

What also showed up quite clearly in Lipset and Schneider's analysis, a result important for my argument in this book, were the cross-industry and even cross-company differences in public attitudes toward business. It is quite possible that there can be high levels of confidence in the system as a whole, though lower levels of confidence in some institutions and the particular officials in office. Watergate, Vietnam, and the sixties seemed to take more of a toll on public confidence in institutions and individuals than in systems.

Rather than God and the goodness of work, contemporary capitalism "appears to derive its legitimacy less from the ascetic features of the Protestant ethic than from secular values such as individualism and economic efficiency" (McCloskey and Zaller 1984, 127). Legitimacy, or public support for economic, social, or political practices, depends on the perceived consonance of these practices with the wider value structure. McClosky and Zaller's poll data suggest that the perception of derivative political benefits, notably democracy, also contributes to capitalism's legitimacy. To these one must add social responsibility, a value first explicitly assumed by American business executives in the early part of this century in response to the questioning of corporate legitimacy that characterized the Progressive era. At this time corporations began voluntarily to recognize responsibilities to constituencies (stakeholders), including employees, customers, and the community, through public statements and the adoption of a variety of social policies. Ethical issues had occupied business and society before, yet these were largely resolved in the idea of the market, the injunction to selfishness, the belief in the futility of social policy, or what became the ruthless combination of social Darwinism. Even exceptional business people, like Andrew Carnegie, did not urge other-regarding behavior as a business practice. It was something for the captain of industry to do once he had accumulated his wealth, and in conformity with the self-help doctrine: "the best means of benefiting the community is to place within its reach the ladders upon which the aspiring can rise" (Carnegie 1887, 28). Carnegie built 2,507 public libraries.

The acknowledgment of social responsibilities also raises public expectations about corporate behavior. Social responsibility becomes a criterion for evaluating corporate performance. In a recent British poll, members of Parliament, "captains of industry," as the 151 board members from the largest 500 U.K. companies were called, and editors in the broadcast and print media responded to the statement: "that industry and commerce do not pay enough attention to their social responsibilities?" (*Index to International Public Opinion* 1993, 9). Even 32 percent of the captains of industry agreed. Respondents faulted businesses for their treatment of the environment, with 83 percent of the general public and a clear majority of business executives, some 59 percent, agreeing with the proposition that "British companies do not pay enough attention to their treatment of the environment." Although there is support for social responsibility, there is evidence that competitive performance is generally regarded as the top priority. In the same poll, 60 percent of the general public, 78 percent of MPs, 97 percent of business executives, and 89 percent of the editors agreed that: "The main responsibility of companies is to perform competitively even if this means reducing the number of people they employ." One would anticipate a similar response if the question were posed directly in terms of social responsibility rather than employment. Further, there were very high levels of agreement with the proposition that "large companies are essential for the nation's growth and expansion." Some 78 percent of the British public, 87 percent of MPs, 88 percent of executives, and 78 percent of editors made this association between large companies and economic efficiency. Fortunately American polls use the same item, revealing that 84 percent of the American public were in agreement with the proposition in 1989 (Lehne 1993, 43).

Note that in reporting these findings we have moved from the more abstract and readily acceptable business system to business institutions, specifically large companies. With room for improvement in some areas, there appears to be considerable public support for these companies and considerable agreement between the mass public and political and economic elites about business priorities. For a more detailed understanding of business legitimacy, comparing business with other important institutions is helpful. Table 3.1 presents the average percentage of respondents over a fifteen-year period who have indicated they have a great deal of confidence in a variety of institutions. Business institutions occupy a middling position. Banks and financial institutions, at least before the scandals in the savings and loan industry, elicited a similar level of support to organized religion. Major companies do substantially better than television, Congress, or organized labor.[1] Riding high in public confidence is the scientific community, presumably because of the importance of expertise in the broader value structure and because scientists are perceived as in pursuit of knowledge rather than material self-interest.

---

1. These data are from National Opinion Research Center surveys. Gallup has a similar set of items concerning confidence in institutions. One notable difference between the two surveys is that, in the latter, organized labor does about as well as business. This difference may result from Gallup using the more negative prompt "big business," as opposed to "major companies" (Gallup 1994).

The averages reported in table 3.1 are useful in comparing support across institutions, yet one also needs an appreciation of the differences resulting from polling at different times. Considerable yearly variations emerge in public confidence in specific institutions, including major companies and their leaders. For major companies public confidence dipped to a low of 19 percent (in 1975) of the public indicating that they had a great deal of confidence and rose to a high of 31 percent on two occasions (1974 and 1984) over a fifteen-year period (Niemi, Mueller, and Smith 1989, 98–105). From their analysis of yearly variations in confidence in leaders of various institutions for the 1966–1980 period, Lipset and Schneider find that changes in the unemployment rate and the inflation rate account for 65 percent of the variation in confidence in the leaders of major companies, 69 percent of the variation in confidence in congressional leaders, and 60 percent of the variation for the executive branch, with unemployment being the most important of the two explanatory variables in the model (Lipset and Schneider 1987, 64). These economic factors have less impact on confidence in the leaders of other major institutions, including organized labor. Increases in unemployment and inflation coincide with declines in public confidence in business institutions. While the public may expect less from business in depressions as David Vogel argues, these correlations suggest that no straightforward relationship exists between the political power of business and economic performance. If public confidence in business declines, it is easier for elected officials to consider measures opposed by business interests. Also what captures attention in

Table 3.1.   Public Confidence in Political and Economic Institutions in the United States (mean percentages for 1973–88)

"I am going to name some institutions in this country . . . would you say you have a great deal of confidence, only some confidence, or hardly any confidence at all in them?"

Institution	Great Deal	Hardly Any
Scientific community	41	6
Military	34	14
U.S. Supreme Court	32	14
Organized religion	31	18
Banks/financial	31[a]	13
Major companies	25	14
Television	16	26
Congress	15	21
Organized labor	12	30

Source: Niemi, Mueller, and Smith 1989, 98–105.
[a]1975–88

this analysis is that political leaders appear to be held about as accountable for economic performance as business leaders.

If support for the business system is generally high, and support for business institutions respectable in comparison to other institutions, how do business executives fare in comparison with people in other occupations? Public assessments of the fairness and honesty of business executives put them below pharmacists, doctors, dentists, the clergy, and college teachers. Yet, in 1990 at least, they were above newspaper reporters, senators, lawyers, members of congress, state and local politicians, and union leaders. Bankers do even better than business executives, finding a birth between funeral directors and television commentators. Those perceived to have the lowest ethical standards are stockbrockers, insurance sales people, advertising practitioners, and car sales people (Gallup 1991, 23). As with confidence at the institutional level, the degree of expertise and other-regardingness seem to be important factors in these sorts of assessments. The community standards are knowledge and unselfishness.

We can, with this evidence, sustain a weaker version of the ideological power of business argument. Business interests, whether conceived as part of an economic system, as institutions, or as individuals, enjoy a relatively supportive climate of opinion. In some respects, business institutions and executives seem to have a more secure place in the public mind than political institutions and politicians, at least in the United States. But what of the strong version, and the claim that business interests have advantages over other interests in shaping public preferences?

The influence on young minds of boy scouts, teachers, ministers, mothers, and others is what sociologists call the process of socialization. Ultimately it is to these sources that we must go for a more complete understanding of where our opinions come from. Here the focus is more short term and on the forces that can shift the public's policy preferences. The media are, for the most part, the means by which the public receive information about policy issues. Of the "agents" of socialization, the media are the most immediately accessible to the business message.

The experimental social science of Shanto Iyengar and Donald R. Kinder provides good evidence on the considerable influence of television in determining the political agenda. They show that manipulating television coverage of problems produces changes in the importance of those problems to viewers. Supporting Lindblom's argument, Iyengar and Kinder argue that "with respect to those matters that Lindblom called the grand issues . . . there is mainly dead silence" (Iyengar and Kinder 1987, 133). Lindblom, recall, had claimed that on the grand issues like private enterprise or the distribution of income, business officials "try, through indoctrination, to keep all these issues from coming to the agenda of government" (Lindblom 1977, 205). In related work, Benjamin Page, Robert Shapiro, and Glenn Dempsey examined the effect of actors and sources in network news stories on responses to policy preference items in national surveys of public opinion. In their effort to isolate the major factors involved in short- and medium-term changes in public opinion, they find that news commentators, "experts," and popular presidents, in that order, have the most impact on policy preferences. On the other hand "groups perceived to represent narrow interests generally have no effect, or even a negative impact, on public opinion" (Page, Shapiro, and Dempsey 1987, 39). The lesson, not lost on business interests, is that influencing policy preferences is possible, particularly if one can harmonize one's position with expert opinion and if one links one's interests with other interests and the "public" interest. The libertarian, Paul Weaver, believes corporations have learned this lesson too well (Weaver 1988, 18). Note, too, the consistency between the finding that experts and the nonselfish have the most impact on policy preferences and the importance of these same factors in determining public confidence in institutions and public assessments of occupations. Finally, John Zaller presents evidence and argument to show that public preferences are determined by "the flow of information in elite discourse." He summarizes recent research on public opinion in the following way: "If one takes it to mean any situation in which the public changes its opinion in the direction of the "information" and leadership cues supplied to it by elites, indeed, there is not much to argue about. Not only the present study, but several others provide abundant evidence of this sort of elite domination" (Zaller 1992, 311). So we know from this research that public preferences are shaped, that the media play a critical role in this process, but business influence depends in part on being able to ensconce the message in the values of expertise and unselfishness.

For the larger issues, friendly expertise may be available, and supportable, in a variety of conservative think tanks, for example, the Heritage Foundation or the American Enterprise Institute (AEI) in the United States. The latter organization, set up in 1943 as the American Enterprise Association by a group of business people led by Lewis H. Brown of the Johns-Manville Corporation, had as its purpose informing the public and policymakers of business priorities. Deriving about half of its funding from corporations and one-third from foundations, it remained true to this purpose in the last decade, targeting its publications "not only at Washington's policy community but at journalists, business executives, and other opinion leaders" (Smith 1991, 174–83, 270–71). Recent or current scholars include Norman Ornstein, William Schneider, Jeane Kirkpatrick, and Michael Novak, who frequently provide the expert commentary on social and political issues for news programs.

In the United Kingdom in 1942, the year of William Beveridge's report on social welfare policy, Aims of Industry was set up and funded by business people to "anticipate the need to combat the false ideologies of the left, and to establish an understanding of the need for freedom and free enterprises" (quoted in Cockett 1994, 72). In the 1950s, the Institute for Economic Affairs (IEA) was created "to propagate sound economic thoughts in the universities and all other educational establishments" (quoted in Cockett 1994, 131), and in the 1970s the Centre for Policy Studies (CPS) and the Adam Smith Institute (ASI) were formed, about the time the Heritage Foundation was set up in the United States. According to Cockett, "the IEA had provided the general theory and principles, and the CPS had won a party-political constituency for those principles, the ASI found a niche for itself as the policy engineers to develop practical policy proposals which could translate those principles into practice when the Conservative Government came to power" (283). Cockett views Friedrich von Hayek's returning the idea of the market to England in 1931 (when the former colleague of Ludwig von Mises took a position at the London School of Economics) as the intellectual point of origin for these think tanks and sees a real division of labor in their various contributions to the long march of the idea from intellectual isolation to hegemonic Thatcherism. In 1979, some twenty-one companies were identified as contributing to the CPS, and thirty-five companies were identified as contributing to Aims of Industry (*Labour Research* 1980). On the eve of Thatcher's first government, such firms as B.A.T. Industries, Glaxo, and the Rank Organisation were financially supporting the think tanks.

For the narrower issues, the more direct approach is to hire, contract, and develop a reputation for specific expertise. Rentokil, a British company providing environmental services and pest control, deliberately fosters a close and cooperative relationship with the media, in part based on a reputation as a source for expert information. This company is often in the news, and "is frequently consulted by the BBC Natural History Unit and other programme makers" (Jefkin 1993, 275). Its public relations is "directed at educating clearly defined publics and establishing Rentokil as the authority to which the media will refer on any matter relating to its areas of business" (274). Rentokil is exceptional—but as a company to be emulated. Rentokil was tenth on the 1994 *Financial Times* list of Europe's companies most respected by European managers (June 27, 1994), and no doubt by British pests. By establishing itself as a useful source of information in this way, even when "truth" and "interest" are not in harmony, it may be difficult to disentangle one from the other.

Just as the boundary between expertise and self-interest becomes uncertain, so does the line between the firm's interest and the community interest. In earlier periods, religious injunctions or the laws of economic science relieved business people of wider social concerns. In the twentieth century, managers claim to serve a number of constituencies and define and pursue community interests. Business magazines rank firms on this social dimension of their activities, which may take the form of gifts to hospitals, schools, or universities, sponsorship of the arts, or even political education, notably Mobil's marathon newspaper campaign on the issues of our time. This company has run its own editorials on the editorial pages of leading newspapers since 1971. In these ways the interests of the firm and the community become less easy to distinguish. Profit making is shuffled in with science and social responsibility.

Concomitantly, the representatives of profit, business people, defer, when they can, to representatives of science or the community as corporate prolocutors. They may even defer to cartoon characters, as did the management of the sugar company Tate & Lyle, Ltd., with the "Mr. Cube" campaign against the threat of nationalization. An endearing sugar cube, taking on the postwar Labour government, argued that prices would go up with government ownership. In the insurance industry's 1994 struggle to shape public preferences on health policy in the United States, the public, in the form of two individuals named Harry and Louise, not insurance sales agents, argued the industry's case on television. To the extent that editorial pages and air waves are for sale, business interests enjoy access, and they seem well aware of the importance of avoiding the appearance of being narrowly self-interested.

Beyond advertising, there is some division of scholarly opinion on whether news commentary itself contributes to the friendly political climate for business. Describing the situation in the United States, Richard Lehne argues that "business organizations are perpetual targets of journalists who demonstrate that companies fail to live up to the society's ideals" (Lehne 1993, 49). In his study of the American media, on the other hand, the sociologist Herbert J. Gans claims that news coverage treats business interests very favorably (1979, 46). While corporate America has been fertile ground for the investigative reporter, from Upton Sinclair to Mike Wallace, how does one come to a more general characterization about the "flow of information?"

Content analysis of British television news coverage of the economy suggests that this coverage generally favors conservative understandings of economic relationships and business over unions. Examining news treatment of the causes of economic crisis in Britain in the 1970s, the Glasgow University Media Group found that the explanation of inflation referred to most frequently, both by interviewees and by commentators and reporters, was that it was produced by wage increases. This explanation was consistent with Chancellor Dennis Healey's view and the basis of the Labour government's Social Contract policy. Alternative explanations were underrepresented. The Glasgow University Media Group claims to "have empirically established that, at least with regards to industrial and economic stories, the overwhelming use of inferential frameworks, routines, and presentational techniques which favour one side of industry rather than the other exist" (The Glasgow University Media Group 1980, 414). Coverage is not necessarily deliberately one-sided. As the British Annan Committee on the Future of Broadcasting argued, great value is placed on what is visually exciting, and so, for example, the activity of striking, while perhaps not presenting the strikers in the best light, often makes for better television than a presentation of the issues behind the strikes (408).

We can approach the question of the flow of information from another direction. To address a variety of empirical issues I use data collected through mail surveys of British business associations, large firms, and unions. In a survey questionnaire mailed in the spring of 1988 to forty-seven major employer and business groups, fifty-nine trades unions with more than 5,000 members, and the top 100 industrial firms in the United Kingdom (see appendix A), survey respondents were asked to rank the media overall, and the major national daily newspapers individually, in degree of sympathy for their organization's views and interests. Table 3.2 shows the percentages of respondents among unions, employer associations, and firms rating the media or a particular newspaper as sympathetic or unsympathetic. Only one of the thirty-eight union respondents to this item saw the media in general as sympathetic. Most of the rest, 66 percent, see the media as unsympathetic rather than neutral. In contrast, only 21 percent of employer groups and 17 percent of firms see the media as unsympathetic. The survey included both the more serious national daily newspapers (*Daily Telegraph, Financial Times, The Guardian, The Independent, The Times*), the serious Sunday papers (*Observer, Sunday Times*), and the tabloids (*Daily Express, Daily Mail, Daily Mirror, Star, Sun*). The *Mirror, Financial Times, Guardian, Independent,* and *Observer* are the only papers to score in double digits on the sympathy rankings for unions. On the other hand, all the newspapers score in double digits for the employer associations and all but two for the large firms. Business perceives *The Financial Times* to be the most sympathetic to business interests. Unions perceive *The Guardian* to be most sympathetic to union interests. But note that for both business associations and firms more respondents view *The Guardian* to be sympathetic rather than unsympathetic. The tabloids, with the exception of the *Daily Mirror,* are all seen as overwhelmingly hostile by the union respondents. As one would expect, a very high correlation (.93) occurs between the employer association and large-firm newspaper sympathy assessments. Business interests generally perceive the newspapers as sympathetic or neutral, and unions generally perceive the newspapers as unsympathetic. If we look at business organizations' own evaluations of the media, particularly in comparison with union evaluations, the results point in the same direction as the content analyses of media coverage, toward a favorably one-sided flow of information on business interests.

The local or regional rather than national markets of most American newspapers makes direct comparison difficult. But there is no basis for expecting that American organizations would assess, for example, Murdoch's outlets in the United States much differently. Parenti argues that in the United States "labor organizations are either ignored or poorly represented in the media" (Parenti 1992, 79). It is implausible, in the absence of a socialist or social democratic party and a tradition of political and intellectual support for trade unions, that media coverage would be less sympathetic to business interests in the United States than it is in the United Kingdom.

Beyond the media's incentive to expand its audience, what accounts for the type of coverage? Sociologists might point out that the top reporters and pundits in the media are themselves members of a privileged group, defined by income and associates, and so share identifiable interests in the policy struggle (see also Fallows 1996, 60).[2] Business analysts might argue that it is not just audience but advertising clients that are important to newspapers and most television channels. Little evidence exists of American network news shows specifically tailoring their coverage to the interests of important advertisers. Rather, local news and network documentaries are more susceptible to pressure and threats from advertisers (Gans 1979, 253). Citing a *Wall Street Journal* article, Michael Parenti claims that "a growing number of corporations along with their ad agencies have issued 'hit lists' of shows they refuse to sponsor. . . . Among the programs were those that did not meet 'family viewing standards,' as well as *Saturday Night Live . . .* and *20/20* with its investigative journalism" (Parenti 1992, 189). Finally, the news media is for the most part privately

---

2. Among others, James Fallows mentions George Will, who "wrote a column and delivered on-air comments ridiculing the Clinton Administration's plan to impose tariffs on Japanese luxury cars, notably the Lexus. . . . Neither in his column nor on the show did Will disclose that his wife, Mari Maseng Will, ran a firm that had been paid some $200,000 as a registered foreign agent for the Japan Automobile Manufacturers Association, and that one of the duties for which she was hired was to get American commentators to criticize the tariff plan. . . . Will had, in fact, espoused such views for years . . . Few of his readers would leap to the conclusion that Will was serving as a mouthpiece for his wife's employers. But surely most would have preferred to learn that information from Will himself."

Table 3.2. Economic Organizations and the Media in the United Kingdom: Percentage of Respondents Rating the Media as Sympathetic or Unsympathetic, 1988

"Which newspapers (media overall) do you consider sympathetic to your organisation's views and interests? For each newspaper indicate your assessment on a scale of 1 (most sympathetic) to 5 (most unsympathetic) with 3 as neutral."

	Unions		Employer Groups		Firms	
	Sympathetic	Unsympathetic	Sympathetic	Unsympathetic	Sympathetic	Unsympathetic
Media overall	3 (N = 38)	66	42 (N = 33)	21	30 (N = 46)	17
Express	0 (N = 35)	97	14 (N = 21)	10	21 (N = 28)	7
Mail	0 (N = 35)	97	18 (N = 22)	14	30 (N = 30)	20
Mirror	69 (N = 35)	11	13 (N = 23)	39	7 (N = 27)	33
Star	0 (N = 32)	84	10 (N = 21)	29	4 (N = 24)	38
Telegraph	3 (N = 35)	83	50 (N = 28)	7	56 (N = 34)	6
FT	22 (N = 37)	8	72 (N = 29)	7	86 (N = 36)	0
Guardian	76 (N = 37)	5	36 (N = 28)	29	32 (N = 34)	21
Independent	32 (N = 37)	11	30 (N = 27)	7	53 (N = 34)	0
Observer	40 (N = 35)	20	23 (N = 26)	35	39 (N = 33)	9
Sun	0 (N = 36)	97	14 (N = 21)	29	13 (N = 24)	33
Sunday Times	3 (N = 35)	83	30 (N = 27)	19	46 (N = 35)	6
Times	0 (N = 34)	79	48 (N = 29)	7	57 (N = 35)	6

owned and is itself part of the corporate world, sharing corporate problems, and pursuing money and power, as well as the public's right to know.

Rupert Murdoch's News International is a good example. His interest in his business led to his pioneering effort to move newspapers off Fleet
Street and champion the Conservative government's policy toward the
unions. Until Murdoch's decision to do battle with the printers, it had
been the British government itself that led the effort to defeat the more
powerful British unions, like the miners. One might note from table 3.2
that the Murdoch papers in the survey, *The Times* and the *Sunday Times*
as well as the *Sun,* are seen as very hostile by the union respondents. Media
companies like News International share problems, policies, and sometimes ownership ties with other businesses.

All the major television networks in the United States are linked,
through ownership, to other business interests: General Electric and NBC,
Walt Disney and Capital Cities/ABC Inc, and CBS and Westinghouse. Do
ownership ties with other business interests compromise the detachment of
the media? This question is sensitive and difficult to resolve empirically.
Parenthetically, in his discussion of television censorship, Parenti cites
specific examples involving both GE and Westinghouse (Parenti 1992,
186–87). One cannot convincingly make conspiratorial assertions about
paying pipers, but nor can one comfortably dismiss these connections with
perhaps a reference to reporters' ethics. A useful exercise in thinking about
the question is to consider how we view other ownership ties with the
media. First, take cases of state ownership and control of the media. This
type of ownership is generally treated with suspicion as government has
identifiable political interests and therefore a stake in the flow of information. One well-known and frequently used comparative measure of freedom uses state control of the media as a negative criterion in the construction of its quantitative indicators (Freedom House 1995). On a different
scale, corporations can have identifiable political interests and therefore a
stake in the flow of information. Both GE and Westinghouse are very large
diversified corporations and operate in various industries subject to heavy
governmental involvement. Both companies have a significant stake in the
policy struggle, can identify political interests, and have PACs that contribute financially to Republican and Democratic candidates in federal
election campaigns.

Second, consider that at least in the United States as a matter of policy the federal government does consider ownership to have serious implications for media companies and in fact puts limits on certain types of
corporations owning radio and television stations. For federal policy the
relevant distinction is whether the corporation is foreign or domestic.
Rupert Murdoch became a citizen for a television station. If who owns

the media companies is an important issue, as this policy presumes, it is not self-evident that nationality is the only or even the most important distinction, nor that domestic ownership has a more benign influence. Domestic companies, too, have interests in the policy struggle, and an interest in the flow of information (the public relations' industry in the United States now monitors the relative favorability of reporters' stories for business interests, and for Hazel O'Leary, President Clinton's former energy secretary).

Even if the public are led to want what business wants, and, as importantly, do not consider or are silent on other issues that are awkward for business, who is to distinguish "true preferences," real concerns, and the "genuine" policy consensus necessary for democracy. The publics' policy preferences are generally favorable to business, and business, at least in some circumstances, has the help of the media in shaping preferences in a probusiness direction, particularly when business can emphasize expert opinion and other-regardingness. The implication is that without business the political agenda would be different. But in drawing this implication we may be accepting figments of an analytical imagination in place of the preferences that we find in reality. Furthermore, to claim that preferences would be different if citizens were not gulled by business's influence implies an intellectual elitism. If the public want what business interests want, then how can business interests pose a problem for democracy? In this interesting way critics of the argument that business has ideological power shift the debate to a conceptual plane and the relationship between preferences and interests. Yet it does make sense to distinguish between preferences and interests, and, as we shall see, the empirical question of who can influence preferences cannot ultimately be avoided.

All preferences are equal, and social scientists should treat them accordingly, as the givens, as exogenous factors, as tastes. Graham Wilson puts this position well: "people who have absorbed a pro-business ideology have a form of 'false consciousness' which blinds them to their true interests. Only those confronted with particularly bizarre ideologies . . . or those such as Marxists who ascribe to an over-arching theory of society and human nature will be happy making such assertions. Most social scientists would be wary of imposing readily their own values on the subjects of their study" (Wilson 1985, 6). Wilson goes on to argue, with reference to Matthew Crenson's *The Unpolitics of Air Pollution,* that the fact that pollution was not an issue for people living in Gary, Indiana, was not necessarily because these people had their preferences shaped by U.S. Steel. He says that people in Gary might believe that pollution controls would interfere with job creation or wage raises. "Such considerations could rationally lead them not to favour pollution control laws" (Wilson 1985,

6). But because people have reasons for not being concerned about pollution control, does not mean that they are free of business's ideological influence.

Successful influence usually depends on providing reasons for a particular alternative and persuading the relevant constituency that the other alternatives will lead to worse consequences for them. Business, like any other political actor, will rarely simply assert the superiority of its position. Even absolute rulers employ divine right. Successful political actors provide reasons for others to think that they have something at stake too. Beyond a fat year for farmers, subsidies for agriculture are necessary so that we are not at the mercy of world markets, so that we can preserve the integrity of rural communities, or so that the government can feed cheese to homeless school children. Beyond a captive market for our car makers, tariffs are necessary on automobiles because of the importance of the domestic automobile industry to the national economy, or because foreign manufacturers are unfairly competing. So beyond the dirty profits of a steel producer, pollution controls will make the domestic industry uncompetitive and workers unemployed. This could be true. The cost of controlling pollution could deter further investment by business. Policymakers in Gary, then, may care about pollution. They care still more about the jobs that may be jeopardized by controlling pollution: "It was feared that the corporation might seek to minimize the costs of pollution regulation by diverting production increases or plant expansion from its Gary mill to other installations subject to more lenient pollution control regulations" (Crenson 1971, 78). If people think about their preferences in these terms, and order their preferences in a way commensurate with U.S. Steel's interests, the company exercises political influence economically.

It is not inconsistent with the view that business influences public preferences and the political agenda to concede that business is persuasive in its arguments. Further, one can concede that even if people are swayed by these arguments, they may still be acting in their own interests. It is perfectly possible for business to control the agenda and for this agenda to be, at least at times, in the wider public interest as well. What is good for Lincoln Savings and Loan may be good for America. Yet it is also possible that people are swayed by arguments to make choices that are not in their best interests.

So we should also concede that at times the individual may have "false preferences." This concession may seem a large one—the language has overtones of "forcing men to be free." All that is required, however, is the admission that the individual would be unlikely to hold certain preferences if he or she knew more or could calculate better. Even with this admission we can still keep company with fairly mainstream social scientists. The lemon eater becomes a vanilla eater because of the discovery that vanilla reduces cholesterol, increases mental agility, and is the flavor of choice for his or her peer group (assuming of course the simple taste for lemon does not outweigh the desire for health, brains, and to fit in socially). The environmentalist's preference for not burying nuclear waste in large underground salt caverns changes when it is found out that the risks are far greater keeping that waste where it is, in rusting rail cars. The Reagan Democrat, concerned about national defense, returns to the fold when it is disclosed that some scientists and the president misled the public about the possibilities of a space-based missile defense system and the immediacy and severity of the threat that the Soviet Union posed. The better-informed analyst knew that the "true" not erroneous preference of the Reagan Democrat was Walter Mondale, a candidate who had a more accurate estimate of the severity of the threat and a defense policy adequate for that threat. William Riker and Peter Ordeshook say that such errors are quite common in voting choices because the costs of becoming informed outweigh the likely benefits of voting. Of uninformed citizens they say, "such citizens frequently make choices which we, as political scientists, do not interpret as being in their best interests. . . . the citizen, faced with the low benefit and high cost of information, may well prefer to remain uninformed and risk an erroneous choice" (Riker and Ordeshook 1973, 30). Recognizing that false preferences may sound like a radical category, it is not a radical analytical step to concede that people can be misled, ill-informed, or too lazy or stupid to know what choice to make to best realize their goals. Recent work by psychologists, with radical implications, suggests that the desire for more money is a false preference (Lane 1991). While people think that money is what they want, the real source of happiness lies elsewhere.

If not a radical step to take, and one that brings us closer to appreciating the complex connection between interests and preferences, one does not want to underestimate the difficulties involved for the researcher in evaluating others' preferences. A critical component of the evaluation is correctly identifying the final goals and priorities of the actors. George Tsebelis, working in the same analytical tradition as Riker and Ordeshook, identifies some interesting political situations where, he argues, actors who are playing games within games only appear to make "suboptimal choices" (1990). To return to one of our examples, the environmentalist's choice for storing radioactive waste above ground in rusting rail cars is suboptimal if it is a "one-shot" game. On the other hand, if we think of it as a nested game in Tsebelis's terms, with the final value being to stop all nuclear power generation, the choice to oppose any type of storage of waste as unsafe, even if it is relatively safe, becomes optimal.

In this way the analyst brings interests and preferences back into line, although here, too, the rational-choice analyst may run the risk of imputing values that the actor does not hold.

Not knowing how best to achieve one's desires is one source of false preferences. More radically, can the desires themselves be said to represent false preferences? At the least a convincing argument can be made that a precondition for asserting "true" preferences would be that multiple streams contribute to "the flow of information." In the examples it was simply assumed that the individual would desire to avoid cholesterol or coming in contact with radioactive material or government misspending but was misinformed about how best to achieve these desires. These seem reasonable assumptions, which is not to deny that in some cases individuals are sometimes knowingly self-destructive. Governments in advanced industrial countries have informed smokers of the risks. But a considerable number continue to smoke. These smokers presumably find the risks to their health counterbalanced by the olfactory, respiratory, and oral pleasures, or smoking's effect of adding a *je ne sais quoi* to their appearance. Unless of course it is the habit of an addict, then such calculations are irrelevant. To the doctor, the preference to smoke may seem a false one—who is the doctor to argue that extending one's life for five years and forgoing the appearance of the Marlboro Man is in the best interests of the smoker he or she wishes to reform? The modern Narcissus' intense and ultimately fatal enjoyment of his own rugged appearance is worth five extra years when he is over the hill. Or, to take another example, the analyst ought to find the homeless person's preference for a new cathedral rather than affordable housing surprising but not false. We cannot question the homeless person putting spiritual shelter ahead of physical shelter, eternal salvation over a temporary terrestrial need. Or can we? To many social scientists the idea of questioning or reordering an individual's desires and distinguishing in this way between false and true preferences seems futile. It is certainly much more treacherous ground on which to base such a distinction than information failure concerning how to achieve those desires.

Desires, beyond the basic, are socially contrived. Different institutions and organizations, whether orthodox economics, Islam, business, or a family, influence what people value. That preferences are shaped by organizations does not make them "false." Imagining a situation in which an individual selects one thing over another free of social influence is difficult. Yet influencing preferences means an organization possesses power. Different organizations have different capacities to influence preferences.

A critical step in persuading someone to make one choice rather than another is the way in which alternatives are posed, as the Gary example suggested. Some organizations may have the capacity to impose a set of alternatives. A business considering alternative sites for a new plant makes the investment conditional on restrictions on union organization. If the organization has the capacity to impose choices, the choice is loaded, but the preference expressed is not false. Yet, we also have qualms about calling this a "free" choice, because of one side's ability to influence the way that the alternatives are posed: the union or your job, your money or your life. All organizations, not just business, have the political incentive, if they cannot impose the alternatives, to frame choices in a way biased to their organizational goals. You must choose between salvation or eternal damnation, private health insurance or "socialized medicine," no growth or environmental catastrophe. Determining whether the choice is real or false is sometimes difficult. As Crenson's work suggests, it may be possible to see whether other communities in addressing similar problems have faced the same choices and experienced the predicted consequences. It may be possible to see if other communities have been less constrained in the way they list policy alternatives.

"If an issue is not raised in a community, there are at least two possible reasons why it is not: Either it is being suppressed or there is a genuine consensus that it is not an issue," says Nelson Polsby in his discussion of Crenson's work (1980, 216). A third possibility is that other political actors do not have the same advantages to raise the issue or to sustain it as an item on the political agenda. John Zaller argues that, "resistance to persuasion depends very heavily on the availability of countervalent communications, either in the form of opposing information or of cueing messages from oppositional elites" (1992, 267). The opposition to business may not be suppressed, but it is often relatively weak. This inequality in organizational capacities, which can plausibly be thought to result in people having a distorted conception of the choices available, can then be said to be a source of false preferences. False preference is a useful concept, without downplaying the difficulties involved in its empirical investigation. The active suppression of dissenting points of view and a free and competitive exchange of ideas, presumably the precondition for a "genuine" consensus, mark the outer limits in the exchange of information. An imperfect competition of political ideas—somewhere between monopoly and perfect competition—is a distinct possibility. That, from the evidence on media coverage, is what we have.

The failure of total social efforts to shape public preferences visible in the Gulag, the exiled Solzhenitsyn, and the astonishing speed with which former young pioneers went their own way as Ajerbaijanis, Armenians, Russians, and Jews suggests the danger of overestimating the degree to which these preferences are controllable, even in systems where power is very highly concentrated. Business interests' incentives and resources to influence public preferences generally exceed those of other interests, yet they fall short of a monopolistic position. Adding uncertainty, we know, too, that the public are ill-informed, that preferences are volatile, subject to today's headlines as well as to shifts in political leadership, and that, within a generally supportive climate of opinion, specific interests, industries, and firms can suffer a sudden collapse in public confidence. When awkward issues arise on the agenda so, too, do the chances of business failure in the policy struggle.

CHAPTER 4

The Second Pillar of Business Power: A Poststructural View of Business Confidence

There is one important problem facing representative Parliamentary Government in the whole of the world where it exists . . . how to reconcile Parliamentary popularity with sound economic planning.
—Aneuran Bevan, last speech in the House of Commons, 1959

If the public and public policymakers do not have the same preferences as business interests, policymakers are still likely to sort through their options in a way favorable to business interests for fear of losing business confidence. The argument that fear of losing business confidence is an important factor in policy-making is only somewhat less contentious than claiming that business exercises ideological influence. In this chapter I discuss why governments ought to be concerned about business confidence, particularly social democratic governments, and develop the empirical case for the presence of a business confidence factor through evidence drawn primarily from social democratic policy-making.

Social scientists usually introduce this factor into explanations of policy-making as a constant, "structural," constraint on the options open to governments. Once introduced, business losing becomes problematic, encouraging the analyst to define away the loss, perhaps by counterposing the long-term interest of the business system to the identifiable interest of any particular business institution. Alternatively, to avoid handling policy losses in this way, scholars may simply ignore this factor. A better approach is to think about business confidence as a conditional rather than constant factor in the policy struggle. Circumstances arise in which policymakers may deviate from the demand to maintain business confidence and pursue policy options unfavorable to business.

Just as evidence suggests that changes in unemployment and inflation cause variations in public confidence in political leaders, voters generally hold elected officials responsible for economic performance and reward or punish them accordingly at election time. Voters do not simply respond to the current economic situation as they see it, they recall earlier economic experiences and imagine the economic future. A comparative study of elections in the United States, the United Kingdom, France, the Federal Republic of Germany, Italy, and Spain, while noting national variations, finds economic voting to be an important factor (Lewis-Beck, 1988). The economy is not the only issue and not the only factor influencing voting decisions. Ideology, religion, class, scandal, and, perhaps, warfare vary in their importance from election to election and from country to country. Yet along with these other elements in the decision, economic voting is a general phenomenon in capitalist democracies.

Through their effect on voting behavior, decisions that concern the distribution and allocation of material resources—like plant openings and closings, levels of investment, production, and wages—have important political as well as economic consequences. Knowing this, governments that wish to win reelection may deliberately try to improve the economic picture to coincide with elections. Evidence for a political business cycle is mixed. Michael Lewis-Beck, who questions the existence of a political business cycle and claims that voters are not so myopic and economic policy not so precise as such a cycle assumes, argues, nonetheless, that politicians "pursue economic policies with an eye to the business cycle, rather than the electoral cycle . . . they still wish to buy votes. . . . Politicians who want to win try more or less continuously to provide economic good times" (Lewis-Beck 1988, 148–49; see also Tufte 1978). Economic voting ensures that governments are acutely sensitive to variations in the major macroeconomic indicators. The significance to political leaders of the signals from the economy places business institutions and membership groups in a very strong position in the policy struggle.

Reciprocally, economists have long recognized the critical importance of the political climate to economic growth and well-being. This important interactive relationship, constituted by both intended and unintended consequences, supports a high level of business interest in politics and a high level of political interest in business. "Economic prosperity is excessively dependent on a political and social atmosphere which is congenial to the average business man," says John Maynard Keynes (1936, 162). Fully eighty years earlier, Karl Marx stipulated political stability as the necessary minimum for business confidence "the aristocracy of finance . . . condemned the parliamentary struggle of the party of Order with the executive power as a disturbance of order . . . in every epoch the stability of the state power signified Moses and the prophets to the entire money market and to the priests of this money market" (Marx 1852, 157). Returning to Keynes, we find a more contemporary account of party influence on business confidence: "If the fear of a Labour Government or a New Deal depresses enterprise, this need not be the result either of a reasonable calculation or of a plot with political intent; —it is the mere consequence of upsetting the delicate balance of spontaneous optimism" (Keynes 1936, 162). Despite the importance of the topic, and the interest of eminent economists, the impact of party of government on "spontaneous optimism" and business attitudes has not attracted much research attention.

In the British context, the expectation is that the Conservative party would have a positive impact and at least the old Labour party (pre-Tony Blair) a negative impact on business confidence. The implication that follows is that social democratic parties are likely to have to work more assiduously to maintain business confidence than conservative parties. In other words, the business confidence factor will be, other things being equal, more salient in their decision making than for the more probusiness party. Related work on the general impact of political parties on policy and interest representation does not support the expectation of a party difference. As Grant Jordan and Jeremy Richardson point out, "many commentators find the matter of who is elected as of less and less importance" (1987, 12).[1] For scholars, partly because the rebirth of corporatist theory encouraged a disciplinary shift in focus to groups and interests and partly because of the growth of single-issue protests in the 1980s, political parties seemed less important to the policy process. Does this also hold for business interests? The analysis of the effect of party of government on business confidence is based on data from a survey sent to the chairs of the top 100 British firms in the spring of 1988 and a survey of the top two hundred British firms in the autumn of 1992 (see appendix A). Przeworski and Wallerstein define *business confidence* as "the expectation by firms concerning government policy" (1988, 22). Clearly business confidence has a nonpolitical component as well, but the focus here is exclusively on its political dimension.

The sum of the scores on three separate items in the 1988 survey provides an aggregate measure of business confidence. The first item assessed the quality of the firm's relations with government on a five-point scale from "cooperative" to "conflictual." The second item prompted respon-

---

1. Stephen Wilkes and Maurice Wright claim: "Even when the complexion of government changes radically, as with the elections which brought Mitterrand and Thatcher, and which confirmed Kohl's chancellorship, in fact, the practical working out of programmes of activity show relatively little change. As British writers, such as Grant, Rose, and Gamble, have recently emphasized, 'when the rhetoric is stripped away the continuity of policies in most areas is what is striking'" (1987, 291). For the textbook version of this view we have this statement in R. M. Punnett's *British Government and Politics:* "When their party forms the Government, particular advantages can accrue to these interests, just as can disadvantages when their party is in opposition. However, the dependence of both parties when in power today upon cooperation with trade union and business interests alike, perhaps tends to nullify this factor to a large and growing extent" (1988, 153).

dents to assess their influence ("very influential, influential, uninfluential") on government, "with respect to government policy of direct concern to your firm." The third item, concerning policy output, ascertained on a five-point scale the degree of agreement or disagreement with the statement: "government policy directly concerning my firm is usually beneficial to my firm." For all three items respondents were asked to differentiate between Conservative and Labour governments. No earlier survey data or comparable alternative source of information is available for the last Labour government. The elapse of time obviously gives cause for caution in the use of the survey results as they reflect the reality of, say, the policy benefits for business from the Callaghan government. But focusing on the partisan nature of business perceptions, the perception or not by business of a party difference in policy benefits is what is significant. It is reasonable to suppose that business confidence will be based on retrospective as well as prospective evaluations of political parties in government. In this way, the business confidence items provide a means of uncovering the political dispositions and degree of partisanship of large firms.

The aggregate scale extends from a lowest possible score of 3 to a highest possible score of 15. The lower the score the more positively business assesses the policy process. Figure 4.1 presents the frequency distributions for firms' confidence in government for the two political parties. The top 100 firms include five nationalized industries, of whom three responded to the survey. Given their special situation, these firms were not included in the analysis of the influence of party that is reported in the figures and tables; when included these firms strengthen the impact of political party. Figure 4.1 provides evidence in support of the view that party of government makes a difference in business confidence.[2] The modal value is 9 for the Conservatives and the distribution is heavier toward the high-confidence end of the scale. For the Labour party the mode is 11, and the distribution is toward the low-confidence end. The impact of the two parties is of the sort expected given the economic interests and value preferences of the parties' core support.

The aggregate measure of business confidence does not mask any discrepancies among the individual items. On each of the items that comprise the scale the mean score is systematically higher for Labour than for the Conservatives—indicating that firms feel that they have less cooperative relations and less influence with Labour and that they derive fewer policy benefits from Labour governments. The impact of political parties is great-

---

2. Some respondents did not complete all of the items. To be included in the aggregate measure, firms had to respond to each of the three items that make it up—giving an $N = 39$ for the Conservatives and $N = 38$ for the Labour party.

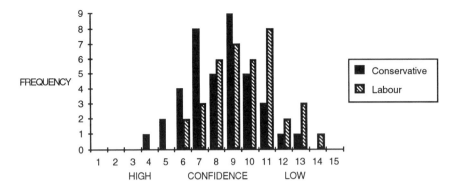

Fig. 4.1.   Political parties and business confidence

est in the important area of policy benefits—on the five-point scale the mean score for Labour was 3.28 and for the Conservatives 2.49. As with discussion of any political attitudes, the timing of the survey qualifies the findings, and it is likely that the distance between the parties on business confidence will vary over time. However, with the 1992 survey there is data for the policy benefits item. Across these four and one-half years and a change of prime ministers, business evaluations of the two parties appears quite stable. The mean scores for Labour and the Conservatives were 3.48 and 2.53 respectively. Reinforcement for these findings comes from a MORI survey of *Financial Times* top 500 companies in March 1992 revealing that about 80 percent of the respondents agreed "that a Labour victory would be bad for the country and industry" (Grant 1993, 137). Business opinion systematically distinguishes between the political parties in the expected direction.

Before drawing the general conclusion that business political confidence is dependent on the program and promises of the party of government and increases with a Conservative government, it is necessary to examine the possibility of interfirm disagreement: that party of government is more significant for some firms than for others. How much real movement on these variables is caused by party of government? Can we reclassify the firms into partisan and nonpartisan categories and attribute the earlier results to the movement of partisan firms?

To pursue this more detailed analysis first we need to establish the presence and size of the partisan and nonpartisan categories. Treatment of business political partisanship in the United States has largely depended on data on election contributions (Burris 1987). Instead of inferring corporate partisanship from corporate behavior, we can get more directly at attitudes through the responses to the survey. The nonpartisan are those firms that gave identical responses for both parties of government on the items that constitute the aggregate measure of business confidence. If firms discriminate between parties on these items, they can reasonably be defined as partisan.

Subdividing the survey data between these identical respondents and the rest produces a nonpartisan group that represents 37 percent of the respondents (excluding nationalized industries) for the 1988 survey, rising to 44 percent for the 1992 survey—that is, those respondents giving identical responses on the policy benefits item. A substantial minority of firms is unwilling to distinguish between political parties in their assessment of various aspects of their relationship with government. The responses of this minority support the view of those scholars who claim that party makes little difference. This nonpartisan category complicates the conclusions one draws about whether political parties make a difference. Parties make a difference but not for all firms.

Market characteristics provide a little help in identifying the nonpartisan. Within the top 100, partisanship does not seem to vary with firm size, though it is possible that the larger a firm, the more impervious it is to partisan considerations. The nonpartisan were almost evenly divided between the firms ranked 1 to 50 and those ranked 50 to 100 in 1988, but the more extensive 1992 survey suggests that size has an important impact. The top 100 firms represent only 56 percent of this sample but 84 percent of the nonpartisan. The MORI poll reported 80 percent of its sample thought Labour bad for industry, suggesting that the nonpartisan are at the most 20 percent of the top 500. Larger size may provide some political insulation to firms. They expect their overall importance to the economy to make both political parties sensitive to their interests.

In line with the British evidence, we can expect the business community in other national contexts to be generally sensitive rather than insensitive to political party change and at the same time politically segmented rather than homogeneous. From this examination of large firms it would be a mistake to draw general inferences about the influence of political parties on other elements of the system of interest representation. Just as it is felt differentially among firms, the impact of a change in party of government is likely to be unevenly distributed on the system of interest representation. Without the power and resources of business, other interests and groups are more vulnerable to party change. An illustration of this imbalance of party influence on the system of interest representation is the treatment of the trade union movement in the United Kingdom by Conservative governments since 1979.

Social democratic or labor parties face an uphill struggle with business confidence, they are also subject to more contrary forces in the policy process. These parties will wish to deliver on their manifesto and follow through on the ideological tenets that distinguish them from their opponents. For social democratic parties there is some tension between the need to maintain business confidence and the other considerations they bring to the decision-making process. For conservative parties, ideology, constituency, and business confidence are more likely to be in harmony. So rather than John Major's or Margaret Thatcher's economic decisions, we will begin with those of an earlier British prime minister, Harold Wilson, as we consider some case evidence on the importance governments give this factor. First we need to think more carefully about how to conceive business confidence in the policy struggle.

Business confidence is sometimes a component of a theoretical argument that postulates the structural dependence of government on business. Structural dependence is thought to work irrespective of the other dimensions of business power. Even without explicit representation of business interests, governments of the right or the left will make policy consistent with these interests. "By returning to Marx's suggestions that the historical process unfolds 'behind the backs of the actors' (including the ruling class actors), it is possible to locate the structural mechanisms that shape the workings of the capitalist states" (Block 1987, 67). By beginning with the view that policy requires policymakers, my contention is that business confidence is an important but conditional influence on policy decisions, and that it is also a consciously articulated and therefore observable factor in the policy process.

What are the conditions affecting the significance of the business confidence factor to policymakers? Social democratic governments are concerned about business confidence not for its own sake, but for the anticipated effects of a loss of business confidence on economic conditions and, in turn, on the public's confidence in the government. Routinely, business confidence is an important factor in the policy process. Nevertheless, in some circumstances, government officials may put other policy concerns ahead of policies that will contribute to their political support. Even if policymakers' primary concern is political support, they know that other factors beyond economic conditions, perhaps quality of life or ethical factors, contribute to public confidence. At any point in time policymakers will weigh the anticipated effect of business confidence against the other items on the political agenda that determine public confidence in their leadership.

While business confidence, through its anticipated effect on public confidence, creates substantial pressure on policymakers to choose one option over another, it is in a sense an intellectual pressure that is dependent on the way the economy is understood. Policymakers may ignore or reject the arguments of the business community, perhaps because they have reason to believe that there are alternative sources of investment, or because there are ways to limit business's investment options and to contain the impact of a fall in business confidence on economic conditions, or even because business's interpretation of the economic situation is erroneous. Policymakers themselves will try to shape the public's appreciation of economic conditions, attaching differing levels of attention and importance to the various signifiers of economic performance and so creating more room for maneuver.

Dennis Quinn and Robert Shapiro—while revealing some frustration with the structural power argument, they say looking for it "is much like using a water-witching stick to dowse a field for underground water" (1991, 868)—construct a test of this and other dimensions of business power. They claim that "structural dependence holds that who governs is irrelevant for business power" and argue that their finding that change in governing party (Democrats or Republicans) has important tax policy consequences is inconsistent with the implications of structural dependence (866). While damaging to the structural dependence argument as it is traditionally conceived, Quinn and Shapiro's finding does not necessarily undermine the importance of business confidence as a factor in government decision making. The conception of structural power tested was never that convincing on a conceptual, let alone empirical, level. Somehow governments were expected to divine the policy ingredients that would positively contribute to business confidence without consulting business. A more compelling account would conceive of the dimensions of business power complementing each other, not working exclusively. Business confidence is not a subterranean influence. It is part of the forensic content of business interest representation and the justification offered by governments, even those of the left, for their policies.

Analysis of the interest representation system often stops at the stage of counting political assets, such as campaign contributions or lobbyists employed. To a degree money talks, but policymakers also need arguments. They need to be able to justify the decisions they make. It is important, therefore, for interest representatives to offer reasons, as well as resources, to policymakers. As all interests try to find a way to project their special interest as a wider public interest in the effort to capture political attention, business representatives will try to put their demands in the context of the national economy by linking them to growth, competitiveness, employment, inflation, or the balance of payments. Further, in normal circumstances, government officials would want to know rather than guess the likely effect of their policies on business confidence, knowing the electoral consequences of variations in national economic performance. Therefore, it is artificial to try to separate "business confidence" from public confidence and business electoral and lobbying activities. The requirements of business confidence at any point are made known through these resources. The needs of business are not self-evident to government officials. They require articulating—by the Governor of the Bank of England, the Business Roundtable, or the CEO of RJR Nabisco. Conceived in this way, business confidence becomes a potentially visible rather than invisible factor in decision making.

We have reason to believe that business confidence is an important factor in policy-making, both from what we know of the significance of political decisions to business and from what we know of voting behavior. How then to add the more direct evidence? It is not enough to examine policy outcomes and attribute business successes to the business confidence factor. But we can examine politicians' explanations of the decisions they have taken. Case selection is always a tricky issue, at least to the degree one wants to move beyond the case evidence to speak more generally about relationships. For our purposes political party remains the most interesting factor and social democratic policy-making the more interesting case. Examining the decision-making process under conservative or more probusiness governments would be less telling, since for ideological reasons alone one would expect a high level of responsiveness to business demands.

The Wilson and Callaghan governments of the late 1970s are certainly worthy of analysis. But their efforts to incorporate the unions in an anti-inflationary strategy and their reliance on the International Monetary Fund are relatively well-known, and their difficult parliamentary situation, ultimately having to depend on the Liberal party, makes it possible to argue that they were restrained by political as much as economic factors in pursuing their policy agenda. For these reasons Harold Wilson's first two terms are a better choice. His narrow victory in 1964 ended thirteen years of Conservative governments. He had been a man of the Labour Left during the years in opposition; he even resigned from Attlee's government over the introduction of prescription charges. Winning another election in 1966, and improving the overall Labour majority in the House of Commons from four to ninety-seven, the Labour government had, in total, almost six years in which to enjoy the uncompromised power that the British political system usually supplies.

It started promisingly: only Harold Wilson's hand on the helm, no coalition partners to placate, and no hostile legislature to manipulate. But the log is disappointing. It records an unheroic voyage through well-charted waters, a perpetual fear of adverse economic currents permitting little more than a glimpse of fresh political territory. The odd squall blowing in from abroad, Ian Smith's unilateral declaration of Rhodesian independence, De Gaulle's awkwardness, or Lyndon Johnson's invitation to join him in Vietnam relieves the Butskellite calm. These things happened to Wilson. He was not looking for excitement. He was preoccupied with his small parliamentary majority for the first two years and with the international competitiveness of British business for the whole period.

The prime minister paid close attention to two economic indicators: the balance of payments and inflation. In 1964, he inherited a large balance of payments deficit of £800 million. In addressing this problem he took the counsel of the City of London in the person of the Governor of the Bank of England and relied on encouraging export industries, cajoling and threatening the trade union movement, and reducing public expenditure. He explicitly rejected an alternative, the early devaluation of sterling, as a dangerous course that might send the wrong message to the financial world, that would not be supported by other countries, and that might spark worldwide economic chaos. Devaluation came in 1967, not, though, as a positive policy choice but as something "forced upon us" (Wilson 1971, 6). From looking at the Wilson years, what comes through, in part because of the political importance he placed on the balance of payments, is the importance not just of domestic business confidence, but in particular the confidence of financial institutions, the City over other sectors, and the confidence of foreign economic actors, public and private. Wilson's policies, reflecting business interests' success in curbing expenditures and identifying unions as part of the policy problem, represented orthodox choices based on orthodox economic priorities and analyses.

In his own words:

> Until we were in surplus it meant that every action we took had to be considered against a background of the confidence factor . . . It meant, and this is not only inhibiting but humiliating for any Government, that things we had decided to do, right in themselves—for example, an increase in old age pensions, even as late as 1969, when we were moving into a strong surplus—had to be timed in such a way as to minimise possible speculative consequences, and whenever possible to coincide with an occasion when some further confidence-winning factor in the monetary field was taking place. (Wilson 1971, 32–33)

> He [the Governor of the Bank of England] was regarded as the voice of the City . . . it was his duty . . . to represent to the Chancellor and

the Prime Minister the things that were being said abroad or in the City; to indicate to the Government the issues on which, in the City's view, it was necessary to win confidence if a disastrous haemorrhage were to be averted.

That was why we had to listen night after night to demands that there should be immediate cuts in Government expenditure, and particularly in those parts of Government expenditure which related to the social services. It was not long before we were being asked, almost at pistol-point, to cut back on expenditure . . . (34)

The economic package we were preparing was approved by Cabinet [July 1965], though there were some extremely tough and unhappy measures in it.

He [the Chancellor] announced that all starting dates for public expenditure, with the exception of industrial building, housing, school-building and hospitals, would be postponed for six months. . . . We announced the postponement of two major measures which had been in our election programme, the proposed income-related guaranteed pension . . . and our proposals for further reductions and removals of National Health charges. . . . At the same time, on the positive side, we announced improved Export Credit Guarantee Department help for medium-term exports and also some reductions in the cost of short-term credit for British exports.

It was a formidable package and was taken as such. Sterling began to pick up, though in the next week or two there were periods when we were doubtful whether confidence had been sufficiently re-established to ensure the security of the pound. (126–27)

What worried me [1967] was the speed with which the confidence factor in industry and in finance—above all international finance—had turned adverse specifically because of the Middle East. Our hard-won recovery in exports . . . was discounted because of our vulnerability to these overseas factors beyond our control. (415)[3]

In February 1966, Harold Wilson intervened in the railways dispute and in such a way as to improve Labour's prospects for the general election in March of that year and to approving comments from the conservative newspapers.

---

3. Sked and Cook say of this period, "Wilson attempted to blame the growing sterling crisis on the Arab-Israeli Six-Day War (although the pound began its slide three weeks before the conflict started)" (1984, 224).

It was most welcome news. The lines were cleared for the election. The Times in its leading article on that Saturday morning, 12th February, began: "All credit to Mr. Wilson for getting the railway strike called off without the payment of any further ransom money." (Wilson 1971, 211)

To the end of his term he wished to avoid inflationary deals with unions, improve productivity, and reduce strike activity, particularly unofficial strikes, with the aim of making British business more competitive. In his own account of those years, Wilson is anxious to put the record straight about his relationship with the unions, denying that "beer and sandwich parties at No. 10," followed by an inflationary hangover, were the order of the day. President Johnson is his witness:

> He [Johnson] was fascinated with our parliamentary problems and our relations with the unions. What really amazed him was that we had secured parliamentary approval and union "acquiescence" for an incomes policy that no democratic country had introduced even in wartime. (Wilson 1971, 264)

An important theme of Wilson's government was the need to reform trade union practices and the relationship between union leaders and members, a concern he shared with Conservative governments, though importantly Wilson's methods were exhortatory rather than legislative.

> I took the opportunity to make a major speech [to the Amalgamated Engineering Union] on productivity and income restraint. In particular I made an impassioned appeal for modernisation of trade union practices: "The sooner your rule book is consigned to the industrial museum, the more quickly the union will be geared to the challenge facing industry and the nation." (226)

Barbara Castle, Wilson's secretary of state for employment and productivity, published the government's proposals on industrial relations in *In Place of Strife* in January 1969. Wilson said, on introducing the legislation:

> The Bill . . . is an essential component of ensuring the economic success of the Government. It is on that economic success that the recovery of the nation, led by the Labour Government, depends. That is why I have to tell you that the passage of this Bill is essential to its continuance in office. (643)

The government used these proposals to prod the TUC into accepting responsibility for dealing with inter-union disputes and unofficial strikes.

Wilson coupled with an acute awareness of the importance of economic performance on the electorate's voting choices an overriding concern to put right Britain's economic problems by doing the conservative if not the right thing (cut expenditure, reform the unions, encourage exports, avoid devaluation). In January 1969 he reports that, "the economic signs were improving and with them came an improvement in the Government's political standing" (Wilson 1971, 605). At the end of the decade he failed to reconcile parliamentary popularity with his approach to the economy, but he came very close.

If there was a single measure of the government's success in managing the economy, it was the trade balance. This measure was not simply imposed on the Labour government, although the problem was a real one. In the 1964 election campaign Harold Wilson focused on the trade deficit in his criticism of Tory economic policies and selected it as the measure of his government's policies. In 1969 he was rewarded with a surplus of £387 million (Sked and Cook 1984, 243). In the 1970 election campaign Labour led in the opinion polls, but there was a gap of a few days between the last polls and the election. It seems likely that this was enough time for a late swing to the Conservatives, perhaps caused by the release of some unfavorable trade figures. Wilson suggests this explanation when he says "the effect of a bad set of trade figures published three days before polling day—and, ironically, since proved to be substantially wrong—must have caused some hesitation and doubt—momentarily, perhaps, but decisively" (Wilson 1971, foreword, 725). The May 1970 trade figures reported a visible trade deficit of £31 million. BOAC's purchase of two Jumbo jets accounted for some £24 million of this deficit, and underrecording errors account for much of the rest. Although the trade figures were inaccurate, done by the statisticians of the Board of Trade, in doing so these civil servants, and BOAC's two jumbo jets, engineered a nice political symmetry, a "hoist with his own petard" ending. The Conservative party won 46.3 percent of the vote over Labour's 43 percent, and an absolute majority of seats in the House of Commons.

Almost exactly eleven years later François Mitterrand led the Socialist party to victory in France. In May 1981 he won the presidency with 52 percent of the vote. A few weeks later the Socialist party won an absolute majority in the National Assembly. With seven years as president, five years before new legislative elections, and the sweeping macroeconomic, industrial, and social reforms contained in his *110 Propositions pour la France,* Mitterrand promised relief from the normal politics of the Gaullist

Republic. In its first year, his government's policies suggested a bold new course. These policies included increases in the minimum wage and social benefits, including pensions, reductions in the retirement age and the working week, the introduction of a fifth week of paid holiday, the creation of tens of thousands of public-sector jobs, the passage of a series of pro-union laws (Auroux laws), and, most spectacularly, the nationalization of a significant part of the French economy, including the steel, electronics, chemicals, aeronautics, and textiles industries, and thirty-six banks. The government financed these measures through borrowing and increasing taxes on employers and the rich. It could anticipate that these tax increases and the increased labor costs associated with their policies would harm business confidence and private-sector investment, but would compensate through public spending on investment in the nationalized industries and by increasing consumer demand.

Unexpected, however, was the rapidly deteriorating condition of France's relationship with the international economy, signaled by a loss of confidence in the franc. Unable to channel consumer demand toward domestic production and without adequate foreign demand for French goods, trade deficits, high interest rates abroad, and low business confidence and investment at home dashed Socialist hopes. Peter Hall comments that "the new industrial policies of the Socialists were all oriented to the longer term; in the short term their effects on business confidence were likely to be negative" (1987, 68). Soon Mitterrand faced Wilson's choice: deflation, financial orthodoxy, and encouraging domestic business, or early and dramatic devaluation. Prime Minister Pierre Mauroy and Finance Minister Jacques Delors took the Governor of the Bank of England's role and advised cuts in spending. Yet visiting Mitterrand after hours were the ministers for industry and social affairs, prime ministers to be Laurent Fabius and Pierre Bérégovoy, recommending socialism and devaluation: "Austerity is not compulsory; in order to fight unemployment, we must temporarily abandon the European monetary system and get growth moving again" (quoted in Nay 1987, 343). The president did not yield to his "evening visitors."

The franc did lose value, public spending was cut, and in June 1982 wages and prices were frozen. The government reduced taxes on business and adopted various other policies to restore business confidence. Austerity was designed to reduce the domestic inflation rate (about 12 percent) and

> to restore the profitability of industry . . . the government deliberately manipulated the costs of austerity in 1982–1984 so that they would be imposed on workers and consumers rather than the corporate sector. Business was to benefit from an increasing range of tax breaks. With

this step, the French Socialists recognized explicitly not only international economic constraints but also the domestic constraints of the mixed economy. If business was not to be nationalized entirely, it had to be persuaded to invest . . . (Hall 1987, 57–58)

By 1986 austerity had brought inflation down and improved the trade balance, while increasing the numbers of jobless. His party losing the March 1986 legislative elections, President Mitterrand appointed the Gaullist Jacques Chirac to mop up what remained of his adventurous first year.

Although begun with gallic flourish, the French Socialist's story is quite similar to Wilson's first Labour government. Mitterrand and Wilson inherited trade deficits and the former a high inflation rate as well. Alerted by the weakness of their currencies, both governments, Mitterrand's more slowly than Wilson's, interpreted the weakness as a signal of the constraints that domestic and international business confidence place on redistributive social expenditures and Keynesian macroeconomic policy. Both governments had an alternative, devaluation, and both chose the more conservative course. Mitterrand and Wilson achieved their conservative priorities, a trade balance or surplus, only to have their governments lose elections.

Is the social democrat in power condemned, almost ancient mariner-like, to repeat the same story from country to country? The subtext of the story is not to keep one's nerve, ignore the representatives of business interests, devalue, and increase public spending when the bottom falls out of domestic and international business confidence, when the trade deficit rises, and the currency wobbles. Though neither Wilson nor Mitterrand cut a very heroic figure, it was not a failure of nerve, more a failure of economic theory. Before being able to resist the demands to restore business confidence, the social democrat needs to move beyond the ideas developed in the interwar period, Keynesianism in one country and the Popular Front in another. An equivalent process would be the way neoliberalism gave Thatcher the strength to defy the old wisdom (some of which business associations voiced to her) about currency rates, trade union power, and privatization in the British context. This theory brought with it a newly appropriate signifier of government policy success—inflation—and provided justification for the policies pursued. Ironically, then, in Thatcher's management of the economy coupled with her success in general elections, if not elections within her own party, lies a lesson for social democrats.

What is politically significant is the electorate's perception of economic performance. With the tools at their disposal, with much economic decision making in private hands, and with the importance of international economic factors, it is difficult for governments to exercise much short-term control over the economy. Personal experience and the information they receive about aggregate economic performance influence the electorate's perception. Lewis-Beck's analysis suggests that "collective economic prospective evaluations exercise, by themselves, a nontrivial impact on individual vote choice" (Lewis-Beck 1988, 66). To influence these expectations governments can, in addition to trying to manipulate the economy, manipulate the release of information about the economy and public priorities in the management of the economy. Tragically, Prime Minister Pierre Bérégovoy, his distorted account of French economic performance in the March 1993 French National Assembly election campaign subsequently exposed, committed suicide, perhaps because of resulting doubts about his integrity. What is most within the control of governments is the context within which the electorate interprets these signs and experiences. Governments can suggest what standard is the appropriate measure of their performance: Wilson and trade figures. They can claim or deny responsibility for aspects of economic performance: Thatcher and unemployment. Perhaps they can convince the electorate that they can "see the light at the end of the tunnel": former Chancellor Norman Lamont and his flashlight, as someone said.

Thatcher illustrates the room that incumbent governments have to maneuver. She illustrates that there are alternatives. Analyses of government survival in West European parliamentary democracies indicate that unemployment is an important factor (Robertson 1983; Warwick 1992). At the same time, and consistent with this argument for a conditional business confidence factor, a recent study by G. Bingham Powell Jr. and Guy D. Whitten presents cross-national evidence to show that political context, in particular the left or right-wing nature of the government, needs to be taken into account in understanding economic voting. Inflation hurts right-wing governments, and unemployment hurts left-wing governments (Powell and Whitten 1993). Earlier postwar Conservative prime ministers were, however, very concerned about unemployment. As Harold Macmillan put it in 1957: "When I am told by some people, some rather academic writers, that inflation can be cured or arrested only by returning to substantial or massive unemployment, I reject that utterly" (quoted in Walker 1977, 28). Yet under Thatcher the unemployment rate increased very sharply from 1979 to 1983. It rose from about 5 percent in 1979 to about 13 percent in 1983, when Thatcher prepared for her second general election without taking direct measures to address this problem.

As one scholar puts it "if there ever was a sure case of a government doomed by economic performance, the first Thatcher government should have been it" (Norpoth 1992, 2). How did she manage to limit the political damage of her miserable performance on this indicator? Although unemployment was the most important election issue, Prime Minister Thatcher's declared economic priority was inflation, not unemployment. For her first year in office the inflation rate rose to over 20 percent. Yet it had dropped to under 4 percent in 1983. Furthermore, her government manipulated the statistics on unemployment, changing the definition to reduce the numbers counted as unemployed. For example, the unemployment level in May 1992 was 9.6 percent, according to the government's count. Calculating the unemployed by the pre-1982 method yields a figure of 13 percent (*Labour Research* September 1992, 10) Between 1979 and 1993 the Conservative governments redefined unemployment thirty times; twenty-nine times to reduce the number counted as unemployed (*Economist* January 23, 1993, 58). Even with this manipulation, the unemployment figures were very bad for the 1983 election. Nonetheless Thatcher was able to reassure a sizable portion of the electorate that these figures were not the responsibility of the government. The monetarist economic theory of the Thatcher government suggested that unemployment was only indirectly under the control of policymakers and that inflation was the prime target for macroeconomic policy. The government argued that powerful trade unions increased the labor costs and, therefore, reduced demand for labor. The Conservatives could also shift responsibility from the government to the poor performance of the world economy. Meanwhile Conservative television broadcasts reminded viewers of the strike wave in the Labour government's final year and claimed that Labour governments had never reduced unemployment (Butler and Kavanagh 1984, 150).

The Labour party was ineffective in formulating the counterarguments. Explaining why the Conservative government "suffered so little from the rise in unemployment," Ivor Crewe says,

> the Labour party lacked credibility on the issue. . . . In the 1940s and 1950s the spread of Keynesian ideas and memories of the wartime economy persuaded voters that Labour's commitment to full employment was credible. In the 1980s, after a Labour government that had presided over a doubling of unemployment, Labour's reliance on old Keynesian nostrums was less plausible. (Crewe 1993, 13)

The Labour party, armed with old ideas of economic management, failed to raise the expectations of the electorate.

As monetarism regenerated Conservative economic policies in the 1980s, social democrats require a similar theoretical regeneration, designed for continental rather than national economies, that equips policymakers to take on relatively high rates of unemployment, and that stiffens their resolve in the face of the demands from business representatives and the Governor of the Bank of England. They require the sort of intellectual lift that "the general theory of employment" provided earlier governments. Braced in this way, social democrats might be able to show the indifference to the policy advice derived from orthodox economics that Thatcher showed to unemployment.

This direction for the argument is implied by treating business confidence and economic voting; that is what makes business confidence interesting to politicians, in a "poststructural" way, although it is nothing more adventurous than Keynes's familiar conclusion to the General Theory about practical men being slaves to defunct economists. The policies to improve or restore business confidence are not self-activating. Policymakers, who consider the policy demands of business interests within the framework of economic theory, chose these policies. It is not that policymakers imagine their own economic reality, windmills remain windmills. The claim is that the economic priorities and policies to cope with this reality are a function of economic theory, causing policymakers to ignore some aspects of economic performance and underline others. The aggregate demand function, Keynes argues, was neglected for a century as a consequence of the theoretical hegemony of Ricardian economics: "Ricardo conquered England as completely as the Holy Inquisition conquered Spain" (Keynes 1936, 32). Prime Minister Thatcher, rejecting Keynes' heretical views, and with the help of business-funded think tanks like the IEA, the CPS, and the ASI refocused policymakers and the electorates' attention on the free market and on unions' interference in that market pushing up the price of labor and causing unemployment.

So in democratic societies, where the power to make economic decisions is to a significant extent privately held, public policymakers will be particularly sensitive to the need to maintain business confidence. Social democratic parties generally experience a lower level of business confidence than conservative parties. At the same time their beliefs, traditions, and core constituencies represent a drag on the electoral tendency to drift into a deferential attitude toward business, and to that extent further encourage partisanship on the part of business. Interruptions to the routine of acceding to business demands in the policy process, when couched in terms of the anticipated wider effects on economic conditions and public confidence in the government, are likely to occur under two circumstances: first, when policymakers put other priorities ahead of the desire for political support; and, second, when policymakers discount business interests' impact on public support either against other factors affecting support or because they have reason to interpret economic performance differently.

CHAPTER 5

The Third Pillar of Business Power (I):
Business Political Finance

The political influence that derives from the incentive policymakers have in maintaining business confidence is complemented by the pressure business institutions and groups exert through participating in democratic procedures. Business interests bring influence to bear through direct financial involvement in the competition between political parties and through the lobbying process. Here the focus is on business financial contributions to parties and candidates for election, arguing that their common purpose and effect are to provide specific benefits for the contributor. In chapter 6, I examine the intertwined lobbying process.

Political systems leave their imprint on business political activities with the financial sums involved, the form that contributions take, and the type of special benefit sought by business people. It is generally the case that the more probusiness the party, the more well-financed it will be. In the United States for 1987–88, some 1,801 corporate PACs spent $89 million, trade associations and professional groups spent a further $82 million, and 301 labor PACs spent $74 million (Federal Election Commission 1989). For the same time period, at the national level the Republican party spent $251 million, and the Democratic party spent $110 million. In 1994, corporate PACs spent $116.9 million, trade associations spent $94.1 million, and labor PACs spent $88.2 million. In that year the Republican party spent $235 million, and the Democratic party spent $130 million (Stanley and Niemi 1995, 141, 164). For the United Kingdom, general expenditures for the 1987 election amounted to £9 million for the Conservatives and £4.7 million for Labour (Pinto-Duschinsky 1989, 206). For the 1992 campaign, party estimates suggest that Labour spending amounted to about 70 percent of Conservative spending (Butler and Kavanagh 1992, 260).

In many democracies the practice is to compensate for the electoral advantage that superior financial resources carry with them with the allocation and distribution of free media time to the competing parties and other public subsidies for election campaigns. In Germany political parties receive, in addition to media time, a reimbursement for each vote. Yet even in that country business political contributions have resulted in scandals like the Flick affair, which involved the company's effort to avoid taxes on the profits made from a sale of stock in Daimler-Benz, donations to political parties, and the resignation of a government minister, Count Lambsdorff, in the mid-1980s. The electoral impact of business wealth is probably largest in the United States and Japan, where media time and gift giving in the Japanese case make elections very expensive, and where the compensating mechanisms are insufficient.

The capacity of business interests to outspend others in the policy struggle is important to the third pillar of business power. But the argument cannot rest on such evidence alone. James Q. Wilson raises this point:

> The fallacy of the Lindblom view is well known to every student of politics: One cannot *assume* that the disproportionate possession of certain resources (money, organization, status) leads to the disproportionate exercise of political power. Everything depends on whether a resource can be converted into power, and at what rate and at what price. That, in turn, can only be learned by finding out who wins and who loses. (Wilson 1981, 37)

Wilson might concede that the superior resources of a political party or a candidate provide an almost automatic electoral advantage, perhaps with the qualification that in the American case research has suggested that such resources work more powerfully for a challenger than an incumbent. But what about his point that just because one establishes that business interests provide more money to politicians, it does not mean that policy made by those politicians will reward those business interests? Clearly he is correct to argue that it is an empirical question, and that one cannot assume such a sequence of events.

To begin with the aims of business interests, what other motivation could there be than the expectation of special benefits? First, not all firms give to politicians. For those that do, they could contribute out of a general political commitment, rather than in anticipation of a specific benefit. One might suppose that underlying the general commitment is an expectation to gain from the election victory of an ideologically sympathetic party. But such a reasoning chain would likely lead potential contributors to see the opportunity to free ride on the contributions of others and so enjoy the fruits of the election victory without their contributions. A general political commitment or an anticipation of a specific benefit is then a defensible simplification of the alternatives. If the former reason is the dominant one for business interests, the existence of a third pillar of business power becomes questionable. With business giving without anticipating a return, the pressures on policymakers are self-imposed.

By looking at the types of firms that contribute, to whom they contribute, and to an extent the auspices under which they contribute, we can make some progress on the problem of why business interests give politicians money. In the United States, corporations or industry associations cannot contribute directly to candidates for elections. They give money through the PACs that they establish. The names of some of the PACs may suggest that their motivation is a general rather than specific commitment. There is Abbott Laboratories' Better Government Fund, Amax Inc.'s Concerned Citizens Fund, American Cyanamid's Good Government Fund, Autozone Inc.'s Committee for Responsible Government, Brown-Forman's Non-Partisan Committee for Responsible Government, Loral Systems' Civic Action Fund, and General Motors' Civic Involvement Program. Yet the money from these organizations tends to flow to certain types of candidates who share, in addition to their dedication to good, better, and responsible government, membership of specific congressional committees, as well as incumbent status. For example, General Motors (including its defense industry subsidiaries) was one of the top twenty financial contributors to members of the Senate Budget Committee, the House Appropriations Committee, the Senate Armed Services Committee, and the House Armed Services Committee. General Motors gave 97 percent of its donations to incumbents in 1989–90 (Makinson 1992, 1273). Targeting members of the powerful committees that can make decisions affecting the contributor's industry is consistent with a strategy of seeking specific benefits from policymakers, rather than any larger political commitment.

When we consider what is at stake, not surprisingly the dominant motivation is specific benefits. How can business people ignore the resources and coercive powers of government? Subsidies, quotas, product standards, local content regulations, tariffs, taxes, or exchange rates have consequences, good or ill, for investors. These consequences create business involvement in politics and generate a variety of responses from businesses. Broadly, the amount of corporate political activity will follow the amount of economic activity and the degree of government involvement or expected government involvement in an industry. So business people are not equally fearful of regulation nor equally interested in government consumption of their products. The variation in their political activity reflects these differences.

Fortunately, a number of studies explore the linkages between these variables (Andres 1985; Boies 1989; Gopion 1984; Grier, Munger, and Roberts 1994; Humphries 1991; Masters and Keim 1985). Whether scholars define the dependent variable as simply the presence or absence of a PAC or as PAC dollars, their work suggests that corporate political activity depends on industry and market characteristics. A variety of hypotheses orient this empirical work including the application of the logic of collective action to the analysis of PAC activity. Firms, it is hypothesized, will form PACs in highly concentrated industries with few large firms, where free riding becomes conspicuous and where they can expect their political activity to make a difference. While the free-rider hypothesis is derived from established theory, it has been disappointing empirically. The use of concentration ratios, a measure of the market share of the largest firms in an industry, raises problems, and when used the results have not been encouraging. Gary Andres found this variable significantly related to the presence or absence of PACs, but only at the 0.1 level (1985). Masters and Keim find that the number of establishments in an industry, an alternative measure of concentration, is related to the presence or absence of PACs, and in the expected direction, but again only at the 0.1 level (1985). In the two more recent studies (Boies 1989; Humphries 1991),[1] these variables fail to achieve even this level of significance.

The resources available to a firm are expected to determine the degree of political involvement. As corporate PACs draw on employee contributions, the number of employees a firm has might be influential in the firm's decision to form a PAC and how much the PAC raises. Firm size, measured either as assets or sales, is often used as an indicator of resources. Firm size also reflects the political visibility of the firm. The larger the firm, the more power it is perceived to have and the more attention it attracts from government and other institutions and groups. Firm size has generally been found to be positively related to PAC formation and activity, whereas the findings for the number of employees are more mixed. The number of employees may be important at some minimum level, but most contributions likely come from management.

The relevance to a firm of government resources and coercive powers is plausibly connected to its political activity. Previous research has focused on regulation and consumption by government and generally suggests that both are significantly related to a firm's political activity. The achievements of this research in explaining this aspect of corporate political behavior remain relatively modest, yet the results are generally consistent with the specific benefits strategy. Those firms with more at stake are more politically active. With more precise, at best firm-level, measurement of these variables, and models that take into account countervailing polit-

---

1. But see also Grier, Munger, and Roberts 1994, who analyze PAC contributions aggregated by industry.

ical spending, the visibility of the corporation, the mobilizing activities of politicians, and control for differences in the ideological dispositions of senior management (see Mitchell, Hansen, and Jepsen 1996), we can expect to explain more of the variance in corporate political activity.

The way in which the money is allocated, as well as the amount spent, is pertinent to the discussion of why firms contribute to parties and candidates. If the motivation is specific benefits, contributions will tend go to incumbents since incumbents may be in a position to deliver benefits immediately and challengers are less likely to win. But if PACs back losers, like the seven incumbent Republicans who lost Senate seats in 1986, they can always donate to the victorious challengers right after the election (Smith 1988, 262). The money also will flow to those with policy specializations relevant to the contributing corporation. The literature on corporate PACs suggests that although there is a general preference for the more probusiness Republican party, the dominant contribution strategy is to give to likely winners, who are usually the incumbents.

Committee membership indicates the specific expertise and policy authority of members of Congress. Table 5.1 shows the top contributors to members of three House committees. From the congressional representative's point of view, committee assignments can make a significant difference to the ease of raising campaign money. In each case the top contributors are those with a direct stake in the committee's deliberations. The clustering of industry contributions on particular congressional committees is what one would expect if contributors have specific benefits in mind. If business executives think that campaign donations influence legislators' activities, then competing business interests must compete in this area too. If a corporation knows that its competitors are contributing, then it will too. This dynamic is vividly demonstrated in the defense industry and with defense industry contributions to the House Armed Services Committee. The stakes are high, given the singular importance of the government as a customer to this industry, and the competitors are relatively few. Sophisticated statistical analyses confirm the picture presented here. Thomas Romer and James M. Snyder Jr. examine the effect of a member's committee assignments and experience on PAC contributions (1994). They find that both changes in members' committee assignments and their seniority have a measurable impact on PAC contributions.

Whether or not the contributions result in benefits, the expectation of this result is sufficiently widespread that even subsidiaries of foreign firms cannot afford to ignore this type of political activity. Note the alarm over this issue, directed principally at the Japanese, that has led to efforts to prohibit PACs of U.S. affiliates of foreign companies. The concern is that foreign firms use political means to secure a competitive advantage. Pat

Choate, a Washington policy analyst and Perot's running mate in 1996, argues that Japanese corporations are heavily and very successfully involved in American politics (Choate 1990). While it is questionable that foreign firms are disproportionately active in American politics, there is evidence of a significant amount of political activity from this source.

Foreign direct investment (FDI) creates affiliates of foreign companies based in the United States. These affiliates can form PACs, so long as these are financed by U.S. citizens or resident aliens and run by U.S. citizens. Relatively comprehensive information on foreign PAC activity for the 1987–88 election cycle is available. The Federal Election Commission (FEC) collects data on corporate PAC activity but not ownership status. Roger Walke and David C. Huckerbee collected data on foreign PACs through a company name search of FEC indexes (1989). Some 7 percent of corporate PACs were formed by corporations wholly or partially owned by foreign corporations for the election cycle 1987–88. Foreign PACs contributed about $3.2 million, or 5.6 percent of total corporate PAC contributions in 1987–88. Foreign-owned PACs made a total of 3,635 financial contacts with federal election candidates in 1987–88. As expected from their leadership in FDI, British companies led all others with thirty-six PACs formed in 1988, up from twenty-four in 1986. Among them these PACs distributed about $988,656 in a total of 1,239 financial contributions to candidates in federal elections. Swiss and Canadian firms come next, spending over $500,000 in 1987–88. While Japan was second in FDI, Japanese firms' political spending put them in fourth place. In terms of U.S. affiliates of Japanese companies contributing to elections, Japan is

Table 5.1. Top Ten PAC Contributors to Members of House of Representatives Committees, 1989–90

	Committee		
Rank	Agriculture	Armed Services	Banking, Finance
1	Assoc. Milk Producers	AT&T	Nat. Assoc. Realtors
2	Mid-America Dairymen	McDonnell Douglas	American Bankers Assoc.
3	RJR Nabisco	Lockheed Corp.	JP Morgan & Co.
4	ACRE[a]	General Motors	Assoc. Home Builders
5	Am. Crystal Sugar Corp.	General Dynamics	Am. Inst. of CPAs
6	Am. Assoc. Crop Insurers	Raytheon	Barnett Banks of Fl
7	Nat. Cattlemen's Assoc.	Northrop	Nat. Assoc. Underwriters
8	Chicago Board of Tr.	Textron Inc.	Credit Union Nat. Assoc.
9	Philip Morris	Grumman Corp.	Citicorp
10	Food Marketing Inst.	Rockwell Intl.	Am. Co. of Life Ins.

Source: Makinson 1992, 130–37.
[a]Action Committee for Rural Electrification

not as politically active in the United States as popular reputation suggests.

If we assume that foreign firms' affiliates adapt to the host political system and target their activity toward specific benefits, it is to be expected that their allocation decisions will be similar to those of domestic PACs, and further that grouping foreign PACs by country will not significantly differentiate their PAC activity. Table 5.2 presents evidence to address these issues (see Mitchell 1995).

Examining the top part of table 5.2 we can compare directly the distribution of all corporate PAC money with the distribution of foreign corporate PAC money in the 1987–88 election cycle. Corporate PACs as a whole gave 80 percent of their contributions to incumbents and 53 percent of their contributions to Republicans (*Almanac of Federal PACs* 1990).[2] Foreign corporate PAC activity closely follows overall corporate PAC activity. Foreign corporate PACs gave 85 percent of their total contributions to incumbents. The concern with legitimacy, and not to be seen to be intervening in the politics of the host country, particularly recommends a

Table 5.2. Comparing the Distribution of Foreign Corporate PAC Money with All Corporate PACs and by Country of Parent Company

A. Distribution of All Corporate PAC Money and Foreign Corporate PAC Money in 1987–88 (by percentages)

	Incumbent	Challenger	Open	Republican	N
All Corporate PACs	80	7	13	53	1816
Foreign PACs	85	7	8	52	119

B. Distribution of Foreign PAC Money in 1987–88 by Country of Parent Company (by percentages)

Country	Incumbent	Republican	N
Canada	87	46	18
Germany	84	68	7
Japan	80	44	12
Netherlands	85	63	9
Switzerland	92	52	10
United Kingdom	85	54	36

Source: Federal Election Commission 1989; Almanac of Federal PACs 1990; Walke and Huckerbee 1989.

2. Note that this source has a slightly higher figure for the total number of corporate PACs than the FEC Report for 1987–88.

strategy of contributing to incumbents not challengers for foreign PACs. Republicans received 52 percent of foreign PAC contributions. This allocation pattern does not reflect the contribution strategies of the Japanese or British parent companies, where business political finance traditionally has been directed almost entirely to the Liberal Democrats in the Japanese case or the Conservative party in the British case. It suggests that foreign affiliates are interested in influencing Congress as it is, not as they might wish it to be. The bottom part of table 5.2 compares the percentages contributed to incumbents and Republicans, grouped by countries with more than five PACs. It reveals a strong orientation toward incumbents, whether the parent companies are Japanese, German, Dutch, or British. While there is more cross-national variability in the proportion of PAC contributions going to Republicans, the differences among the countries are still not very large, and none of the foreign PACs comes close to an exclusive focus on one party or the other, despite the practices of their parent companies. In allocating the money between parties, these foreign-owned firms are about as evenhanded as their domestically owned counterparts. They adapt to the local political economy, and they pursue a strategy aimed at securing special benefits.

Some analysts question whether the "revolutionary" 1994 midterm election represented an important shift in the pattern of corporate PAC allocations. Thomas Ferguson commented that "a sea of money that had for years been flowing reliably to Congressional Democrats . . . abruptly reversed direction and began gushing in torrents to Republican challengers" (1995, 359). But at least in overall terms not much evidence suggests a general shift in strategy. Corporate giving to incumbents declined from 1988 but only by a few percentage points to 76 percent of total corporate giving (for data on 1994 contributions see Stanley and Niemi 1995, 168–69). Republicans received about the same in 1994 as they had in 1988 with 51 percent of the total.

While the evidence on PAC contribution strategies in the United States seems relatively straightforward, the question of why British firms make financial donations to the Conservative party presents more of a challenge to the specific benefits hypothesis.[3] The link between any specific donation and election success or failure is more attenuated, and there are more effective ways of tying elected representatives to outside interests in the British political system.

This analysis of British business's financial participation in the com-

---

3. For this section I draw on an article coauthored with John G. Bretting (1993). The article contains more detailed statistical analysis, the results of which are only summarized here.

petition between the parties focuses on the 1980s. With some recent changes, notably the selection of Tony Blair as leader in 1994, the coming out of New Labour, and the effort to reform the conduct of Conservative MPs in the wake of Lord Nolan's committee, business political investment may seek new channels. There are signs of business interests seriously entertaining the possibility of a more bipartisan approach to British politics. The Pearson group, owner of the *Financial Times,* gave £25,000 to both the Conservative and Labour parties in 1994, and Tate and Lyle, the politically savvy sugar company, gave to the Conservatives, Labour, and the Liberal Democrats (*Labour Research* December 1995, 13). To the extent that the recent changes reduce the probability of deriving specific benefits from the investment, one would also expect a decrease in the level of investment, as measured, for example, by the amount of financial contributions and the retention of MPs as consultants.

Historically, business donations have gone almost exclusively to the Conservatives. Over 50 percent of Conservative party funds come from business donations, yet the "business thinking" behind donating is not obvious. An influential sociological theory (Useem 1984) explains these donations as examples of business activity that is "other-regarding," which is consonant with the notion of a general political commitment. However, solid evidence suggests a narrow rationality in the decision to donate, and that British business people, like their American counterparts, share an orientation toward specific benefits. Where they part company is on the nature of the benefit.

In chapter 4, I presented evidence to show that British firms differentiate between political parties by their policy expectations. Even so the rationality of a firm's financial contribution to a political party is not transparent. If corporate officials perceive a business advantage in a particular party's election victory, they would only contribute in the unlikely circumstance that they calculated the election would turn on their firm's individual contribution. Business thinking should result in the firm leaving to others the support of the Conservative party, secure in the knowledge that they could not be excluded from the improved business climate produced by a Conservative victory. There is a "free rider" incentive not to contribute. While some experimental research supports only a weak version of the free-rider hypothesis, this same research suggests that an individual's education and experience influence the propensity to behave as a free rider (see Marwell and Ames 1981). If any can be expected to free ride besides economists, it is those in the cockpit of narrowly defined utility maximization, business people. To the absence of tangible benefit is added the cost of the contribution itself, though generally a small item in the corporate budget, the risks of stockholder and employee opposition, and of creating gratuitous hostility should the other party win, as well as generating unwelcome publicity. It is clear that some business people are well aware of the potential danger in becoming involved directly in the competition between parties. To allay business executives' fears an organization called British United Industrialists was used as an indirect and more discreet way to make political donations to the Conservative party. Some firms also give to various Conservative party supporting organizations and think tanks like the Economic League, the CPS, and Aims of Industry.

In contrast to PAC contributions to candidates for election in the United States, business donations to political parties in the United Kingdom are not the most direct means of securing access and influence in the political effort to represent the firm's interests. "Under modern conditions" writes Pinto-Duschinsky, "companies, unions, and pressure groups wishing to purchase political influence frequently make payments—direct or indirect—to individual legislators who have already been elected to the House of Commons. Such payments can provide more leverage than contributions to a parliamentary campaign or to a party headquarters" (Pinto-Duschinsky 1981, 238–39). An analysis of the 1994 Register of MPs' Interests found that 82 percent of Conservative backbench MPs shared 276 company directorships and 356 business consultancies. Former ministers are similarly engaged, with the very active David Mellor, MP for Putney, a consultant for twelve companies, four of which are defense manufacturers (*Labour Research* January 1995, 9). The activities of elected representatives on behalf of business interests, notoriously asking questions in the House of Commons on behalf of the owner of Harrods, led in 1994 to the prime minister appointing a senior judge, Lord Nolan, to head a committee to investigate "standards in public life." The outcome was a series of House of Commons votes in November 1995 to end "paid advocacy" (such as putting questions to ministers), to require MPs to disclose their earnings from outside interests, and to appoint a Parliamentary Commissioner for Standards.

The issue of company donations to the Conservative party, an issue that the Nolan committee has avoided to this point, became more sensitive with the Trade Union Act of 1984. This act required trade unions to ballot their membership on union contributions to the Labour party. Current Labour party proposals indicate that a Labour government would introduce legislation requiring shareholder approval for company political donations. British and Commonwealth Holdings, which gave £137,000 to the Conservative party in 1987 and £90,000 in 1988, and which has taken the unusual step of consulting shareholders, had to weather some criticism from that source. In the end the company gave nothing in 1989, and it ceased trading in June 1990.

A further contrast with the trade unions contributing to the Labour party is that the unions have had a very important role in party leadership selection and the annual conference, whereas company donations do not provide corresponding influence in the Conservative party (Pinto-Duschinsky 1981, 238.). So institutional interests would suggest noninvolvement in political campaigns for most firms in the United Kingdom, since elections are unlikely to turn on an individual contribution, there are more direct means of influencing policy, and there are some serious potential costs. The fact that about a third of large industrial firms did contribute to the Conservative party in the 1980s is puzzling.

Industrial category may help to differentiate between those firms that donate and those that do not. The food, drink, tobacco, and construction industries have long ties with the Conservative party (Grant 1993, 143). Second, foreign-ownership status may influence firms' political activity. While the evidence on PACs of United States' affiliates of foreign corporations was not conclusive since only firms that had PACs were examined, the literature on political donations in the United Kingdom provides some support for the expectation that firms may be concerned about the perception of politically intervening in the internal politics of the host country and thus are more cautious politically. Pinto-Duschinsky in his study of British political finance says a "particular feature is the absence of political payments by the British branches of multinational corporations" (Pinto-Duschinsky 1981, 232). Finally, in terms of market characteristics, firm size may be important. As with PAC contributions, firm size is an indication of the ability of the firm to give and of its visibility. The more visible the firm, the more likely it is to be targeted by politicians and political parties. To this point, analysis of both corporate financial contributions in the United States and the United Kingdom has focused on the characteristics associated with the firm or the industry that produces this sort of political activity. Neglected in these analyses have been the efforts of candidates and parties to mobilize support and encourage this activity.

Institutional characteristics of the firm may differentiate the donating firms from the rest. Focusing on financial contributors to political parties, sociologists point to the social networks, interlocking directorates for example, in which corporate officials participate. For Michael Useem it is the extent of corporate interconnectedness, what he calls "the inner circle," that is an important factor in donations to political parties in both the United States and Britain. He says, "The election of probusiness candidates and the success of the Conservative and Republican parties can be a windfall for all large companies. . . . The free-rider disincentive will thus discourage contributions by firms narrowly fixed on their own welfare" (1984, 132). Useem argues that the collective interests of capitalists as a group motivate the inner circle member. The more connected you are to the inner circle, which according to Useem is the key attribute of "institutional capitalism" that has recently replaced "managerial capitalism," the more likely you are to act on the basis of "class-wide" interests, and less on free-rider calculations, and the more likely you are to give to political parties. Contributing to probusiness parties or candidates will produce a better political climate—a benefit from which the noncontributor cannot be excluded: "Consequently, companies with managements attached to the transcorporate network and its overarching political interests are more often found at the forefront of political contributors than firms whose management is less broadminded" (Useem 1984, 132). To these broadminded firms Useem adds some of the narrow-minded: that is, those "corporations especially affected by government decisions. . . . In the United Kingdom, companies most fearful of nationalization by a Labour government, such as large insurers, are among the most generous supporters of the Conservative Party" (132). Although presumably for these narrowminded exceptions, dependent on specific party programs, their contributions will have to be large enough to be expected to make a real political difference.

While Useem places business political contributions in the United States and the United Kingdom in the same category, there are a number of important differences. In the United States campaign finance laws, passed in the 1970s, permit PACs to contribute up to $5,000 to federal election candidates, with no limit on the total number of candidates' they may contribute to, and require that PACs register with, and disclose their activities to, the FEC. Corporations can support the formation and administration of their PACs directly, but they must raise the money they contribute to candidates from voluntary contributions from employees, management, and stockholders. By no means all large American firms have PACs, but there is a larger proportion of these activists in the United States, between 50 and 60 percent of the Fortune 500, than in the United Kingdom.

Some important differences between the political systems are responsible for the greater number of corporate political contributors in the United States than in the United Kingdom. Financial contributions in the United Kingdom are a declaration of partisanship in a way that PAC contributions are not. The individualized, decentralized, and more money-driven style of campaigns in the United States create more opportunities for business involvement and less risk of alienating a whole party, than do the centralized, party-oriented campaigns in the United Kingdom. The traditional weakness of American parties makes U.S. legislators much more open to alternative sources of influence on their activities as representatives. In contrast to their British counterparts, American corporations commonly contribute to candidates from both major political parties, and, as we have seen, incumbency rather than party affiliation is an important criterion for contributions. Because political parties are less disciplined in the United States, and Congress has more capacity to influence public policy than the House of Commons, PAC contributions carry, at least potentially, more influence on policy than contributions to parties in the United Kingdom.

Empirical analysis based on U.S. data alone has provided only mixed support for the inner-circle thesis (see Burris 1987; Clawson and Neustadtl 1989). The "inner circle" may represent too complicated a theory, resting on too "economic" a view of the ways in which narrow-mindedness can express itself. Given these empirical and theoretical doubts, it is reasonable to explore an alternative explanation for business political contributions in the United Kingdom.

Specific benefits have a socially as well as economically defined component, and while Useem is right in arguing that donations generally will not produce a tangible benefit to the particular firm, they may well produce a social benefit to the particular firm's management. In order to improve their chances of receiving an honorary title, a company's senior management may decide to make a donation to the Conservative party. Seeking titles may sound a frivolous pursuit for a successful business person, yet it may ease entry into new influential political and economic positions in the British context. Britain has a lengthy history of honoring industrialists, such as Trollope's Roger Scatherd, who rose from drunken stonemason to railway magnate and on up to knighthood. Even at the inception of capitalism the "covetousness of great riches, and ambition of great honors" and the "perpetual and restless desire of power after power, that ceaseth only in death," was observed by Thomas Hobbes. Coincidentally, one study actually dates the "sale of honours" as really beginning with the Stuarts (Walker 1986, 31). The most notorious modern example is Lloyd George's use of honors to increase contributions to the Liberal party, but one could go back to "Lord Linoleum" of Gladstone's time (Pinto-Dushinsky 1981, 34). More recently, it was the Labour Prime Minister Harold Wilson's resignation honors list of 1976 that provoked public outcry with the inclusion of "financiers or entertainment tycoons whose contributions to national politics were not always immediately apparent" (Sked and Cook 1984, 309).

Under the honors process civil servants present lists of possible names to the prime minister, before the names are forwarded to the monarch for approval. From the political party's perspective, the logic of collective action would suggest using honors as a selective incentive, an organizational response to the difficulty of raising money—though, following Lloyd George, legal considerations inhibit too open or automatic an exchange of honors for donations and thus suggest some discrimination in the use of this selective incentive. Pinto-Duschinsky notes a decline in business contributions to the Conservatives of 24 percent from the 1950s to the late 1970s and a continuing decline in these contributions in the 1980s (1981, 153; 1989, 209), which presumably adds to the Conservative party's organizational interest in finding additional incentives to encourage business contributions.

Useem rightly, then, sees the significance of Mancur Olson's work (1971) in identifying the problem and framing a solution, but he does not focus on the most relevant parts. Corporate officials are not shouldering a collective responsibility. They are anticipating a selective incentive that the party can provide. But what evidence is there that business people expect to improve the chance of their receiving honors by contributing to the Conservatives, and that the Conservative party under Thatcher used honors as a selective incentive for contributing? In James Q. Wilson's terms, how do these contributions exchange for benefits? Documentary evidence, like the letters from Liberal whips in the Gladstone Papers, is too much to hope for, and interview evidence from the contributors is unlikely to be very revealing, given the illegality of exchanging honors for financial contributions. As Hedrick Smith, in addressing the question of what PAC contributions buy, ruefully remarks, "Most politicians handle the entire question with kid gloves. Very few will discuss it candidly for direct quotation, unless they are retired or about to retire" (1988, 257). While not being able to measure the expectation of honors directly, it is possible to examine whether in practice a general pattern of honors accompanies donations—a pattern that would support this explanation. Are those industrialists on the honors lists also those who tend to contribute to the Conservative party? Although not as conclusive as documentary evidence on the contributors' motivations, this approach is similar to the way in which social scientists have had to examine the reasons for PAC contributions and the sensitive issue of selling access and legislative influence.

Analyzing donations given to the Conservative party by any of the largest 500 British companies and knighthoods and peerages received by officials of any of these companies between 1980 and December 1990 reveals that while most firms do not have senior executives receiving honors, the proportion of honors recipients was substantially higher for firms that donated to the Conservative party than for nondonating firms (see Mitchell and Bretting 1993). Only 14 percent of the nondonating firms had officials who received honors, compared to 36 percent of the donating firms.

There are alternative explanations for being honored, which also might account for the link with donations. It is plausible that industrialists with outstanding service get honored for this service. Some of these industrialists may tend to encourage their companies to be politically active and donate to the Conservative party. Broad civic consciousness is the underlying reason for being honored. Thus if those companies whose officials can attribute their honors to their outstanding public service are controlled for, the relationship between donations and honors should disappear. In addition, there are other factors, such as foreign or domestic ownership, industry, and firm size, influencing company donations to the Conservative party. It is also likely that some of these factors influence honors. For example, with firm size, the very largest firms generally do not financially contribute to the Conservatives. For top executives in these firms, especially the top ten firms, knighthoods are almost automatic. Consistent with the selective incentive hypothesis, these very large firms tend not to make financial donations to the Conservative party. Even Sir John Harvey-Jones, former head of Imperial Chemical Industries (size rank 5 in 1987–88), did not destroy his chances for honor, only delayed his knighthood, by publicly criticizing the Thatcher government's economic policies. Yet even when public and charitable service, foreign ownership, and firm size are controlled for, the relationship between donations and honors remains. Although the expected utility, social status or lobbying advantage, differs, in both the United Kingdom and the United States company political contributions can be conceived as, at least in part, narrowly "rational," calculated to deliver specific benefits and not, then, so much a free-rider puzzle.

Some evidence indicates that business executives' desire for social status is not a peculiarly British phenomenon. It is present in the United States, though with different titles. A contribution made to political parties, "soft money," is not covered by the same limitations and disclosure rules that apply to campaign contributions. Both individuals and corporations donate large amounts, often over $100,000, in this way. Large contributors and fund-raisers for the successful party, often in a more open way than their British counterparts, might well expect an ambassadorship to a foreign country, rather than a seat in the House of Lords.

With respect to British firms' contributions to political parties, the evidence suggests that this money converts into status rather than power. PAC contributions in the United States, in a more direct way, are about power. Do they work? Elizabeth Drew recounts the 1980 election of Charles Grassley, Republican senator for Iowa, who defeated the incumbent senator, John Culver, with the help of substantial contributions from oil and chemical companies. Culver was being punished for supporting a bill requiring these companies to clean up toxic waste through superfund contributions. And she quotes a lobbyist, "when issues are not issues of conscience—and most of them are not—and their district or state doesn't have a clear interest, if you raise enough money you can keep them from doing anything" (Drew 1983, 21, 89). Another close observer of Washington D.C. remarks that "most lobbyists and legislators are smart enough to use language vague enough to deny illegal vote buying," and quotes a lobbyist, "you never talk about political money in the same conversation as you discuss a legislative issue" (Smith 1988, 256). This type of evidence encourages interest in addressing the problem in a more systematic way.

Earlier analyses of the relationship between the distribution of PAC money or lobbying efforts and congressional voting patterns produced mixed results (Frendreis and Waterman 1985; Grenzke 1989). Yet more recently analyses that use a wider definition of the dependent variable, not just committee or floor votes, are confirming the political importance of financial contributions. Ease of measurement is one of the attractions of using congressional voting to operationalize political power, but it is merely one dimension of representatives' activities that PACs are interested in influencing. Because it is the most highly visible of the representatives' activities, because they have a voting "record" and therefore a desire to be consistent, and because representatives must be highly sensitive to any suggestion that their votes are for sale, voting is the most difficult dimension to directly influence (Hall and Wayman 1990; Snyder 1992, 16). As far as it is used to measure influence, voting, then, constitutes the stiffest test for the analysis of the impact of PAC money. Prior to the vote, PACs will focus on encouraging those who may well be already favorably disposed to their political interest to commit time, staff, and effort to see that interest prevail. They may also give to those who will likely oppose their policy position in an effort to reduce the intensity of opposition. Instead of voting records, Richard L. Hall and Frank W. Wayman measured legislators' participation on three issues on the basis of interviews with congressional staffers and the committee and subcommittee markup records (1990). Analyzing members' participation on the 1982 Dairy Stabilization Act, the 1982 Job Training Partnership Act, and the 1984 Natural Gas Market Policy Act, they found that contributions were influential. Hall and Wayman investigated both the mobilization and demobilization effects of PAC contributions, finding that money has more impact in encouraging the participation of those already likely to support the contributor's position than it has in discouraging the participation of those likely to oppose it (1990, 814).

Corporate PACs will at times desire representatives' intervention in their corporation's interactions with federal bureaucrats, usually a much less public but nevertheless very important concern for corporations. Further, in focusing on a single vote, analysts might misinterpret the strategy and influence of those PACs that take the long view in their effort to cultivate friends in Congress (Snyder 1992). In 1991 the Senate Banking Committee faced a difficult issue, whether banks should sell insurance in other states, that pitted two generous contributors against each other. For the 1986, 1988, and 1990 election cycles banking, insurance, and securities PACs distributed over $12 million among the members of the House and Senate Banking Committees and the House Energy and Commerce Committee. Members of the Senate committee had received about $1.6 million from commercial banks and about $1.5 million from the insurance industry. The contribution patterns, "show how industries develop long-term relationships with the panels with which they do business most often" (Alston 1991, 2315). Alternatively, analysts have studied a specific policy area, for example, tax policy, and found changes in business taxation to be related to the political success or failure of the probusiness party and to PAC activity (Quinn and Shapiro 1991). When influence is defined and measured in these more sophisticated ways, analyses tend to confirm what the intuition that business would not continue to contribute if it were not getting something in return suggests, that PAC money does indeed convert into power.

One finds the most compelling evidence of the conversion of money to power in the direct corruption of public officials, the informal polity. Despite their considerable advantages in the representational process, corporations seek to corrupt public officials. The costs are potentially so high that the aim is invariably to provide an individual firm with an exclusive benefit. Firms in the defense industry, relying as they do on government orders, are likely to be important players in the informal polity.

No political or corporate culture is completely resistant to this type of corruption. Swedish business's international reputation was built on safe cars for the middle classes and on financially encouraging good intellectual and moral behavior from the rest of the world. Yet Nobel and Volvo now keep company with Bofors who, with their efforts to secure an arms contract, can claim a role in bringing down a dynasty in the world's most populous democracy. With Rajiv Gandhi as prime minister, high Indian government officials received millions of dollars in bribes from Bofors in that firm's attempt to sell howitzers to the Indian army.

The defense industry in the United States has recently been associated with domestic corruption. Bendix, Boeing, Grumman, IBM, Loral Corporation, Martin Marietta, Raytheon, RCA, Rockwell, United Technologies, and Unisys have all been implicated in various efforts to gain illegal advantages in the effort to secure the Pentagon's business. Defense contractors hired consultants, often former employees of the Defense Department, including one former assistant secretary of the Navy, to obtain classified information on Pentagon budgets and rival bids. Exposure of this corruption has resulted in prison terms and substantial criminal and civil fines for some of these corporations. It is difficult to dismiss this behavior as aberrant, given the number of "blue chips" implicated. Irrespective of the integrity of the individual business person or the values of the specific corporate culture, if one's competitors are cheating, an individual firm can refuse to do so only at great cost. The moral quandary for the corporate executive tempted by inside information is a little like the choice facing the athlete who is tempted by steroids. Both executive and athlete operate in an uncertain world with imperfect information on what competitors are doing to enhance their performance. Resisting temptation when competitors yield means they are likely to lose the competition. This sort of corruption is firm initiated, but contagious, and is therefore often an industrywide problem. Both the athlete and the executive need to be confident that their competitors are not cheating. The solution is in urine tests, frequently and externally administered.

Another recent American example of business corruption is the notorious case involving the Lincoln Savings and Loan Association, five U.S. senators, and over $1 million in campaign contributions. Charles B. Keating Jr. gave substantial amounts to four Democrats and one Republican to secure their help in his interaction with federal regulators. Senators Alan Cranston, Dennis DeConcini, John Glenn, John McCain, and Donald Riegle Jr. received money, and in Republican John McCain's case Bahamian holidays, in exchange for their help in delaying the seizure of Lincoln Savings and Loan. They interceded for Keating in meetings with officials from the Federal Home Loan Bank Board. A Senate Ethics Committee investigation of their activities on behalf of Keating resulted in little more than some public embarrassment to the senators—the leniency of their colleagues suggesting that this sort of activity in exchange for contributions is not so unusual. The senators defended their activity as constituency service, and Alan Cranston spread the blame: "How many of you . . . could rise and declare you've never, ever helped—or agreed to help—a contributor close in time to the solicitation or receipt of a contribution? I don't believe any of you could say never" (quoted in de Leon 193, 158). As Dennis F. Thompson points out, it is the connection between the contributions and the politicians' intervention that is corrupt, rather than the contributions or interventions in themselves. The Keating Five case is an example of what Thompson calls mediated corruption: "the use of public office for private purposes in a manner that subverts the democratic process" (Thompson 1993, 369). This case provides a nice example of what is missed if analysts define congressional representatives' usefulness to business interests by their votes alone. It is as good an example as one is likely to get of how both contributors and representatives view the exchange for contributions in much more positive terms than simply "access."

Italian businesses paid billions of dollars in bribes and contributions to Italian politicians and political parties to secure public contracts. The "clean hands" investigation has implicated the country's political parties, particularly the Christian Democrats and the Socialists, top politicians including former prime ministers, and the country's leading corporations, including Fiat. Among rich representative democracies, only Japan can rival this level of corruption. The wealth of Japanese business and the Liberal Democrats' grip on power were the important contributors to the corruption. Leading Liberal Democrat politicians in Japan received cut-price shares from the Recruit Company. The ensuing scandal led to the resignation of Prime Minister Noboru Takeshita and the Socialists winning the 1989 upper house election.

In both Japan and Italy political power in the postwar period has not alternated between political parties. It has been restricted to one party or a generally stable coalition of parties. As Lord Acton suggested with his aphorism about power and corruption, such monopolies of political power encourage bribery—party officials can exploit their position without fear of losing political power to a competitor. Business people who are dependent on the public sector, even at the local level, may face a situation in which they may feel they have little alternative but to give in to the extortionate demands of politicians.

Direct business corruption most immediately damages other firms, taxpayers, and the democratic integrity of public officials and the political system. There is a general incentive for corruption, given the importance of government decisions for business, but some political systems may be more susceptible to business corruption than others. The variation across political systems is important as a guide to which systems are most successful in controlling this behavior and thus for any attempt at political reform. Among democracies, a dominant political party and expensive campaigns, which increase politicians demand for money, are the most obvious factors that would favor corruption. However, not even generous public subsidies for political parties can immunize a system. Despite the per vote system of remuneration political parties enjoy in Germany, the Friedrich Flick Group contributed money to three political parties, most of it going to the Christian Democrats, in exchange for help in avoiding taxes. Japanese parties receive funds based on seats in the legislature, traditionally favoring the Liberal Democratic Party (LDP), and even Italian parties received public funds from 1974 until 1993. Public subsidies to political parties and politicians and restrictions on campaign spending are probably as easily justified on grounds of electoral fairness as a defense against corruption.

This evidence on business's financial involvement in politics puts the third pillar of business power in sharper relief. It suggests that business interests' pursue a strategy of donation aimed at various but quite specific benefits, and that with this strategy resources are converted into power or status. James Q. Wilson's second question, the rate of exchange, is not one that has been addressed with much precision. While he frames it in a simple way, who wins and who loses, it is a very difficult question. To be sure, success in the pursuit of honors is an all or nothing thing. A captain of industry does or does not become a knight of the realm. Few political processes have quite such unambiguous outcomes, and the participants know this. They will not expect total victory.

While underscoring the advantages of business interests in the policy struggle, this discussion of business financial involvement in politics also hints at a direction for the search for the conditions of business failure. We should not expect business interests to be outspent. The limit to this type of power is not financial. It must lie in the politician's susceptibility to financial incentives. This susceptibility is driven by the content and visibility of the particular issue in the policy struggle. Some issues, issues where their conscience is on display, carry politicians out of the reach of financial influences and perhaps out of the reach of the other resources business interests bring to the system of interest representation.

CHAPTER 6

The Third Pillar of Business Power (II): Associations, Interest Representation, and the Descent from Heaven

Business financial support for probusiness parties and candidates is one dimension of business political participation. Business interests, either individually or collectively, also participate directly in the policy struggle. Business associations and corporations resort to a variety of methods to influence politics. In this chapter I use a mix of evidence, including data from published sources on lobbying activities in the United States, survey data, and information from particular policy cases, to assess the political importance of business associations and the political self-reliance of corporations in directly representing their interests in the political process.

There are three major routes for business interest representation. Firms may represent their interests directly to government, or they may have their interests channeled through either an industry-level trade association or through a national businesswide association. The political importance of business associations varies across political systems. It is worth exploring this variation and the implications for business political influence before considering the significant amount of political activity originating directly from corporations. The argument is that no straightforward connection exists between the political power of business and the political importance (cohesion and inclusiveness) of the leading business federation. In some respects institutions such as corporations actually have representational advantages over membership groups and federations in the policy struggle. In addition to internal pressure from within the business community, the position of a business association is dependent on other elements in the political system, principally labor and government, and its power can only be assessed in its relation to these other elements. To illustrate how some of the major elements of business political activity fit together, and to return again to James Q. Wilson's troublesome question about the conversion of resources to power, I finish the discussion of the third pillar of business power by describing a particular case of a business interest successfully influencing the policy struggle.

In Britain the most inclusive business association is the Confederation of British Industry (CBI), although the Institute of Directors can claim to speak for a significant segment of the business community. Social scientists have credited the CBI with considerable authority and describe a relatively centralized system of business representation, at least when the point of comparison is the United States. David Vogel writes: "America continues to differ from other capitalist nations, not only in the resources companies devote to affecting public policy, but also in the decentralized nature of that participation" (Vogel 1987, 111). Michael Useem says that "no single American organization can claim the near monopoly over expression of the business viewpoint that the Confederation of British Industry has come to command" (Useem 1984, 71). When one's comparison is with business organizations in other European countries, the role of the CBI seems more modest. An analysis of business representation in seven countries concluded that, "in the Anglo-American democracies where comprehensive business associations tend to be poorly integrated and in competition with one another, individual, very powerful business persons often enjoy informal and frequent access to key policymakers" (Coleman and Grant 1988, 484). Wyn Grant argues that in Britain "business remains politically weak," in part because of the failure of the CBI "to get business leaders to think strategically in political terms" (Grant 1993, 18–19). In comparison to continental associations, the CBI is weak, but it is important to distinguish the political power of business interests, in the sense of being able to achieve their goals in the policy struggle, from that of their peak association.

Among the major industrial countries, the United States has the least authoritative businesswide associations. Three associations can lay claim to speak for American business. The National Association of Manufacturers, formed in 1895, represents mostly small manufacturing firms. The Chamber of Commerce of the United States, established in 1912, has the largest membership, the largest staff, and is the most encompassing of the three associations. The Business Roundtable, formed in 1972, represents the views of large corporations. Its membership is more exclusive than the other associations, composed as it is of the top executives from 200 large corporations. The contrast with Austria, Sweden, or Germany is stark.

In Austria, all firms are members of the Federal Economic Chamber. With Austria's "neocorporatist" political system, this business association plays an important role in economic policy-making and a central role in the business community. "Austria's business community relies," says Peter Katzenstein, "probably more than the business community of any other advanced industrial state, on the services and political contacts provided by its peak association" (1984, 138). In Sweden, the Swedish Employers'

Association (SAF) represents thirty-five industry associations and 45,000 firms (*Europa Yearbook* 1992). Formed in 1902, four years after the Swedish trade union confederation, the SAF has a historically important role in the development of industrial relations and economic and social policy in Sweden. In Germany, the most important national business association is the Federation of German Industries (BDI), which represents the views of thirty-nine industry associations on economic policy. These industry associations in turn organize approximately 90 percent of western German industry. Two other business associations operate at the national level, the Confederation of German Employers' Associations, which focuses on social and labor issues, and the Association of German Chambers of Industry and Commerce (DIHT), membership in which is compulsory for businesses, and which deals with commercial issues and the interests of small business. This substantive specialization produces generally harmonious relationships between the associations (Dalton 1993, 246; Conradt 1993, 101).

It is reasonable to expect that the greater the centralization and inclusiveness of business associations, the more the government is interested in negotiating with them. A cross-national comparison of these associations in terms of their access to government and depth of policy involvement provides support for this expectation (Coleman and Grant 1988). It is, however, quite different to equate the political importance of these associations with the political strength of business. The fact that we find these associations strongest in social democratic or "social market" systems should make one wary of such an equation.

In explaining the differences in the strength and cohesion of business organizations, in keeping with my general approach in this book that to understand business one has to understand antibusiness, and as part of the argument that the strength of national business associations is not the same as the political strength of business, the contention is that one important determinant is the relative strength and cohesion of national union organizations (see also Windmuller 1984). In support of this claim, one could note that the apex of CBI authority was the social contract years of the mid- to late 1970s—also the apex of union power in Britain, whether measured by union density or union access to policy-making circles. The cohesion of business representation is, then, a defensive reaction to labor cohesion. If the union confederations weaken, we can expect national business associations to weaken as well.

As a crude test of the organization-is-counterorganization hypothesis, we have enough information to rank these organizations by their degree of unity and inclusiveness for a small number of countries. In an effort to increase objectivity, I rely on other scholars' rankings as far as possible. The business centralization rankings draw mainly on Coleman and Grant's (1988) analysis of business associations in Austria, Canada, Germany, Italy, Sweden, Switzerland, and the United Kingdom. In order to measure union cohesion, David Cameron's organizational unity of labor score is used (1984).[1] Table 6.1 shows the rankings for those countries for which there is data on both business and labor associations. Unfortunately, these rankings include neither the French nor the Japanese business confederations. More systematic evidence for this relationship requires more precise comparative measures of the degree of unity of the national organizations of business and labor and information on more countries. Austria achieves the highest ranking on both business and union cohesion, and the United States the lowest on business cohesion and next to lowest on union cohesion. Overall, the fit between the two sets of rankings shown in table 6.1 appears quite good, with Italy as the most obvious anomaly.

Also critical for the hypothesis is the timing of the organization of labor and business. If business organization is a defensive reaction to labor organization it is expected that, at whatever level of cohesion, labor organization precedes business organization. Complicating this test are the historical changes experienced by different organizations representing business and labor, as well as the institutional discontinuity forced by World War II on some countries. In Germany, for example, both trade unions and employer organizations date back to the nineteenth century. Lending support to the hypothesis, Ronald Bunn says "circumstances leading to the formation of the early German employers associations are to be found in the latter half of the nineteenth century, more particularly in the emergence of the trade union as a persisting and intruding factor in the relations between employer and the employee" (Bunn 1984, 169). As in Britain, 1868 was an important year in the history of German unions with the formation of two confederations at that time. The Central Association of German Industrialists was founded in 1876 and the Federation of Industrialists in 1895 (see Jaeger 1980, 138; Campbell 1992).

In Italy,

> the first attempts to build employers associations took place in areas such as the Milan and Turin regions, where industrialization already had deeper roots and was moving fairly rapidly and where trade unions were more militant and better organized than elsewhere. . . .
> Italian history confirms the thesis that both the structure and the ini-

---

1. For a detailed and critical discussion of measures of union strength, including Cameron's index, see chapter 7.

tiatives of employers associations tend to parallel those of the trade unions. (Martinelli and Treu 1984, 264)

After World War I, Confindustria supported the Fascists, and the trade unions were suppressed. In the postwar period the unions reemerged but split into three major ideological confederations in 1950. In Sweden, a general strike in 1902 led to the founding of the SAF in that year with "its primary purpose to insure its members against loss of income due to strikes and lock-outs" (Skogh 1984, 152). With respect to timing, the expected pattern appears to hold at least for the countries in table 6.1. Windmuller argues that "at the central level the creation of overarching bodies for broad representational, political, and legislative purposes lagged behind the rise of national trade union centers by roughly ten to twenty years" (1984, 3). Nevertheless, other factors are likely to be at work in accounting for business association strength and cohesion in addition to union organization.

First consider Japan, where labor is comparatively weak and yet the national association of business, the Keidanren, is powerful. Set up in 1946, this organization includes among its members all the major trade and industry associations. Japan forces us to recognize that these organizations have other functions than countering union initiatives. While scholars differ over the economic significance of Japan's approach to economic and industrial policy, it has followed a distinctive path in the postwar years. A centralized and authoritative business association facilitates planning in a non-command economy. In a sense the Keidanren is the Ministry of International Trade and Industry's (MITI) collaborator, and a natural corollary of the Liberal Democratic governments' traditionally interventionist economic thinking.

Table 6.1. Crossnational Rankings of Business and Union Cohesion

	Business Cohesion	Union Cohesion
1	Austria (1946)	Austria (1945)
2	Sweden (1902)	Sweden (1898)
3	Germany (1950)	Germany (1949)
4	Italy (1910)[a]	United Kingdom (1868)
5	United Kingdom (1898/1916)[b]	United States (1881 AFL)
6	United States (1895 NAM)	Italy (1906 CGL)

Source: Coleman and Grant 1988; Cameron 1984.
Note: Dates in parentheses are founding dates for union or employer confederations.
[a]Renamed in 1919.
[b]The Employers' Parliamentary Council was formed in 1898 and the Federation of British Industry in 1916.

One can account for France's Conseil national du patronat français (CNPF), "a rather imposing and exceptionally well-staffed confederation" (Ehrmann and Schain 1992, 182), in a similar way. Like Japan, in France labor is weak, and the government has had an interventionist approach to the economy. French governments' well-known efforts at economic planning in both the Fourth and Fifth Republic encouraged the CNPF, which was set up in 1946 to represent large firms, to assume an influential position. Further illustrating the importance of the economic approach of the government to interest groups, Mitterrand's dash for socialism excluded the CNPF. Yet "by the end of 1983, the influence of the CNPF had nearly returned to its usual levels" (Wilson 1987, 101). Similarly, in Italy in the 1950s though labor was divided, "Confindustria and the government marched step in step to a tune of fiscal austerity, low wages, and union repression." The relationship subsequently changed with the increasing importance of the public sector in the 1960s, Agnelli's leadership of Confindustria in the 1970s, and the championing of market forces in the 1980s (Spotts and Wieser 1986, 209–10). Two principal factors in the relative centralization and authority of a national business association are, then, the level of union centralization and the government's approach to economic policy-making. These factors can be expressed as a corollary to the iron law: who says organization says counterorganization and complementary organization.

Both of these factors influenced the position of the CBI in the 1980s. Prime Minister Thatcher's approach to the economy departed from that of earlier governments, both Conservative and Labour, and this change in approach, coupled with the declining fortunes of the TUC, accounts for the diminished role of the CBI in the 1980s. The scholarly disagreement over the role of CBI over the years may reflect, in part, these changes.

What of the other routes for business interest representation? The survey data suggest that individualized firm contact with government is extensive in Britain and not restricted to large and famous companies. Although these firms are for the most part members of the CBI, which has a staff of 300 or more and a large London office, they frequently initiate their own contact with government. The CBI is a somewhat unusual organization with both associations and firms as members. Despite the government's intention to have it be the authoritative representative of business, the data suggest that the role of the CBI has been overestimated. This conclusion rests not on an examination of small business or financial institutions, always on the margins for the CBI, but on an examination of trade associations and large industrial firms—its core constituency.

When asked, in 1988, to indicate the frequency of direct and group mediated contacts with government the responses produced the pattern displayed in table 6.2. Generally, among large firms in Britain the practice is to deal directly with government, rather than to rely on groups to represent their interests to government. The frequency of firm contact with government falls steadily as mediation and representational centralization increases. Some 68 percent of large firms always or often contact government directly, 46 percent always or often contact government at the industry level through trade associations, and only 24 percent always or often rely on the peak organization, the CBI. At the other end of the table, the number of firms that never contact government directly is zero, rising to 7 percent that never contact government through trade associations, and 21 percent that never use the CBI. It is part of the overall pattern that the number of firms not responding on these three items also increases as centralization increases, from one not indicating how often it contacted government directly to ten not indicating how often they used the CBI. To summarize these findings, if one scales the responses to the question of how often firms use the different modes of contact on a range from "always" as 1 to "never" as 5, the mean values are 2.2 (very often) for direct contact, 2.8 (quite often) for trade association contact, and 3.4 (sometimes) for CBI contact.

It is probable that the type of issue influences the choice of contact route, whether directly or through the peak association. The 1988 survey included employer associations and unions with more than 5,000 members, as well as the top 100 firms. Of the forty-seven business groups sent a questionnaire, about 77 percent responded to the survey.[2] One trade association respondent explained that,

> on those issues which affect business as a whole we tend to rely on the CBI and to put our views through them . . . where an issue is of special relevance . . . or where a general policy has a particular impact on our industry we would make separate representations to the government.

However, a surprisingly high 50 percent of associations, whatever the issue, "always" contact government directly. Although among individual firms only 13 percent always make direct contact, one-fifth never rely on the CBI. A considerable amount of business interest representation, even on "businesswide" issues, is not channeled through the CBI.

Data from the 1992 survey of large firms suggest a similar pattern of

---

2. Business groups that identified themselves as representing both small and large businesses were the largest category of respondents. Most of the respondents represented the manufacturing sector, followed by the service sector and the financial sector.

business political contacts. Respondents were asked to estimate the average number of times per year they contact government directly, through a trade association, or through the CBI on policy issues of concern to their firms. Comparing the three routes, 34 percent indicated that they contacted government directly ten or more times a year, 27 percent indicated that they used a trade association ten or more times a year, and 9 percent used the CBI ten or more times a year. Of the industries represented in the 1992 survey, utilities were the most likely to contact government directly. Yet it is generally the case that firms, whatever the industry, will use this route.

The increasingly common practice of firms hiring their own political consultants fits with the self-reliant pattern of political activity revealed in the survey data. According to a House of Commons' select committee report, the political consultancy industry grew very rapidly in the 1980s. In 1989, this report estimated that there were thirty political consultancy companies. In Britain a political consultant is likely to be a former civil

Table 6.2.   Business Interest Representation: Frequency of Direct and Mediated Contacts (by percentages)

Firms: "How often is your contact with government direct, through the CBI, or through a trade association?"

	Direct	Trade Assoc.	CBI
Always	13	2	0
Often	55	44	24
Sometimes	28	35	29
Rarely	4	12	26
Never	0	7	21
Total	100	100	100
	(N = 47)	(N = 43)	(N = 38)

Industry/Trade Associations: "How often is your contact with government direct or through the CBI?"

	Direct	CBI
Always	50	0
Often	38	12
Sometimes	9	54
Rarely	3	15
Never	0	19
Total	100	100
	(N = 34)	(N = 26)

servant, MP, or member of a minister's staff (House of Commons 1991, ix–x). Business interests are their most important clients (Grantham and Ure 1990). For the 1992 survey, 52 percent of the respondents indicated that their firms hired political consultants. The respondents were asked the reason for employing consultants. Most indicated that they chiefly employ consultants for informational purposes. About one-third of those who hire consultants indicated that the purpose was to represent the firm.

In the sense that the decision to hire political consultants is not entangled with the social aspirations of senior managers, it is a purer measure of firms' political interest and activity than financial donations in the case of the United Kingdom. Also, whether or not the firm hires political consultants is likely to be an item that survey respondents can address confidently—more confidently than, say, estimating the average yearly amounts of contact with government.

As expected, large firms and firms that consider government heavily involved in their industry tend to hire political consultants. Approximately 79 percent of the firms that hire political consultants are in the top 100— 56 percent of respondents. Some 57 percent of all the firms in the survey are in the heavy government involvement category ("How heavily is government involved in your firm's industry? Please circle the appropriate number on the scale from 1 = very heavily to 5 = not heavily"). Such firms, respondents circling "1" or "2" on the five-point scale, represent 72 percent of the firms that hire political consultants. In sector terms, the food and brewing industries are particularly likely to hire political consultants. Perhaps most interestingly, no direct relationship exists between the decision to hire political consultants and the decision to donate to the Conservative party. This finding is consistent with the "members interests" analysis reported in chapter 5 and underlines the importance of sorting out the different dimensions of business political participation and the argument that financial donations in the British political system are an analytically separable category of activity.

Firms that institutionalize their political activities in a specific department of the corporate bureaucracy, often referred to as government relations or public affairs departments, tend to be firms that hire political consultants. About 86 percent of the firms in the 1992 survey that have government relations departments also hire political consultants. One might think that for firms that have developed their own political expertise the hiring of outside political consultants would be superfluous. However, Wyn Grant quotes a parliamentary liaison officer in a government relations department justifying the hiring of political consultants in the following way: "Consultants roam about the outside world, they have more informal contacts, they can duck and weave in a more political way than would be possible for us" (Grant 1993, 100). For large firms, the firms most likely to have government relations departments, the cost of hiring political consultants is a small consideration, and the importance of public policy to the firm outweighs any redundancy in political activity.

In 1988, about 42 percent of the top 100 firms indicated that they had government relations departments. By 1992 the figure for the top 100 had risen to 50 percent. Of all firms in the 1992 survey, 33 percent indicated that they had "a government relations department or unit." As size decreases below the top 100, very few firms have such divisions. In Britain this bureaucratization of political activities is a recent corporate development dating from the mid-1970s. In the United States public or government affairs offices have been a common organizational feature of corporations for some time—at least since the 1950s (Salisbury 1984, 70). Only one exceptional British firm indicated that it had established such a department prewar, after which 1974 was the earliest indicated date for establishment.

Harold Wilson's relations with the financial sector might lead one to expect limited independent political activity from financial institutions. In Wilson's first term he could describe the Governor of the Bank of England as the "voice of the City." Whatever the situation in the 1960s, in the 1990s commercial banks, financial institutions, and insurance companies are not willing to rely entirely on the governor to represent their views to policymakers. These institutions are about as likely as firms in other sectors to hire political consultants and form government relations divisions. About 35 percent of the respondents in the financial sector indicated that their institutions had government relations departments, and 48 percent hired political consultants.

A government relations department makes a considerable difference in the firm's chosen mode of contact. Analyzing the use of direct government contact by firms with government relations divisions and those without produces a strong and significant association between these two variables: it is likely that the politically active firms establish these departments and the departments increase their activity. Firms with government relations divisions also tend to make use of trade association and CBI contacts somewhat more heavily, although this relationship is not statistically significant. While encouraging firms to increase their use of all modes of political contact, this bureaucratization has its largest impact on direct contact.

Industry-based trade and employer associations are members of the CBI, yet they, too, independently interact with the government. Asked, in 1988, whether they often, sometimes, rarely, or never met with civil servants, as expected, 86 percent of employer groups indicated that they often met with civil servants.[3] For ministerial meetings the corresponding figure was 47 percent. About 57 percent also said they often used parliamentary lobbying. When asked to assess the effectiveness of these and other activities on a scale from most effective to least effective, 58 percent rated meetings with civil servants most effective. In contrast only 10 percent of these respondents rated parliamentary lobbying as most effective.

A related item in the 1988 survey asked business groups at what point they participated in the legislative process. Inclusion at the early stages of the policy process enhances a group's effectiveness. As table 6.3 shows, with a Conservative government 71 percent of business group respondents said they participated both when the principles and the details were discussed. Only 3 percent indicated they never participated. Although unlikely to underestimate their importance, the responses of these business associations suggest that they have a high level and quality of participation in the policy process, independent of the CBI, and even under a Labour government.

These findings have a variety of wider implications both for characterizing the policy process and for research approaches. To summarize, for large firms the most important representational route (in terms of use) is direct contact. At the group level, trade association rather than peak association contact is more common. In other words, the less encompassing the interest organization the more frequently it is used. The firms that contact government most regularly have recently begun to bureaucratize their political activities in government relations divisions, which serve to maintain and possibly increase that activity. Large firms and firms with heavy

Table 6.3. Business Group Participation in the Legislative Process (by percentages)

"Under a Conservative/Labour government, with respect to legislation of direct concern to your organisation, at what point does your organisation usually take part in the legislative process? Indicate which is most appropriate: When the principles of legislation are being discussed, etc."

	Conservative	Labour
Principles	14	14
Details	11	14
Both stages	71	66
No stage	3	6
Total	99%	100%
	$N = 35$	$N = 35$

3. See chapter 8 for further discussion of these data.

government involvement in their industry, illustrated best by the food and brewing industries, also tend to hire political consultants. Industry associations themselves regularly interact with government, with civil servants and ministers, and irrespective of party of government are involved in the legislative process. Thus in order to understand the nature and scope of business political activity in Britain, the focus must be at the firm level, as well as at the industry level or the businesswide, peak organization level. This focus on individual firms and industry associations complicates the task of data collection because of the increased amount of data required and the difficulty of accessing it.

Over two decades since its creation the CBI still disappoints its creators. Obviously, like any organization of its size and structure, the precondition of finding broad agreement among its members constrains the freedom of the CBI to choose issues to pursue. Adding to this intrinsic weakness and accounting for its lack of authority in the 1980s is Thatcherism. A principal component of this ideology is what political scientists Ivor Crewe and Donald Searing called "statecraft" or the "ideal of strong central government." They list trade unions, local government, the nationalized industries, universities, the civil service, and the BBC among the institutions over which the government has asserted its autonomy (Crewe and Searing 1988, 364). The CBI deserves a place on this list too.

The decline of CBI influence corresponds with the decline of some of the tripartite institutions constructed in the 1960s and 1970s and Thatcher's hostility to the "corporatist" ethic of consensus. The strain between the CBI and Thatcherism became public drama in 1980 with the director general's famous, according to him misconstrued, conference speech reference to a "bare-knuckled fight" with the government. Among business groups, Thatcher appeared to have most resonance with the more conservative and less inclusive Institute of Directors. Trade union officials claimed that the government does "not just refuse to listen to us or the NEDC [National Economic Development Council], they do not listen to the CBI or the employers" (TUC 1982, 539). Meanwhile, member companies not only opted for direct contacts with government but some even left the CBI—Lucas and Rover, for example. The position of the CBI in business representation is more limited than is often supposed.

Its position is limited by the nature of the issues, as it has always been. Infrequent but important businesswide public policy, like worker representation or trade union legislation, presents the CBI with temporary opportunities to increase its role. But when presented with potentially influence-enhancing issues like the incrementally legislated trade union policy, the CBI was still only a marginal actor in the Thatcher years. In contrast to the high regard firms have of their influence on policy of direct concern to the firm, to return to the question raised earlier, when asked about the role of "employer organization pressure" in the sequence of trade union legislation, they credited such pressure with very little influence. When asked, "why did the Conservative government make the trade union legislation of 1980, 1982, and 1984—list employer organization pressure, the ideology of government leaders, and in response to public opinion in order of importance," most firm respondents selected government ideology as most important. Only one respondent selected organization pressure as most important. Even employer organizations credited government ideology and public opinion, not organization pressure, for the trade union policy. Trade unions overwhelmingly focused on government ideology in their responses. On this issue, government policymakers took action guided by a vision, which had been incubating in the think tanks, of the correct functioning of the economy, and a strategy, consistent with an economist's view of collective action, directed at individual choices. Chapter 7 discusses this policy in detail, showing the applicability of rational choice theory to the design of public policy in this domain and the policy's important consequences in diminishing the economic and political influence of organizations that might countervail business interests. The policy was in line with business interests but was not the result of contact and guidance from business groups.

Moving to an issue on which the CBI actively campaigned and had the support of its members, rate reform, the government nevertheless rejected its proposals, "largely on the grounds that they were submitted too late." The CBI felt it had been "penalised unfairly" (*Financial Times* March 7, 1988; *Financial Times* March 8, 1988). Reversals of this type enhance individual firms' confidence in a self-reliant representational strategy, not just in matters of "direct concern to the firm," but possibly in relation to businesswide issues as well. This diverse evidence, when combined with the developing capabilities of firms themselves to contact government, suggests that it is time to revise assessments like the following: "the CBI, since its founding in 1965, has assumed an undisputed role as the chief voice of industry: the CBI's growing enrollment of many leading financial and retail firms has further legitimized its claim to be the chief voice of business as well" (Useem 1984, 71).

The decline of the CBI under Thatcher coincided with the decline of the TUC. Unions in the United Kingdom suffered a precipitous decline in membership in the 1980s, and the government excluded the TUC from the policy-making process. While Thatcher's concern for "statecraft" is a major factor in both cases, it is reasonable to suppose, and to take up the argument made on the basis of the cross-national evidence, that removing the TUC from the policy process reduces the importance of its counterweight, the CBI. Although considerable explanatory emphasis has been placed on Prime Minister Thatcher's approach to economic policy in understanding the decline of the CBI, it was her successor who administered le coup de grâce to British corporatism, and closed down the NEDC, a creation of an earlier type of Tory prime minister. While it might have been established in the summertime of French indicative planning, it had much earlier origins in Macmillan's own ideas about macroeconomic management: "The National Economic Council, with all the facts before it, would survey the whole field of economic activity, and, in consultation with the responsible representatives of the government, formulate a comprehensive plan for general guidance." The council was to be appointed in consultation with affected interests (Macmillan 1938, 290). So much for that. But there are some signs that with John Major as prime minister the influence of the CBI has increased. In part, this recovery is attributable to another change in the view of the role government should play in the economy within the government—or at least a more tenuous attachment to the neoliberal views of the 1980s. Even if the CBI becomes more significant in the policy struggle, large firms and trade associations are likely to continue to pursue independent political representation, particularly in matters of direct concern.

What difference does this decentralization make, and does it matter that firms rather than groups are representing business interests to government? A policy process characterized by narrow or specialized rather than encompassing interest representation is one that will detract from, rather than contribute to, general economic well-being, or so some political explanations of macroeconomic performance maintain. While scholars have attributed Britain's poor economic performance to all sorts of things, they have repeatedly pointed to overly influential special interests, although unions rather than business usually provide the focus of attention. Mancur Olson draws on British evidence and the characteristics of the unions to develop the argument that "the highly encompassing organization will in its own interest seek socially efficient policies, whereas very narrow common-interest groups never have an incentive to take the interests of the larger society into account" (Olson 1983, 24). The British evidence on business interest representation, that the more encompassing an organization the less use the firm makes of it, should be as disturbing to Olson as the characteristics of labor interest representation.

Business interest representation in Britain is, in Robert Salisbury's framework, institution rather than group dominated. Consequently, decentralization has direct implications for the power of interests. Decentralization certainly amounts to political weakness for the CBI, but its weakness does not mean that business interests are weak politically. The bureaucratization of political activities in large firms further encourages institutional dominance. Salisbury argues that institutions have a number of advantages over membership groups in representing their interests. Institutions have hierarchical structures, and the need to seek member approval does not constrain decision makers in the adoption of policy positions and the disposition of resources. Institutional interest representation is also likely to be "far more durable and persistent in policy-making circles . . ." (Salisbury 1984, 75). Institutional dominance becomes especially significant when one considers that the major opposing interests to business in the policy process, recognizing the cleavages within the business community, can only achieve representation through membership-based groups—trade unions or consumer and environmental groups. Although Salisbury does not put it in these terms, the fact that among the organizations he considers "institutions" the business corporation is the most significant, suggests that he is providing another angle from which to view the "privileged position of business." The decentralization of business representation to institutions rather than groups leads, then, to the rejection of the equation of decentralization with political weakness.

With interview data, Graham Wilson presents interesting and comparable evidence from the United States that shows the importance of corporate political activity in contrast to associations' activity. His survey of Fortune 500 companies reveals that the great majority of his respondents regard direct contact between corporate officials and legislators as much more important than trade association contact (Wilson 1990). As in Britain, corporations rather than associations are the source of most business political activity.

Although lobbying is a common activity for corporations generally in the United States, as with PAC contributions it is the lobbying of foreign, notably Japanese, corporations that has attracted disproportionate attention. In the 1980s, Toshiba Machine Company assisted the Soviet Union in obtaining classified submarine technology. Learning of this, the U.S. Congress threatened sanctions against Toshiba. Not relying on Japanese government representations alone, Toshiba marshaled their American employees in a letter-writing campaign, hired a group of well-known lobbyists, and drew on the support of American corporate customers to effectively counter the threat (see Choate 1990, 7–11; Prestowitz 1988, 265). Rather than evidence of "undue" Japanese political influence as both Clyde Prestowitz and Pat Choate see it, the Toshiba case illustrates how a foreign company can successfully adapt to the host political environment.

It is true that Japan's companies and business organizations hire more Washington lobbyists than those of any other foreign country. Canada's business interests are the second most frequent hirers of lobbyists. As the amount of foreign direct investment broadly constrains PAC activity—without any foreign direct investment there can be no foreign PACs—trade becomes the major relevant economic relationship underlying non-U.S. affiliate foreign lobbying. It is the size of the economic stake, not the nationality of these business interests, that drives lobbying activity. Japanese lobbying is congruent with its position as the largest exporter to the United States. Canadian lobbying is congruent with its position as number two exporter.

Table 6.4 shows the ten countries from which the United States imports the most, and the number of businesses, governments, and other organizations from these countries that hire Washington representatives. While governments that retain representation in addition to embassy staff and other organizations were included in the totals for each country, since they, too, may represent their nation's business interests and because of the difficulty of determining the purpose of an organization by its name, the great majority of interests listed are business interests. Some of these interests retain more than one individual or organization to represent them. Leading the way among business organizations is the Korea Foreign Trade Association with eleven individuals and organizations representing its interests, closely followed by Toyota Motor Sales, Seagram and Sons, Matsushita Electric Corporation, and Hitachi.

In general, the data suggest that the more economic activity from a particular country, measured by the size of U.S. imports from that country, the greater is that country's political activity, measured by the number of that country's interests with Washington representatives. Japanese interests are most numerous, but in proportion to the size of their eco-

Table 6.4.   U.S. Imports (1988) and Foreign Interest Representation in Washington: Top Ten Countries

	Imports ($ Billions)	Interests Represented	Interests/Imports
Japan	93.168	144	1.5
Canada	81.434	62	0.8
FRG	27.420	45	1.6
Taiwan	26.526	22	0.8
Korea	21.209	37	1.7
United Kingdom	18.740	60	3.2
France	12.699	32	2.5
Italy	12.278	19	1.5
Hong Kong	10.810	6	0.6
Singapore	8.226	5	0.6

Source: *Washington Representatives* 1990; International Monetary Fund 1989.

nomic stake they are not as notably overrepresented as some other countries: France and the United Kingdom, for example.

On consideration, it should come as little surprise that firms are economic institutions before they are national institutions, and that in similar situations they respond in similar ways, whatever their country of origin. They are politically active because they have the available resources and they have much at stake in the political process. Just as foreign firms are politically active in the United States, so American firms are politically active abroad. Particularly since the Single European Act, American and Japanese corporations have become very active in Brussels. Sonia Mazey and Jeremy Richardson argue that "Japanese and American groups are among the most effective EC [European Community] lobbyists. Especially influential is the EC Committee of the American Chamber of Commerce (Amcham), which represents eighty US organizations including multinational (sic) such as ITT, IBM, Allied Signal Inc., Colgate Palmolive, General Electric, General Motors . . ." (1993, 7). They also note the effectiveness of individual American firms lobbying the European Union (EU).

A much-discussed lobbying technique is to employ former government officials to represent the corporation's interest. Again, Japanese use of this technique in the United States excites passion (see Choate 1990), yet the idea of a "revolving door" between government and industry is a familiar part of descriptions of American politics. The implication is that the ability to employ former government officials produces distinct lobbying advantages for the employing organization.

One of the more extended scholarly treatments of the revolving door is to be found in Heinz, Laumann, Nelson, and Salisbury's recent research (1993). Their book merits close attention because it presents new empirical material on a lobbying technique that is likely to confer a particular advantage to business interests—simply because those interests provide most post–public-sector career opportunities—and because one of the principal conclusions in the book is that the revolving door is of small consequence. The authors present survey evidence on Washington representatives' career backgrounds, on the time elapsed since executive or legislative employment (for convenience referred to as government employment or experience), on the reasons for employment, on the frequency of former employees contacting former employers, and on the issue of who you know versus what you know. The interview data are for 1983 to 1984 for the agriculture, energy, health, and labor policy areas and include the responses of Washington representatives, employers of Washington representatives, and government officials. Analysis of this data leads the authors to dismiss concern about the revolving door as the stuff of "horror stories" and "contrary to our experience" (1993,

126). But one can argue that the evidence presented is more open to interpretation.

Representatives were asked if their previous government experience was helpful and in what ways. The majority of respondents, 87 percent, found the experience helpful. The authors report that experience was more likely to be seen as useful in familiarizing the respondents with the issues (70 percent) and the policy process (80 percent) than in providing helpful contacts (48 percent for administration contacts and 59 percent for congressional contacts), "what you know outweighed who you know" (Heinz et al. 1993, 122–27). Nonetheless, a significant proportion of the respondents affirmed that their experience provided contacts in the administration or in Congress. None of this data would seem too damaging to the revolving door hypothesis. Overwhelmingly, respondents find their government careers useful to them as lobbyists. Certainly more chose the safer answers concerning knowledge of the issue and the process, yet perhaps surprisingly large percentages of respondents were willing to report that their experience provided contacts. More importantly there is no reason to think that developing a "what you know" advantage is inconsistent with the revolving door, as seems to be suggested. Whether former government employees trade on their knowledge or the contacts, or both, is secondary to the fact that they have an advantage over those without that career experience, and that the anticipation of knowledge as well as contacts make government officials an attractive recruiting pool for private organizations seeking influence in Washington.

The proportion of representatives who contact an agency and who were former government employees is at its highest in energy policy and for contacts with the House of Representatives—18 percent (Heinz et al. 1993, 120–21). The authors treat the question of the quality as well as the quantity of contacts. Maybe the few contacts made by former employees have much greater policy influence. They have data on reported success on policy events, income levels, and prominent representatives known by the respondents, but in comparing former employees with the others they "find there are few statistically significant differences between these two groups" (121). Somewhat puzzling in this regard is an analysis reported later in the book where government experience is found to have an effect on success (349–50).

The authors define prior agency employment "broadly"—any section of a department, any experience in the House, constitutes prior employment for contacting the department or the House. However, they systematically exclude the impact of useful knowledge and contacts generated by previous government employment outside the department or branch that provided the actual employment. It is possible that former employees had extradepartmental, extraagency, or extrachamber ties of relevance to their lobbying work. It might also be interesting to examine not just the presence or absence of former employment but the time factor. The expectation is that the longer the representative served in an agency, the greater the influence on lobbying activities.

Respondents from interest organizations were asked to rank fourteen reasons for hiring. They ranked government experience below experience in the lobbying industry as a reason for hiring and above elite educational background or party affiliation. At best the evidence here is inconclusive since the authors say that government experience was not a "dominant criterion" but was also not "irrelevant" (Heinz et al. 1993, 121–22). Further it is plausible to suppose that these organizations employ different criteria for different hires in the organization. It would be relevant to know what priority interest organizations place on hiring at least one person with previous government experience.

Of the respondents with federal government experience, the average length of employment was seven years and the average time elapsed since government employment was eleven years (Heinz et al. 1993, 118). With these data representatives' government experience is characterized as short and relatively old. At the same time the significance of this characterization for the revolving door is diminished when the authors present data on degree to which government experience "decays in usefulness" (125). These data suggest that both knowledge of the policy process and even contacts have a good shelf life.

About 46 percent of their sample of lobbyists have had federal government experience, and 9 percent have had state experience. This figure is compared with the 50 percent in Milbrath's study, and the 86 percent of the organizations in Schlozman and Tierney's study with at least one representative with federal experience (Heinz et al. 1993, 116–17). Again, this evidence cannot be construed as damaging the revolving door unless one interpreted the hypothesis to mean that government experience would be universal among lobbyists. Further, it may well be that the Schlozman and Tierney approach (1986), which assumes the importance of roles in an organization, is superior. Heinz, Laumann, Nelson, and Salisbury find that only 8 percent of the sample, or one-fifth of those with government experience, actually "revolve" in the sense of moving back and forth between their lobbying and government careers (Heinz et al. 1993, 119).[4]

---

4. The authors later state, "The revolving door between government employment and work as an interest representative—one of the mechanisms through which interest groups are thought to influence the agencies that regulate them—appeared in the career histories of only 5% of our sample" (1993, 379). If the 5 percent refers to actual revolvers, it is inconsistent with the 8 percent actual revolvers reported on p. 119.

Only when the authors interpret the metaphor in this literal way does the evidence presented permit any confidence in rejecting the revolving door as an important feature of interest representation in Washington.

Heinz, Laumann, Nelson, and Salisbury's work is helpful in thinking about some of the relevant questions for research, yet another dimension of the revolving door hypothesis is the question of the impact of the prospect of future employment in industry on the incentives of current government officials. One study, investigating this "career incentive," found that in three of four agencies studied, "the existence of pro-industry policy incentives deriving from industry job opportunities was confirmed to varying degrees" (Quirk 1981, 163). Paul Quirk also used survey data and interviewed the government officials themselves, that is, those least likely to admit to such incentives.

This lobbying technique is not an exclusively American phenomenon and is significant enough to tax conceptual imagination elsewhere. It is a practice Japanese firms employ in their home political environment and with which the French have long been familiar. Avoiding the confusions of a "revolving door," the French refer to this phenomenon as *pantouflage:* "bureaucrats who had proved their goodwill toward the business community to slip (pantoufler) into lucrative positions in that community" (Safran 1985, 105). An extraordinary 47 percent of the chief executives of the largest 125 French companies in 1993 were former civil servants, usually having received their training at the Ecole Nationale d'Administration (Bauer and Bertin Mourot 1995, 70). But in describing the career corridor from public to private sector, conceptual kudos must go to the Japanese for the term *amakudari,* which translates as "descent from heaven." In 1986, 252 civil servants made this descent—most coming from the Ministry of Finance, followed by the Ministry of International Trade and Industry (Koh 1989, 235–37).

A civil service career in Britain, never described as heavenly, at least used to approximate what the Japanese would refer to as lifetime employment. Evidence suggests that this is no longer so true. Between 1979 and 1984, 1,404 officials went from the Ministry of Defence to the defense industry (*The Guardian* July 17, 1985), and between 1985 and 1995 approximately 2,000 MoD, or members of the armed forces, were hired by business interests including British Aerospace, EDC-Scicon Defence Ltd (subsidiary of GM), GEC-Marconi, Lockheed, McDonnell Douglas, Siemens, Westland Helicopters, Rolls Royce, and Price Waterhouse (*The Guardian* January 25, 1995). In the United Kingdom there are some rules governing how civil servants switch from public to private employment. Civil servants require the approval of a committee of the cabinet office if they plan to accept a private-sector job within two years of their employment as civil servants. Ministers, however, are not restricted in this way. Perhaps at one time ministers were willing to trade-in their cabinet seat for elevation to the House of Lords and looked forward to turning statesman-like reflections into memoirs. Now they trade-down for a seat in the board-room. Of thirty-one ministers who served in Prime Minister Thatcher's cabinets, nineteen descended to the private sector—accumulating among them fifty-nine company directorships and often far higher salaries than they received as ministers (*Labour Research* October 9, 1990). Some former cabinet ministers have found employment with companies that their government privatized—creating the appearance of a do-it-yourself revolving door. Sir Norman Fowler, a former secretary of state for transport, joined the National Freight Company—privatized February 1982. Peter Walker, a former secretary of state for energy, joined British Gas—privatized December 1986. Norman Tebbit, a former secretary of state for trade and industry, joined British Telecom—privatized November 1984. Lord Young, secretary of state for trade and industry from 1987 to 1990, joined British Telecom's rival, Cable and Wireless—privatized October 1981 to December 1985 (White 1991; see also *The Observer* June 17, 1990). In contrast to her former colleagues, the former prime minister has behaved more decorously—Lady Thatcher and her considerable memoirs.

These comparative data on the widespread practice of employing former government officials suggest that there are obvious advantages to this practice for interest groups. They can expect favorably predisposed government officials, lobbyists with detailed procedural knowledge, and, with the government contacts ex-officials bring to the private sector, a significant gain in access to the political system. Business gains additional leverage in the process of interest representation to the extent that government officials, elected and appointed, envisage future careers in the private sector and thus develop a very personal stake in the government's interaction with the business community. For government officials, bright futures are probably less easy to envisage in the trade union or public interest movements. A favorable policy toward business, thus adorned with potential personal benefits, becomes increasingly attractive to government officials as they move up the public career ladder and begin to contemplate their alternatives. From a public perspective these very same business advantages represent an influence inimical to democratic government and the principle of political equality.

Whatever route business interests choose to represent their interests, they employ a fluid mix of activities to persuade or "lobby" government. A specific policy case, the brewing industry's successful stand against a government effort to increase competition in the industry, illustrates some of the activities used in the British political system.

In the spring of 1989 an uncommonly public rift developed between the brewing industry and the Conservative government. If disagreements arise between a probusiness party and business interests, the likely source is general ideological rules on the correct running of a market economy clashing with actual business practice. A core principle for neoliberals is competition. Competition among large numbers of buyers and sellers preserves the public interest in an economy driven by self-interest. Business people may work up some enthusiasm for the principle of competition. In their working day they seek ways to hinder, exclude, or collude with their competitors. Consequently, the "antitrust" policies of well-meaning governments, because of business opposition, are difficult to enforce. In the United States, the Sherman Act of 1890 prohibited "every contract, agreement, or combination in the form of a trust or otherwise in restraint of trade or commerce among the several states or with foreign nations." This policy, tougher than antitrust policies elsewhere, has been difficult to implement in a consistent way, and observers, noting that increased concentration rather than competition has characterized the subsequent development of many industries, use antitrust policy as an example of symbolic politics (see Arnold 1937; Edelman 1964). Of course, legitimizing symbols, like sacred cows, occasionally do get in the way in a modern economy.

In March 1989, the Monopolies and Mergers Commission (MMC) completed its report on the brewing industry in the United Kingdom. It characterized the supply of beer as a complex monopoly and made several specific recommendations to increase competition within the industry. The MMC investigates mergers, monopolies, and restrictive practices on the basis of referrals from either the Department of Trade and Industry or the Office of Fair Trading. In 1986 the Office of Fair Trading requested an MMC investigation of the brewing industry. Lord Young of Graffham, secretary of state at the Department of Trade and Industry in 1989, and who was "converted" to Thatcherism by the think tank the CPS and believed that "economic liberalism as preached by Joseph and Thatcher offered a practical solution to Britain's economic difficulties" (Cockett 1994, 259), said, with his peculiar use of language, that he was "minded to implement" the recommendations of the MMC on the brewing industry. The central proposal was to make the six largest brewers, Allied-Lyons, Bass, Courage, Grand Metropolitan, Scottish & Newcastle, and Whitbread sell 22,000 public houses. Other recommendations included ending the system under which brewers made loans to independent "free-house" owners, who in return sell only the lender's beer (*Financial Times* July 11, 1989). Lord Young's apparent willingness to follow through on these recommendations outraged the big brewers, not least because they had "traditional historic ties" to the Conservative party. Allied-Lyons, Whitbread, and Scottish & Newcastle even contributed quite generously to the party, both before and after this policy issue arose on the agenda. But persuading the government to change course required more active measures.

The biggest challenge for the brewers, as they sought to alter the government's position on the MMC report, was to maintain unity. Though the six national breweries had a clear common interest in opposing the recommendations, there were aspects of the MMC report that might appeal to the more aggressive smaller regional breweries. Nevertheless almost all the small brewers opposed the MMC recommendations. Their solidarity in the face of this hostile government involvement in their industry was variously attributed to the national brewers' share holdings in the smaller brewers and some "arm-twisting," the work of the association, and a sort of industry esprit de corps (*Independent* July 18, 1989).

Both firms and the industry association, the Brewers Society, participated in the effort. In 1989 at least five MPs had direct ties to either the association or one of the big brewers. The weight of the House of Commons in the legislative process is not the only way to assess the importance of ties with MPs. Legislators can improve access to the executive. As the Select Committee report put it, "Clearly a lobbying company which is able to call directly upon the services of Members, particularly, perhaps, in arranging meetings and other contacts with fellow Members, or with Ministers or civil servants, has a perceived advantage over its competitors" (House of Commons 1991, vii). Members of Parliament Neil Hamilton (one of the MPs involved with Al-Fayed, owner of Harrods, and the "cash for questions" scandal that led to the Nolan committee) and Allan Stewart were political consultants for the Brewers Society, and Members of Parliament Gerrard Neale, Sir Dudley Smith, and Roger Gale worked in a similar capacity for Allied-Lyons, Bass PLC, and Scottish & Newcastle.[5] Member of Parliament David Shaw was a director of Hoskins Brewery PLC, a smaller brewer. Whitbread and the Brewers Society also retained professional parliamentary lobbying firms. These in turn retained MPs. Ian Greer Associates (also involved in the Harrods affair), with Whitbread as a client, retained Member of Parliament Michael Grylls, for example. Constituency ties, notably the presence of a local brewery, linked other MPs to the industry. Robert Neame, of Shepherd Neame brewery, argued in *The Faversham Times* that the MMC recommendations might doom the village pub. Roger Moate, MP for Faversham, sponsored an early day

---

5. *The Investors Chronicle* (June 16, 1989) lists Sir Paul Dean as a consultant for Grand Metropolitan, yet Sir Paul's entry in the *Register of Members' Interests 1990* declares merely that he is a "consultant on pension schemes."

motion in the House of Commons, a device to signal opinion in the House. The motion opposed the Conservative minister's acceptance of the MMC recommendations, and ninety-three Conservative MPs signed (see *Financial Times* July 12, 1989; *Independent* July 18, 1989).

Indirectly, the industry pressured elected representatives through a campaign to shape public opinion. The advertising for the "Be vocal—it's your local" campaign cost about £6 million. The brewers, through this campaign, broadened the adversely affected interests to include drinkers and employees—gaining, as a result of a fear of loss of jobs in a more competitive industry, the support of the Transport and General Workers Union. Perhaps, more importantly the Bishop of Truro claimed "the pub is the centre of village life which has served local needs as nothing else has, including the church. I find myself comparing this phenomenon to the dissolution of the monasteries" (*Financial Times* July 12, 1989; *Independent* June 15, 1989). An opinion poll released by the brewers suggested that a majority of drinkers, while presumably not opposed to dissolution, were as content as the bishop with their local. This public opinion campaign was thought to secure the brewers an invitation to a meeting at the Department of Trade and Industry from the minister in May 1989. According to the brewers, "the agenda changed. . . . Lord Young told us that if we did not like the proposals we should come up with suggestions ourselves." The brewers also enlisted the support of civil servants in the Ministry of Agriculture and Fisheries, the "sponsoring" ministry for the brewing industry. The breadth of their support buoyed them sufficiently to reject Lord Young's first effort at a compromise proposal. In July, perhaps as a result of pressure from Prime Minister Thatcher, Lord Young gave way on the central recommendations of the MMC report. He abandoned the proposal to force the sale of pubs and permitted loan ties to the national brewers, although the big brewers had to let some of their pubs have the status of free houses (*Financial Times* July 11, 1989; *Financial Times* July 12, 1989).

We can draw some general lessons from the brewers' tale. It is a cautionary one for overzealous ministers—Lord Young left the government in 1990. Even when a probusiness government pursues policies justified by a core principle of neoliberalism and has the support of expert opinion (MMC), it can still be successfully challenged by business interests. For business interests the case illustrates the importance of business unity in industrywide policy issues. At the same time lobbying activity could play on divisions within the government, the Ministry of Agriculture against the Department of Trade and Industry, and divisions within the governing party. Business interests and political consultancy link MPs to the brewing industry. The case also illustrates the importance of widening the adversely affected population. Casting the issue as one affecting the national heritage, the pub in this case, was an effective way of generating public support. Of course many of the Thatcher government's policies were unpopular—for example, the abolition of the Greater London Council, privatization of electricity and water, and the poll tax. The Thatcher government continued with them anyway. With brewing, unpopularity worked in conjunction with significant business political activity.

The level and ease of access for representatives of business interests in their interaction with elected and appointed political officials are a result of the advantages business organizations derive from their superior resources and their control of the economy, although this factor was only a marginal one in the brewers' case. There is, in addition, a "sociological" dimension to business overrepresentation that focuses on the elite social and educational background of business and political leaders. Similar manners, accents, and habits, developed in the educational and social institutions that they share, aid communication between the representatives of the business and the political worlds. Eton, or a Parisian lycée, Oxbridge, Ivy League, or the Ecole National d'Administration stock an educational pool that both government and business institutions hold in common. Connections of this sort may have helped the brewers: "I know the local brewery people socially," said a Conservative MP, "when they are your friends it is difficult to resist their arguments. Like hundreds of other MPs up and down the country, they have open access to me. They have my home telephone number and know my wife and children" (*The Independent* July 18, 1989). In its composition, the Establishment links business, political, and opinion leaders. It rarely includes union leaders or consumer advocates. It provides alternative settings for communication in addition to the conventional democratic arenas. Within democratic arenas members of the Establishment interact familiarly. One can grant these additional advantages to business representation, without subscribing to notions of conspiracy that often accompany concepts like Establishment or "power elite." Nevertheless, in this book my theoretical interest is less in the sociological denominators of business and political life and more in the resources, motivations, and incentives that contribute to an advantageous political position for business in the struggle over public policy.

The variety of routes available, and the mix of activities and incentives at work, complicate the representational process. We cannot assess business political effectiveness in national policy-making simply in terms of the effectiveness of the national business association. Indeed the strength of these types of associations is dependent on the government's approach to economic policy-making and the relative strength of the union movement, rather than a reflection of the political strength of the business interests in general in a political system. While the activities associated with the lobbying process are, in a representative democracy, available to all interests, large firms are able to make the best use of them. The political activity of their membership associations should be viewed, at least for the larger firms and those in industries with heavy government involvement, as but a supplement to their own political activity. These firms are also better placed than most other organizations to manipulate the incentives that motivate government officials. Further support and refinement of this argument depends on an examination of the resources and activities of interests opposed to business.

PART 3

Business Opposition

CHAPTER 7

Business Divisions, Collective Action, and Countervailing Power

The times have changed in nothing more than in the rapid conveyance of intelligence and communication . . .
—Sir Walter Scott, *The Heart of Midlothian*

The public support for the business system, the political importance of business confidence, and the superior political resources and organization of business interests are the pillars of business political power in capitalist democracies. Yet even if one examines these pillars closely, a true appreciation of their strength and their critical position in the democratic structure is possible only when they are surveyed in relation to that structure's other elements. They may seem to have a less critical position when the position of other groups becomes part of the perspective. The more weight that unions and other adversarial groups and organizations carry, the less is left to business.

Countervailing power, "the neutralization of one position of power by another," is for John Kenneth Galbraith the contemporary solution to "the problem of economic power" (Galbraith 1954, 1). He argues that the development of unions in conjunction with the concentration of economic power in the modern corporation is the clearest example of how countervailing power operates. He also includes the divisions within the business community as examples of the same dynamic: the countervailing power of oligopolistic retailers to their oligopolistic suppliers. Later critics of the argument that business carries disproportionate weight in the policy-making process are largely content to elaborate on Galbraith's thesis. They too point to rival organizations like unions and to offsetting business interests.

For all their current difficulties connected to expanding international markets, unions remain central to any general analysis of the opposition business interests face, and, as the critics of the argument that business carries disproportionate weight implicitly recognize, without them the democratic structure is lopsided. In part 3, beyond the analysis of business divisions, I explore the national variations in union resources, power, and capacity to countervail business power. I argue that these organizations are themselves highly sensitive to political change and vulnerable to hostile public policy. A common theoretical thread to this discussion is the relative difficulty of organizing large numbers as opposed to small numbers for political action. For the relationship between unions and governments, union movements characterized by fewer, more monopolistic unions tend to exercise more power in national policy arenas. For the relationship between unions and members, reducing the authority of and coercive powers of unions reduces their ability to organize the work force and encourages free riding. This relationship is examined with a case analysis of public policy toward unions in the United Kingdom. I pick up the thread again in the next chapter by examining the relationships among unions, business, and governments in the context of expanding the labor market and the number of unions to organize it. At best we can speak of business being resisted to varying degrees but not countervailed, as far as the latter term suggests some balance of power. But first we must address the prior question of whether business political power is self-correcting.

All observers of business power, at least from Marx forward, are aware of the divisions within the business community, among finance, service, and manufacturing, between retailers and their suppliers, or between domestic and foreign-owned concerns. But these business divisions likely compartmentalize political as well as economic activity, suggesting indifference rather than conflict between business interests in the political arena. Cross-industry political conflict would seem most likely over barriers to market entry and where industry boundaries become fuzzy or when such barriers have direct consequences for other industries, as in the case of tit-for-tat tariff disputes. Within-industry competitive political activity would be most likely to occur over government procurement decisions.

George Stigler criticizes Galbraith's argument in terms of the division between retailers and suppliers. He points out that large-scale retailing actually developed in those sectors, shoes and confectionery for example, where "concentration of production was relatively low." Conversely, where production was concentrated, automobiles and cigarettes for example, there were not countervailing large-scale retailers. Stigler also notes with respect to the growth of American unions that, with the exception of the railroads, the major unions were organizing quite competitive industries (1954, 11). Where there is "bilateral oligopoly" there is no reason to suppose that this relationship will be competitive rather than cooperative, and therefore there is no necessary beneficial affect on price or for that matter democratic politics. Stigler mentions "movie film production-exhibition" as an "area of perennial collusion" and goes on to fault Galbraith for not offering any explanation of "why bilateral oligopoly should in general eliminate, and not merely redistribute, monopoly gains" (Stigler 1954, 13). Neither history nor theory offers much to support Galbraith's thesis.

Sometimes businesses accomplish collusion through horizontal or vertical integration. The huge Japanese financial keiretsu—which group firms around a large bank and integrate through stockholding, loans, and regular meetings of company presidents—carry this collusion to the highest level. Examples of these keiretsu include Mitsui, Mitsubishi, Sumitomo, Fuyo, Sanwa, and Dai-Ichi Kangyo, and which between them, account for about 28 percent of Japan's GNP (U.S. General Accounting Office 1993, 82, 86). Other keiretsu, notably in the automobile and electronics industries, integrate vertically. In Germany, the largest banks have substantial investments in large German firms and, through seats on the supervisory boards of these firms, a say in management decisions. Even in Britain, where some observers see a gulf between finance and industry, links do exist through nonexecutive (outside) directorships. Wyn Grant, in his authoritative study of business and government in Britain, argues that the differences between finance and industry have been exaggerated (1993). Finally, transnational corporations, as they create an interlocking international pattern of ownership ties and collaborative projects, obscure business divisions following national lines: the "who is us" phenomenon.

Beyond examining institutional ties among corporations, survey evidence contributes to our understanding of whether the exercise of business power falls into a pattern of off-setting conflict. For the United States, the empirical research on this issue is quite consistent. Business persons generally do not identify other business persons as their adversaries in the policy process. Kay Schlozman and John Tierney found that almost 90 percent of their respondents from corporations named other corporations as an ally; only 23 percent also named antagonists among the business community (1986, 284–85). They conclude that "cooperation with the business community is far more commonplace than conflict" (Schlozman and Tierney 1986, 400–401). Heinz, Laumann, Nelson, and Salisbury also present evidence suggesting that the adversaries business interests identify are not other businesses but unions and environmental groups, depending on the policy domain (1993, 256–58). In his analysis of congressional testimony, sociologist Mark Mizruchi found that, "firms were approximately four times as likely to agree with one another as they were to oppose one another" (1992, 251). In their analysis of PAC contributions, Tie-ting Su, Alan Neustadtl, and Dan Clawson argue that business is politically cohesive enough to represent an important force in public policy (1995). Getting at this issue in a somewhat different way, the 1992 survey of large British firms presented respondents with a list of other organizations they might meet in the policy process and asked whether they were usually in agreement or disagreement with these organizations. Responses to this item are shown in table 7.1.

These data do not reveal a pattern of off-setting conflict within the business community. The item isolates the more enduring distinctions within the business community: firms, industries, associations, and country of ownership. For firms, either within the same industry or from other industries, the levels of policy disagreement are low. Levels of disagreement are even lower with respect to trade associations, as expected if such associations only adopt policy positions on issues on which they can develop consensus among their members. The level of disagreement with the CBI is low and attributable to that organization's task of representing the businesswide view. Correspondingly, and as expected, relatively high levels of agreement occur on domestic policy among firms within the same industry and business associations. The level of agreement with the CBI is lower than some scholars would have led us to expect but is consistent with the other data presented on the limited role of the CBI in the policy process. The level of agreement drops off sharply for firms in other industries and foreign firms. With these categories of firms the modal response is that they are neutral or irrelevant in policy disputes. In other words, business interests are generally compartmentalized in their political interests, not in conflict.

What of those cases of conflict? Does this conflict, where it occurs, compensate for the underrepresentation of nonbusiness interests? The

Table 7.1.   Firms and Other Interests in the Policy Process: Percentage of Respondents Indicating Agreement or Disagreement, 1992

"Generally speaking, in disputes over domestic public policy affecting your firm, with which other organisations is your firm in agreement or disagreement? Please circle the appropriate number on the scale from 1 = usually in agreement, to 3 = neutral or irrelevant, to 5 = usually in disagreement."

	Agree	Neutral	Disagree	N
Business Community				
Business associations	81	16	4	57
CBI	65	31	4	55
Same industry firms	72	19	9	54
Other industry firms	40	52	8	50
Foreign firms	24	65	10	49
Other Interests				
Environmental groups	39	37	24	54
Consumer groups	38	43	19	53
Trade unions	24	60	16	55

defense industry, perhaps united on the need for a large defense budget, provides occasional examples of intense, even corrupt, interfirm conflict at the stage of distributing defense spending across specific weapons systems; feast-or-famine decisions for defense firms are also decisions that have significant consequences for nonbusiness interests, notably taxpayers. Such conflict does not in itself damage the claim that business is overrepresented, for the conflicting business interests win or lose, they do not cancel each other out. Internal business conflict cannot itself act as a surrogate for the representation of other interests, though one may find some correspondence of views on some issues at certain times, the clergy and the brewers, for example, and there may be a democratic payoff in business organizations using resources to pull other interests with friendly views into the policy struggle. The data indicate that conflict, where it occurs, is most likely with foreign firms. The position of the domestic firms may facilitate the expression of citizens' interests in employment; foreign firms may facilitate the expression of their interests in consumption. Internal business conflict is no substitute for alternative interests and values being independently represented in the policy process, but it may selectively ease such representation.

The perception of disagreement with nonbusiness interests reported in table 7.1, while significantly higher than the level of disagreement within the business community, seems nevertheless relatively low. The perception of trade unions' role is particularly interesting. It is reasonable to suppose that business would be more divided in its perception of consumer and environmental groups than of trade unions. One would expect business to be more uniformly opposed to trade unions. Some firms, like The Body Shop, are aggressive supporters of various environmental causes. A plausible interpretation of the high level of "neutral or irrelevant" responses for unions is that it is evidence that Thatcher achieved her goal of marginalizing unions in the policy process. The finding that more respondents saw unions as agreeing with them over policy than disagreeing is attributable to unions' current industrial as well as political weakness, to the diffusion of Japanese doctrines of personnel management, and to the diffusion of continental notions of "social partnership." Anxiety about international competition and the future of domestic industry induces compliance from unions. For the first time, and two months before the survey was administered, the head of the TUC invited his "social partner," the director general of CBI, to address the annual conference. The responses of senior managers on this item in the 1992 survey fit with the low estimation of the power of unions in public opinion polls after more than a decade of Conservative government.

A strong union movement is important to the quality of democracy.

There are, of course, a variety of issue groups, as well as church and community organizations, that represent alternative values to those of business interests in the policy debate. Perhaps in comparison to groups like these, unions may seem scandal prone and less worthy, rooted as they are in the rival interests that emerge in the hierarchy of the workplace, rather than in the struggle for the larger good. Yet these same narrow interests give unions an organizational extension and continuity that other groups lack, and they have the ability to expand the policy debate beyond choosing from among business values and the implementation recommendations of experts.

Even with their decline, trade unions remain the most consistent challenge to business interests and values, at the workplace and in the national political arena, and in this way can give meaning to the formal rules for collective decision making that are minimally necessary for democracy. Democracy may not be the primary objective, but it is a complementary one (Chartism). Historically, trade unionists have been at the forefront of the struggle for democracy and commonly are among the first to get locked up by nondemocrats.

Finally, and very importantly, unions' decline is as a national institution in an international economy. Their commitment to improving the security and conditions of work is as relevant as ever, and the idea of the self-regulating market is more "starkly utopian" in the international context than it was in the national context (see Polanyi 1944). The historical mirror to our age is the struggle to adjust to a national market in the nineteenth century. As national markets developed, and labor became urban, competitively priced, and removed from traditional sources of support, the political struggle crystallized to a choice between efficiency and humanity, and a variety of organizations including trade unions, social democratic parties, communist parties, and fascist parties capitalized on the opportunities created by this development. The change to continental and more international markets again pits efficiency, or reengineering and downsizing, against humanity and creates a parallel political uncertainty. There is opportunity for both reactionary (nationalistic, protectionist formulae) and reformist responses to the effort to re-commodify labor in a self-regulated market writ large. To the extent that unions can address the significant organizational challenge of cross-national and cross-cultural unity, they offer protection from the market, the "decommodification" of labor, and common standards of employment not defined by the lowest national standard of employment.

Karl Polanyi describes the nineteenth century achievement:

> They achieved what had been intended: the disruption of the market for that factor of production known as labor power. Such a market

could serve its purpose only if wages fell parallel with prices. In human terms such a postulate implied for the worker extreme instability of earnings, utter absence of professional standards, abject readiness to be shoved and pushed about indiscriminately, complete dependence on the whims of the market. Mises justly argued that if workers "did not act as trade unionists, but reduced their demands and changed their locations and occupations according to the requirements of the labor market, they could eventually find work." This sums up the position under a system based on the postulate of the commodity character of labor. It is not for the commodity to decide where it should be offered for sale, to what purpose it should be used, at what price it should be allowed to change hands, and in what manner it should be consumed or destroyed. (1944, 176)

Even if some human beings take Mises' deductive, unbearably cruel advice and act as *labor,* in an international economic system their equilibrating flow is moated and trenched politically and culturally. For advanced industrial countries there are profound "short-term" externalities to an international labor market including falling employment and social protection standards, the anxious anticipation of a free fall in such standards, and rising social resentment and its political manifestations. Policy responses that define the problem as a lost period of corporate social responsibility or as reconditioning the commodity through education are inadequate.

As political systems react to a more international economy, we can expect false starts in the effort to provide social protection equivalent to the Speenhamland Law, the popular parish-based effort to guarantee a living. "During the most active period of the Industrial Revolution, from 1795 to 1834, the creating of a labor market in England was prevented through the Speenhamland Law" (Polanyi 1944, 77). In the international economy, organized labor first seeks social protection on national lines through barriers to trade, perhaps in coalition with weaker performing corporations. This form of protection, like Speenhamland, may buy time, but it is no substitute for organizing for the international institutions, the social corollaries to the Single European Market, and NAFTA. Insofar as they are successful, that is, insofar as corporations know their competitors have to observe the same standard of social protection, trade unions even offer corporations relief from the unpleasant choices they are presented with by unconstrained market forces. Corporate greed and rootlessness attract attention, particularly when downsizing CEOs accept huge financial packages as incentive. Yet corporations have less scope for social responsibility as they position themselves to overcome competition in expanded markets, opportunistically seeking political protection, concentration, and cheap tricks to, in Marx's metaphor, "batter down Chinese walls." In this context trade unions, revitalized and international, remain relevant and normatively appealing.

Revitalization is a very difficult task, however, particularly given the national contexts in which some union movements find themselves. Although universal partners in the industrialization process, the fortunes of unions vary wildly across time and national boundaries. Business does not face a uniform challenge to its power, from period to period or country to country. The usual measure of union power, union density, or the proportion of the work force in unions ranges from about 10 to 15 percent in France and the United States to over 80 percent in Sweden. It is much easier for employers to substitute nonunion for union labor in the United States than it is in Sweden. Consequently unions are generally in a much weaker position at the workplace and command significantly less attention in policy-making circles in the United States than they do in Sweden.

While there is general agreement that union density, the proportion of the work force organized in unions, is an important element of union strength, social scientists are only beginning to identify the other critical elements. That union density is not the whole story can quickly be appreciated by comparing the influence of unions in Britain and Germany. For much of the postwar period union density has been higher in Britain than in Germany, although German unions have sustained at least as important a political and economic role as British unions. An influential theory of group-government relations directed our attention to the degree of hierarchy and monopoly present in an interest structure and to the degree of institutionalized access to policy-making circles, wrapping these characteristics together in the concept of corporatism. Yet there is a developing interest in disaggregating corporatism as part of an effort to understand the specific characteristics of labor movements that produce political and economic influence (Cameron 1984). In particular there is an interest in the relative "concentration" of union movements.

Union concentration or monopoly is comparable to the notion of industrial concentration for business and reflects the monopolistic or competitive nature of a country's union movement. Union concentration is important to unions' political influence for two principal reasons. First, the larger the number of unions, the smaller is each union's share of the membership pool. For unions, as for other groups, members are an important political resource. Second, increasing the number of unions increases the difficulty of achieving a common political position. There are other dimensions of union power, including institutionalized access to company decisions (German codetermination) or national policy-making circles (the Swedish remiss process). Yet concentration, in addition to union density, is likely a very important component of union power. If a high proportion of the work force belongs to the union movement, and if it is highly concentrated, then institutionalized access to the policy process and influence on policy outcomes will follow.

Complicating the definition and comparative measurement of the term is the role of national centers or confederations of unions. In some countries there is one center, in others unions cluster around two or three centers. It is generally supposed that increasing the number of centers decreases the cohesion of a union movement. Even so there is uncertainty about how to combine these elements of concentration, the number of unions and the number of centers, into a single measure of union concentration. The presence of only one center is not an unequivocal sign of union concentration. In the United States, far more significant than the apparently monopolistic AFL-CIO is the multiplicity of unions contained under that one confederation, as well as the large number of unions that are not affiliated with the confederation. Correspondingly, more than one center is not necessarily indicative of significant internal competition within the union movement. If the centers originate in political, ideological, or religious differences, rivalry among the centers is likely. In France, three major centers have organized the labor movement: the Force ouvrière (FO), the Confédération générale du travail (CGT), and the Confédération français democratique du travail (CFDT). The FO broke from the communist CGT in 1947 to represent a noncommunist alternative. In Italy, the communist center (CGIL) also coexists with two other major centers. It should be noted, however, that these Italian unions were able, at least for a decade or so, to suppress their political and ideological differences with their agreement, in 1972, to a more unified front. This agreement preceded a period of heightened union influence during the 1970s.

Yet, generally, if the centers are functionally distinct (for example, separate centers for salaried employees) or perhaps even "regionally" distinct (for example, the Scottish TUC), their roles in organizing the work force are likely to be compartmentalized, and relations between the centers are more likely to be harmonious. If the centers are ideologically distinct, then rivalry is likely. Cameron alludes to this point (1984, 170), but he does not recognize this third element, the *type* of confederation, in his coding of the organizational unity of national union movements as would be appropriate. To an extent the three elements, the number of unions, the number of confederations, and the type of confederations, are interrelated in that if there is rivalry among confederations there is also likely to be a proliferation of unions, since all compete for scarce members. The FO (twenty-seven affiliates), the CGT (thirty-four affiliates), and the CFDT (twenty-three affiliates) each have energy industry unions, for example. Given the difficulty of knowing the degree of rivalry among centers, the lack of a clearly stated operational rule for combining the center element with the number of unions element to form a concentration index is not surprising.

With the uncertain impact of confederations, there is something to be said for a more straightforward approach to operationalizing and measuring the important concept of the concentration of a union movement. Treating all confederations equally is unsatisfactory, and incorporating a third element, the type of confederation, is too complicated. Instead, why not reduce the analysis to the simplest and least equivocal element, the total number of national unions organizing the work force? In contrast to the difficulty of knowing the significance of centers for concentration in any particular case, the number of unions is indisputably a central theoretical element of the concept of concentration that should hold in all cases. What Mancur Olson says of firms in an industry applies to unions: "The high degree of organization of business interests, and the power of these business interests, must be due in large part to the fact that the business community is divided into a series of (generally oligopolistic) 'industries,' each of which contain a fairly small number of firms" (Olson 1971, 143; see also Golden 1993, 440). To continue the parallel, the firm, not the industry association, is the critical unit in the measurement of industry concentration or monopoly, so the union, not the association of unions, becomes the basic unit for the measurement of union concentration or monopoly. As the number of competing unions grows, membership shares decline and interunion cohesion suffers. The more unions, the more divided the movement, the harder it is to reach common authoritative positions. As the number of unions expands, so the chances of central control diminish. Other organizations, including governments, have a correspondingly diminished incentive to negotiate with any individual union. Internally, fewer larger unions can hope to enjoy scale economies in the costs of running the organization. So the larger the total number of unions in a country, the lower the concentration assessment is for that country— even if a large proportion of those unions are in one confederation. The number of unions as the measure of concentration has the additional advantages of simplicity and meaningfulness, reflecting a directly observable characteristic of labor movements.

Data on two principal dimensions of union strength—density and concentration—for seventeen countries for 1980 are presented in figure 7.1.[1] The great variation in union strength, even among relatively similar

---

1. The best available single source for information on national union movements is the *Europa Year Book*. The density data is the average for the 1965 to 1980 period provided in Cameron 1984. For a full discussion of this analysis see Mitchell 1996.

economic and political systems, is illustrated in figure 7.1. Concentration is measured by number of unions, an inverse scale with lower scores meaning higher levels of concentration. Using concentration and union density to identify the stronger union movements, the bottom-right quadrant of the graph, we find that we have successfully rounded up the usual suspects. Sweden, Norway, Belgium, Denmark, and Austria all score at or above 50 percent on the density scale, and roughly 50 or lower in number of unions. It is in these countries that business interests will find the stiffest resistance in the policy struggle. In the top-left corner, where unions are weakest, it is no surprise to find the United States.

So how do these resources convert into policy influence, to return once again to James Q. Wilson's question? One can argue that national economic performance as measured by unemployment or inflation indica-

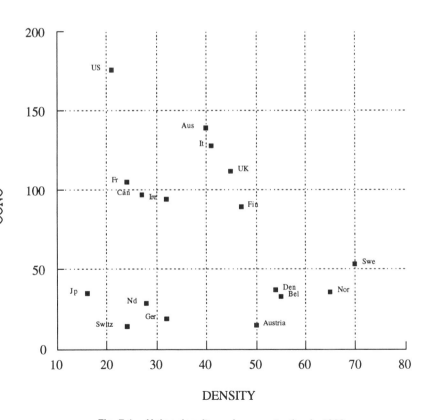

Fig. 7.1. Union density and concentration in 1980

tors is a way to test the relative influence of the organizational characteristics of union movements. Other political scientists have shown some interest in accounting for differences in national economic performance in terms of the structure and degree of union participation in national economic policy-making (Lange and Garrett 1985; Jackman 1987; Golden 1993). But these sorts of indicators may not provide the best test of coordinated union action or union power, since the determinants of economic performance are so diverse and the theoretical issues are quite complicated. It is less problematic and much more relevant to my concerns in this book to examine how the variation in union strength affects the policy struggle, rather than the more distantly related indicators of macroeconomic performance. The strength or weakness of union movements might be reflected at the company or industry level in wage levels and health and safety conditions, and in national politics, as Polanyi pointed out (1944), in the development of labor market distorting policies, like welfare policy, for example. Michael Goldfield, in his account of the increasingly unfavorable position of unions in the United States, says, "a strong, organized labor movement is often a key determinant in the passage of social legislation; conversely, the lack of strong social welfare programs in an economically developed capitalist country is often due to the weakness of organized labor" (Goldfield 1987, 27). Welfare policy provides a more direct test of the conversion of union resources into political influence than national differences in macroeconomic performance. Does welfare policy deviate furthest from market norms in those countries where unions are strongest?

A useful cross-national measure of welfare policies can be derived from these policies' "capacity to de-commodify" labor. Gosta Esping-Andersen describes decommodification as "emancipation from market dependency"—presumably the raison d'être of labor movements. In its operationalization, decommodification amounts to a measure of the relative generosity of welfare policies. Esping-Andersen calculates decommodification scores for a variety of countries based on benefit rates and the eligibility criteria (1990, 47; see also Swenson 1989). These independently collected data increase the objectivity of the analysis of the measures of union strength. Esping-Andersen focuses on the party variable in explaining decommodification. While acknowledging that "trade-unions may also influence policy," he omits them from the analysis "because trade-union strength is empirically substitutable by party strength" (Esping-Andersen 1990, 111). Socialist or social democratic parties use power to legislate social policy. The working class, it seems, collects its political and industrial strength behind a common policy agenda.

From figure 7.1 it is readily apparent that the stronger union movements are in countries also associated with generous welfare policies. Using Esping-Andersen's decommodification scores to measure welfare generosity for seventeen countries, the correlations with concentration measured by numbers of unions (−.78) and density (.60) are high. The negative sign for the number of unions indicates the direction of the relationship is as expected: the more unions, the lower the decommodification score. Including these variables in a multiple regression model, both concentration and density are significantly related to decommodification, with concentration having the greater influence.[2] While the analysis is based on a small number of cases, it provides strong support for Polanyi's historical account of the nature of union interference with national markets, showing that variations in union strength have an important positive relationship to the relative generosity of the welfare state. By extension the analysis indicates the varying capacity of union movements to resist business interests.

Unions do not present a uniform challenge to business and exhibit their weakness or strength in the outcomes of collective bargaining or through the policies that governments pursue. In broadly similar economic and political environments, these are all nations enjoying comparable levels of well-being, market economies, and basic democratic rights of association and speech; this variation in union power is quite remarkable. The particular weakness of American unions holds one's attention.

Why is it that on the North American continent the evolution of economic and social life has followed a different path? Although adrift from Europe for two centuries, we are nonetheless surprised to find the distinctiveness of the political and economic forms that characterize America. Of particular note is a political party system largely untouched by the ideological migrations that have swept Europe in this century and the stunted and less political trade union movement. A moveable frontier, a heterogeneous population, and a history without feudalism proved inhospitable surroundings for the European ideas of class solidarity and the justice of redistribution and for the successful and linked development of a socialist or social democratic party, a strong and legitimate trade union movement, and a timely and comprehensive welfare state; so the argument goes.

The fortunes of unions and left-wing parties are obviously interconnected. Cross-national studies have shown a strong positive correlation between the strength of unions and socialist parties. David Cameron, interpreting this correlation, says, "whether a nation's government is dom-

---

2. The simplified measure of concentration, the number of unions, actually performs better than Cameron's index in this analysis. For a more extensive treatment see Mitchell 1996.

inated, over the long run, by leftist or non-leftist parties depends very much on the organizational structure of the labour movement" (1984, 167). Just as plausibly we might turn the relationship the other way around. The strength of unions is itself dependent on the political success of the left and the establishment and maintenance of a friendly legal environment for union activity. One recent study finds that "a large share of cross-national variation of unionization rates can be explained with two variables: the cumulative impact of leftist governments and the size of the labor force" (Wallerstein 1989, 493). The size of the labor force is important because to achieve comparable union density figures, unions in large labor markets must incur the costs of recruiting many more members; Michael Wallerstein argues that unions in large labor markets accept a lower unionization rate. One feature of this argument is that unions, through their recruitment strategies, are seen as instrumental to their own success or failure. In the American case, both factors that inhibit union organization, the lack of supportive governments and the large size of the labor market, are present.

Their focus on industrial and economic goals and their historical reluctance to form stable political alliances and positions, as well as their weakness, distinguish unions in America. The absence of a working-class oriented party in the United States limits union options. In the United States, the concentration on the workplace rather than the political arena is itself encouraged by an underdeveloped welfare state, where even the secondary union interests of health insurance or pensions have been part of the negotiation with employers, rather than public policymakers. Elsewhere, unions couple industrial and economic goals with broader social and political goals. They sponsor, affiliate to, or work closely with social democratic or labor parties to accomplish these goals (United Kingdom, Germany, Austria, Sweden). Alternatively, unions may subordinate their economic and industrial goals to political goals—the opposite of American unions. Historically, these unions may even owe their existence to political parties, and the presence of a large Communist party exerts a major influence over the political dispositions and divisions within the trade union movement (France and Italy). The head of the CGT typically has had an important position in the French Communist party hierarchy. These three broad types of political strategies are not precisely illustrated from one nation to the next. In France, for example, the FO ("a union not a party") approximates some American unions in its traditionally anti-communist "apolitical" stance.

If stable relations with social democratic parties contribute to union strength, too little or too much politics is not good for unions. To simplify, too little politics (United States) betrays an ignorance of the fact that a union's well-being is in important ways dependent on public policy. Too much politics (France) multiplies unions, may mean the sacrifice of union organizational interests for political purposes, and may make it difficult to work with the party of government. In the 1980s, the decline in membership of the largest confederation (CGT), corresponds to the political decline of the French Communist party (PCF), which has seen its percentage of the vote fall from 20 percent in 1978 to 9 percent in 1993. While the Socialist party held the presidency from 1981 to 1995, distinguishably socialist economic and social policies lasted for only about the first year.

Explanations of union strength that incorporate political factors usually do so in terms of the presence of supportive social democratic governments or, to a lesser extent, the ideological divisions within union movements. The particular misfortunes of unions in the 1980s in Britain or the United States remind us that the degree to which right-wing governments create a hostile political and economic environment is also important. The anti-union policies of these right-wing governments can have consequences as important for unions as those stemming from the union-supporting policies of left-wing governments, though the policies of right-wing governments have been neglected, or "unoperationalized," by social scientists in the analysis of union strength. Michael Goldfield's account of American labor history is somewhat of an exception. He includes right-wing government in his analysis, though he is not persuaded of its significance: "While the independent effects of labor law and public policy may indeed be real, they may also be largely a reflection of the interrelations between unions and capitalists . . ." (Goldfield 1987, 189). We can construct this argument for a neglected independent variable, the policies of right-wing governments, within the framework of an equally neglected theorist, Mancur Olson, where the analysis of unions is concerned.

Despite Mancur Olson's lengthy discussion of unions in *The Logic of Collective Action,* academic studies of unions have ignored or downplayed the analytical utility of this approach.[3] Olson's application of an economic approach contributes to our understanding of union responses to membership losses, and it delineates some basic strategic considerations for market-oriented governments designing policy to weaken unions and anticipates aspects of the political argument (neoliberalism) for government policy.

Olson shows how large membership organizations like unions rely on compulsion and coercion to maintain their size and eliminate those who would enjoy the collective benefits but do not wish to bear the individual

---

3. See Crouch 1982, 67; Barry 1970; Goldfield's bibliography does not include Olson's work; see also Wallerstein 1989, 494–95.

costs, the free riders. "By far the most important single factor enabling large, national unions to survive," says Olson, "was that membership in those unions, and support of the strikes they called, was to a great degree compulsory. . . . Compulsory membership and picket lines are therefore of the essence of unionism" (1971, 68–71). Compulsion is exercised through the closed shop, the internal discipline of the organization, and picketing activities, which force members and nonmembers to bear the costs of a strike. Without compulsion nonmembers, who do not share the cost of union membership, can benefit from better working conditions and higher wages won by the union threatening or using strike action. Without the threat of such coercion, union demands will be empty. Olson also describes the ways in which an anti-union policy will be defended:

> There are of course many intelligent arguments against unions and the union shop. But none of them can rest alone on the premise that the union shop and other forms of compulsory unionism restrict individual freedom, unless the argument is used to cover all coercion used to support the provision of collective services. There is no less infringement of "rights" through taxation for the support of a police force. . . . The debate . . . should center not around the "rights" involved, but on whether or not a country would be better off if its unions were stronger or weaker. (88–89)

Finally, rational choice theory suggests how unions will respond to these sorts of policies. Deprived of compulsion, large organizations like unions will emphasize the "members only" benefits that they supply. Under this theory, organizers build large membership organizations on the basis of restricting or structuring the individual choices of members or potential members. The choices made by individuals will reflect their economic self-interest comparison of a union job against no job or, if the union cannot achieve that level of control, of membership benefits against membership costs, principally time and membership fees. Olson's work can be crystallized into five propositions about how governments will act, through operating on individual choices to weaken large organizations like unions, and how these organizations will respond:

1. Government policy will be designed to expand individual choices and limit organizational compulsion and coercion of nonmembers.
2. Government policy will be designed to weaken internal organizational authority over individual members.
3. Government policy will be designed to increase organizational

costs and the perceived costs of membership to current and potential members.

4. Government policy will be defended in terms of "individual freedom" and "national well-being."
5. Unions will respond to their organizational weakness by offering noncollective goods or selective incentives.

With this attention to the "logic" of policy, the empirical focus is an examination of the content of particular policies toward unions.

Unions are an integral part of the economic and political culture of a country, shaped by years of independent struggle, not just by legislation. Yet as often as not we identify milestones in that struggle by legislation, by Wagner, Taft-Hartley, or Trade Disputes acts. Recent Conservative governments' policy toward unions has been capsuled in a series of statutes and spread over more than a decade. As the 1988 survey data suggests, the neoliberal goal of reducing unions' economic and political power guides this tactical "step-by step" approach, which follows the hard-earned experience of Prime Minister Heath's disastrous frontal assault on union power with the 1971 Industrial Relations Act.

Running through this sequence of legislation are the issues of the closed shop, restricting striking and picketing, increasing organizational costs, and increasing the role of the union members in decision making. For a closed shop setup after 1980, the 1980 Employment Act stipulated the support of 80 percent of those entitled to vote, effectively making those who do not bother to vote count against the closed shop, and it widened the grounds for individuals' choosing not to join unions. The 1982 Employment Act made existing closed shops subject to periodic secret ballots, requiring majorities of 80 percent of those entitled to vote or 85 percent of those actually voting. Mopping up after a decade-long legislative onslaught on the unions, the 1990 Employment Act finally outlawed the closed shop.

The 1980 act narrowed the definition of lawful picketing to picketing at or near the picket's place of work. Otherwise injunctions and damages are possible. In 1982, trade unions as well as union officials became liable for damages and injunctions. Total membership determines the amount of damages for which a union can be liable, with a maximum of £250,000 for unions with over 100,000 members. Contracts requiring the use of union labor became illegal. The 1988 Employment Act's most radical measure was to provide the individual union member protection from union discipline if he or she refused to strike, even if a majority of members had approved the strike by secret ballot. The 1990 act made unions liable for claims of damages for all secondary strikes, made unions liable for unofficial strikes, and denied strikers fired for unofficial strikes an appeal to an industrial tribunal. The 1993 act permits citizens, whose access to services is threatened by union strike action, to seek injunctions against unions.

The main themes of the 1984 Trade Union Act were union democracy and union political expenditures. It made secret ballots for strikes compulsory and introduced ballots for trade union leaders at least every five years and union political funds (used to support the Labour party) every ten years. The 1988 legislation created a Commissioner for the Rights of Trade Union Members. This commissioner provides individual union members with financial help for legal actions against unions. The 1988 act made compulsory postal ballots for presidents, general secretaries, and both voting and nonvoting members of executive committees. The 1993 Trade Union Reform and Employment Rights Act required postal rather than workplace balloting of members before strikes and that the union give the employer a week's notice of strike action. This law also required unions to get periodic consent from members for the "check-off" system of paying union subscriptions. The check-off system, where companies deduct union dues from pay checks and pass them on to the union, is fundamental to union financing in the United Kingdom. The 1993 act is likely to make the check-off system more "porous," confronting members with the tangible cost of membership in a legal environment that has made it more difficult for unions to deliver benefits. Some members, as a result, decide not to pay. The consent requirement increases the cost for the company of providing this administrative benefit for unions and creates an incentive for companies to opt out altogether. Other methods of collection are not as comprehensive and will entail the unions bearing more of the administrative costs. A CBI survey of 318 companies with unions found that "changes in the check-off arrangements made by companies . . . point to further but not wholesale falls in trade union membership" (CBI January 1995).

The CPS, the conservative think tank founded in 1974, is credited with making trade union policy a priority for a Conservative party committed to the idea of the market (Cockett 1994, 274). As early as 1978 Thatcher was making plans to defeat the miners' union (see *Economist* May 27, 1978). Before assuming office, Conservative policymakers viewed trade unions as too powerful and too political. The legislation since 1980 directly addresses these problems by imposing internal reorganization designed to weaken the authority of union leaders and membership majorities in favor of dissident minorities and individuals and constraining external activities.

Following a similar strategy, the earlier American legislation that was designed to weaken organized labor targeted unions' abilities to compel and coerce. The Taft-Hartley Act followed a great strike wave and a decade of union growth stimulated by the Wagner Act, circumstances similar to the pre-Thatcher period in Britain, with the union-friendly Labour policies like the Employment Protection Act of 1975, and the "winter of discontent" strike wave that closed the decade and presaged a precipitous decline in union membership. The Taft-Hartley Act permitted the abolition of the closed shop by individual states or, for a weakened closed shop, if the majority of the membership agree. The threat of financial penalties and legal action restricted picketing, secondary action, and unofficial strikes. The Landrum-Griffin Act of 1959 provided for secret ballot elections for union officials every five years. British legislation excludes provisions for special boards or courts, the legal enforcement of collective bargaining, making strikes of government employees illegal, and denying union office to Communists. With respect to government employees, strikes are illegal only for the police, members of the armed services, and merchant seamen at sea in British waters. The attempt to rid GCHQ (the intelligence monitoring center at Cheltenham) of unions is the nearest Conservative governments came to acting in this area. From time to time the government has also expressed interest in removing the right to strike of workers in "essential industries" where "unions have the power to hold the nation to ransom," corresponding to the Taft-Hartley provision for calling off strikes in national emergencies.

How effective has Conservative policy been in weakening British unions? Union membership, as we have seen, is one dimension of union strength. Since 1980, union membership has declined year-by-year. Thatcher's years in office coincide with the most sustained and precipitous drop in union membership in the postwar period. That the decade prior to her assuming office was the best in the postwar period for union recruitment and was marked by highly visible union industrial and political victories make the consequences of Thatcher's policies for British trade unions more dramatic. From 1972 until 1979 union membership increased yearly; every year after 1979 union membership declined. While very high levels of unemployment characterized Thatcher's first two terms, even a fall in unemployment toward the end of the 1980s only slowed, it did not halt, further membership decline. Consequently, one cannot attribute union fortunes during this period entirely to the business cycle. Union density for 1991 was 33 percent, dropping over 22 percent since 1979. Richard Freeman and Jeffrey Pelletier provide a statistical analysis of data through 1986 that gives an important role to Thatcher's union legislation in the decline in union density in the United Kingdom in the 1980s (1990). Conventional, pluralist accounts of the political process direct our attention to the activities of groups and the effect on government. Thatcher's trade union policies, inspired by a particular view of the proper functioning of the economy, fostered by the work of business-funded think tanks rather than specifically demanded by business interests, and sharpened by the bitter experience of her Conservative predecessor, Edward Heath, in this policy area, illustrate the reverse dynamic, the effect of government on groups.

Clearly the variable "right-wing government" includes more than the union-specific legislation. In addition to the sequence of legislation targeted at unions, other elements of Thatcher's program contributed to union decline, notably privatization of the strongly unionized public sector in Britain, as well as her own determination to tackle the "enemy within." Further, while unemployment is not directly related to union strength in this period, her governments' willingness to tolerate very high levels of unemployment in the pursuit of other economic goals provided an unfavorable environment for union efforts to fight government policy. The parallel to the Conservative governments' achievement in reducing union power is the effect on American trade unions that the Taft-Hartley Act had in curtailing growth after the surge in membership produced by the Wagner Act.

How does the experience of British unions in the 1980s match that of unions in other countries? Thatcher's policies were pioneering, and other countries came to adopt her imperatives of privatization and unfettered market forces. However, throughout this period other international trends were damaging to unions. But if this analysis is correct we would expect her impact to reveal itself in cross-national comparisons of union membership.

Reporting differences and differences in treating retired and unemployed union members mean that the figures are often not readily comparable. In most countries membership data come from the unions themselves. In the United States this data comes from a survey. Figures from the International Labour Office and from the *Monthly Labor Review,* adjusted for comparability, are reported in table 7.2. A grim picture for unions generally emerges from table 7.2. Unions across the industrialized world felt the hostile economic trends, the high levels of unemployment, the decline of traditionally highly unionized industries, the increasing size of the private and service sector, the increase in part-time and female employment, the relative mobility of business, and the spread of Japanese management techniques. Of these trends, the increases in part-time and female employment are those to which unions can most easily respond. In the United Kingdom, union density for part-time workers is about half the rate for full-time workers, but part-time employment grew from 20 percent of the work force in 1983 to 28 percent in 1993. Unions do lower union dues for part-timers—but they could explore other recruitment strategies tailored to these types of workers. The question is whether the cost of these strategies is worth the membership gains. Most of these part-timers are women (80 percent). In EU countries, with the exception of Denmark, women generally are less likely to be members of unions than are men. The Dutch union federation, the FNV, launched a recruitment campaign in the mid-1980s focusing on women (FNV 2000) and appears to have had some success. Union density in that country was 29 percent in 1985 and increased to 35 percent in 1993 (see *Labour Research* March 1990, June 1993, September 1993). Whichever series one examines, the United Kingdom has experienced the largest negative difference in union density over this period. (Note that the MLR series understates the decline, since 1988, not 1989, data are used for the United Kingdom.) In no other country has a union movement faced such an implacably hostile government.

Shifts in public attitudes toward unions underline the success of Conservative policy. In 1978, 82 percent of a MORI poll agreed that "trade unions have too much power in Britain today." In 1993, only 24 percent agreed with this statement. One of Thatcher's cabinet ministers went so far as to say that, "In the context of a thousand years of British history that [taming the unions] will be seen as a significant event beyond calculation" (*Sunday Times* May 12, 1985).

Table 7.2. Union Density Cross-Nationally, 1980–89

Country	ILO			MLR		
	1980	1989	Difference	1980	1989	Difference
Australia				40[a]	34[b]	−6
Denmark				76	75[c]	−1
France	18	10	−8	19	11	−8
Germany	36	32	−4	36	33	−3
Italy				53	47	−6
Japan	30	26	−4	31	26	−5
Netherlands				35	28	−7
Sweden				80	84	+4
Switzerland				33	28[d]	−5
United Kingdom	55	39	−16	51	41[b]	−10
United States	21	15	−6	22	16	−6

Source: ILO data from *Economist,* April 3, 1993. MLR data from Chang and Sorrentino 1991, 50.
[a]1982
[b]1988
[c]1990
[d]1986

As the key legislation was already in place, Ronald Reagan's effect on American unions was less dramatic than Thatcher's on British unions, and his claims to historical significance probably lie elsewhere. Yet Reagan, too, served as an inspiration to the private sector as he fired the nation's air traffic controllers when they went on strike and made hostile appointments to the National Labor Relations Board. By the late 1980s, a sharp increase occurred in illegal firings of workers "for exercising their rights to organize," and there were fewer union representation elections (*Business Week* May 23, 1994, 78). Unions lost cases in the Supreme Court—for example, a 1984 decision permitted a company to break collective bargaining agreements under the bankruptcy law. They lost in government agencies as well. During the Reagan and Bush terms, the OSHA "was a hands-off agency—and work-days lost to injuries jumped from 58 per 100 workers in 1983 to 86 in 1991" (*Business Week* May 23, 1994, 78). Union density in the United States dropped from about 21 percent in 1980 to 15 percent in 1990.

To an extent density is destiny for unions. Yet through recruitment activities they are not completely at the mercy of favorable or unfavorable labor markets and friendly or unfriendly governments. With financial services, cheap mortgages, discounts on cars, travel clubs, and credit cards, British unions are hoping to address recruitment difficulties. Most unions and the TUC are shareholders in the Unity Trust Bank, established in 1984, which offers a personal pension plan for union members. The General Municipal Boilermakers (GMB) general workers' union was the first to offer a credit card in 1988. Unions are also providing services—for example, access to lawyers and accountants—for their members.

The aggregate membership data do not suggest that these sorts of selective incentives have been effective, although it could be that the situation would have been still worse without them. Only with data on the individual member's decision making could one estimate with any confidence the effect of these selective incentives. Olson is not sanguine about noncompulsory unions: "It seems difficult to find more than a few examples of large unions that have supported themselves primarily by providing noncollective benefits . . ." (1971, 73). The success of these sorts of incentives depends on their value and presumably on the existence of substitutes available to nonmembers. The more common these sorts of selective incentives become, perhaps with other membership groups besides unions offering them, the less recruitment advantage they will confer on any individual union. The pressure of market forces to innovate and seek imaginative and more expensive new packages for members will be continuous.

Although these selective incentives are new in content, and some British unionists oppose this "business unionism," unions have anticipated, for some time, the lessons of rational choice theory applied to collective action problems. Returning to the issue of American union weakness, at the beginning of this century unions in Britain and other European countries offered significant welfare benefits to union members. American unions were more reluctant to get involved in this sort of activity. In 1910, when the Labour party received the same percentage of the vote (6 percent) as the Socialist party did two years later in the American presidential election, union density was 10 percent in the United States, 13.8 percent in Germany, and 14.6 percent in the United Kingdom. In 1920, union density was 45 percent in Germany, 45 percent in the United Kingdom, and yet only 16.7 percent in the United States (Bain and Price 1980). With a comparable level of density before World War I, unions became weak in the United States in part because the government, unlike European governments, did not implement social policy through union administrative structures. In particular, the American unions did not develop systems of providing unemployment benefits for members, and the American government did not implement measures to cope with the problem of unemployment. Many European countries had central or local government-assisted union unemployment benefit schemes during the early years of the twentieth century, but, as scholars at the time noted, there were no similar efforts in the United States.

Generally, American unions had not provided welfare benefits, including unemployment benefits, to nearly the same extent as European unions. Very few private union schemes provided the administrative structure on which government could build. As late as 1916, only three national unions in America paid unemployment benefits: the Cigar Makers, the Deutsch-Amerikanischen Typographia, and the Diamond Workers (Smelser 1919, 130). In contrast in Britain in 1904, 81 of the 100 most important British unions paid some form of unemployment benefits (Gilson 1931, 34). In Germany, unions used unemployment insurance as a means to counteract "fluctuations of membership." In 1898, 12 unions offered this selective incentive, increasing to 27 in 1904 and to 41 in 1910 (Perlman 1968, 90–91).

During this period in Europe it was the general practice for governments to assist unions that had unemployment benefit schemes, making the unions less vulnerable to membership erosion in depressions and offering a "selective incentive" to join or remain in the union. In 1901, the city of Ghent began to subsidize organizations that had unemployment benefit schemes. Most of these organizations were trade unions. Over the next two years, Belgium saw eighty-four municipal funds set up to assist union unemployment benefit schemes. Beginning in 1907, the central government also began providing subsidies. France, Denmark, Norway, Czechoslovakia, Finland, Spain, The Netherlands, Switzerland, Germany, and Great Britain launched similar initiatives before 1920. The Ghent system was the model because it was easy to start; it encouraged workers to provide for themselves; it was simple and cheap to administer, relying as it did on existing union structures; and it was expected to reduce fraud (Cohen 1921, 89).

At the beginning of World War I, a variety of German cities, including Cologne, Strassburg, Stuttgart, Mannheim, and Leipzig, had adopted the Ghent system (Cohen 1921, 143). Despite Bismarck's interest in social welfare policies in the late nineteenth century, his country did not establish a national unemployment policy until 1927. Britain set up the first compulsory unemployment insurance scheme in 1911. The Liberal government enacted a compulsory scheme in spite of, rather than because of, pressures from unions and their political supporters. Prior to this act, the trade union movement had been "suspicious of government welfare activities that would invade a province regarded by the unions as their own" (Gilbert 1966, 279). The Webbs, in their minority report of the Poor Law Commission, opposed "compulsory unemployment insurance on the ground that it might prove injurious to the interests of the trade unions . . ." (Gilson 1931, 40). In the end, the act reflected union interests by adding a provision for a Ghent-type arrangement. Central government subsidized the unemployment benefit expenditures of trade unions. Another provision of the act permitted unions to administer the state benefits.

Union unemployment insurance as an inducement to join or remain in a union appears to have encouraged a growth in membership. In 1902, the Ghent fund had an affiliated union membership of 12,239. In 1907, the figure was 17,426. In 1920, the Belgian government intervened to increase the membership of those unions paying unemployment benefits by providing a daily allowance to unemployed members of unions affiliated with municipal funds and denying poor relief to workers who did not belong to such organizations. Membership increased from 126,000 in 1913 to 800,000 in 1921 (National Industrial Conference Board 1932, 30). In the policy debate over unemployment in Sweden prior to World War I, the Social Democrats supported "Ghent-type insurance as an aid to unionization" (Heclo 1974, 73).

In Denmark, Norway, and Britain, where there are available union membership figures and where central governments introduced subsidies at one point in time (the impact of local government subsidies in different cities that started subsidies in different years would be difficult to isolate), these policies seem to have had a positive effect on union membership—although we can only look at membership gains and losses and not examine members' reasons for their actions. In each of the three countries the year of introduction marks substantial increases in the rate of membership growth, although the effect is more dramatic in Norway (+62 percent in 1906) and Britain (+22.3 percent in 1911) than in Denmark (+10.8 percent in 1907). While in Britain and Denmark these were the highest annual growth rates for the three years preceding the year of introduction and the three years following the introduction, in Norway union membership actually increased by 73 percent in 1905, was at 62 percent for 1906, 54 percent for 1907, and 21 percent for 1908. That American unions did not develop unemployment insurance in a similar way to European unions and could not take advantage of government subsidized union employment schemes may have contributed to the comparatively slow growth of American union membership in the early twentieth century. The Ghent-type system provided unions with government subsidized selective incentives for union members.[4] During the first decades of this century the lack of these unemployment benefits is part of the explanation for the comparatively low level of union membership in the United States.

This analysis has relied on the application of rational choice analysis to problems of collective action in its unmodified form. But in at least one area, union members' approval of political funds, British trade unionists responded to "purposive incentives," or inhabited the "world of morals" as Peter Swenson puts it (1989, 11) and consequently dealt a significant defeat to Conservative policy based on the "logic of collective action." The 1984 law requiring ballots on union political funds resulted in a remarkable union-by-union vote for retaining these funds, which represent about 80 percent of Labour party income. A negative vote would have prohibited the small individual contributions to these union political funds. In conjunction with a very active union campaign in favor of these funds, union members voted in a "political" rather than "economic" way. Ten years later union members again voted overwhelmingly to retain these funds, and a number of unions that had not had funds have since voted to set them up.

The Conservatives defended their union policies as a means of advancing the cause of "individual freedom," of ensuring that the rights of union members are "fully developed so that they provide the ordinary member with the effective protection that he or she is entitled to enjoy in a free society" (*Trade Unions and Their Members* 1987). The 1980 act widened the unfair dismissal definition, which previously was sustained only in terms of religious objections to unions. "Deep convictions" became grounds for not joining a union. But the government could not

---

4. For analyses showing the positive impact of the Ghent system on postwar levels of unionization see Rothstein 1990; Western 1993.

advance this policy on the basis of the individual freedom argument alone, without running into the inconsistencies Olson's discussion anticipates. Secretary of State for Employment Michael Howard, in the Second Reading debate for the 1990 act that ended the closed shop, described it as a "hammer blow for the freedom of the individual" (House of Commons 1990, col. 38). However, he brings the defense of government policy in line with proposition 4 and rescues the government's position from relying solely on the individual freedom claim in the following way: "the aim of all government legislation had been to curb union power, particularly over individual members, *where it was damaging to the interests of the country as a whole*" (*The Independent* January 5, 1990), as Olson anticipated (1971, 89). Unions raise the cost of production, make British industry less competitive, and create unemployment, according to the government's neoliberal ideology.

Olson's logic, identifying as it does the principal difficulties that large membership organizations face, allows us to anticipate right-wing government strategy that has as its goal the weakening of just such a type of organization. A major element of Conservative policy toward the unions, as well as American policy in the 1940s and 1950s, was to eliminate the ability of unions to compel and coerce individuals, as suggested in proposition 1. Most directly, the Conservatives progressively abolished closed shops, outlawed union labor requirements, and constrained the ability to strike. The commissioner is an institutional symbol of the effort to weaken unions' ability to compel and coerce. Undermining union discipline of members who refused to strike weakened the internal authority of union leadership (proposition 2). This attack on organizational authority encourages rational individuals to respond to the economic incentive not to bear the cost of union membership but to enjoy the collective benefits that are won by unions. At the same time, these measures make it more difficult to realize these collective benefits. The policy increased the costs of union participation by limiting the time off from work allowed for trade union duties and the organization cost of collecting union dues (proposition 3). The government justifies the pursuit of the policy in terms of individual freedom and national economic goals (proposition 4).[5] Unions have responded to their organizational weakness in the way predicted. They have begun offering packages of selective incentives to members (proposition 5). From the union perspective, the alternative, less expensive, and probably more effective remedy to selective incentives is union-friendly government action. Hostile policies are reversible, but such action

---

5. For an assessment that credits the Thatcher governments with a somewhat more modest impact on unions see Marsh 1992.

becomes increasingly difficult for national governments to contemplate, even for social democratic or Labour governments, without assurance that governments of other countries will move in a similar direction.

As business interests will not generally countervail themselves in the policy struggle, attention must focus on the capacities of opposing interests. The diverse experiences of union movements illustrate the national variation in countervailing power. Even the bastions of union strength have had to face such factors as higher long-term rates of unemployment, the disposition to privatize, and the corporation with increased mobility. The comparatively sudden decline in union resources in the United Kingdom puts in particularly sharp relief among the general union-hostile economic and political trends the importance of the strategic interaction with governments for the well-being of these organizations. The anti-union ideas of the Conservative party in the 1980s, positioning the United Kingdom for competition in the Single Market, resulted in a sequence of policies that had an important impact on union activities. With these hostile trends business will be less effectively resisted and fail less often in the policy struggle.

CHAPTER 8

Business, Unions, and the Policy Process

So far the determinants, dimensions, and consequences of union power have been considered but without direct comparison with business interests and without discussion of how unions participate in the policy process. By examining the pattern of participation with data from the survey of British business and unions, we can compare the positions of these organizations, directly drawing out the implications for the thesis of countervailing power. What we find is an asymmetrical pattern that favors business interests, a pattern that holds when we extend the analysis from the national to the international arena. In the international arena, labor is at a particular disadvantage because of the impact of the expanded labor market on union concentration and coordination.

There are fewer routes for labor representation than for business representation. Trade unions can contact the government directly, or they can channel their views through confederations like the TUC. From the survey data, individual unions tend to rely more heavily on the TUC than do trade associations on the CBI. Increasing the number of active interests complicates representation. Individual firms, unlike individual members of trade unions, are an important source of political activity. Their participation in the representation of business interests adds an additional direct route to government and two indirect routes through the CBI and through trade associations, creating a more dispersed, circuitous, pattern of representation than is to be found on the labor side. In terms of flows, the major contrast is between the CBI and the TUC. The TUC is a more important junction in the representation of labor interests than is the CBI on the business side. Trade unions tend to route representation through the TUC, whereas firms and trade associations tend to circumnavigate the CBI, making more use of direct contact. In the survey the frequency of contact for each route was indicated on a scale with "always" as 1, "often" as 2, "sometimes" as 3, "rarely" as 4, and "never" as 5. The mean score for trade union use of the TUC to contact government was 2.7 on the five-point scale. Firms and trade associations or employer groups are in surprisingly exact agreement over how little of their contact with government they route through the CBI, both with mean scores of 3.4. Consequently,

Thatcher's exclusion of both the CBI and the TUC in the 1980s was felt much more severely on the labor side than the business side.

To this point, government has been referred to as the destination without any more precise definition. A general characteristic of parliamentary constitutional structures is that interests direct their attention and activity first toward the executive rather than elsewhere. Distinguishing among three types of activity depending on whether it is aimed at the executive, the legislature, or public opinion, Punnett says that "pressure on the Government and the Civil Service is the most direct and most important sphere of influence . . ." (1988, 152). The survey data support this ordering. As part of the survey, business associations and trade unions were asked to indicate how often (often, sometimes, rarely, never) they use various types of activity to influence government policy. The frequency of use of various types of activity and the percentage of respondents rating, on a five-point scale, each activity as "most effective" are shown in table 8.1. Unions and business groups direct most contacts at the executive. The relative ease of making written submissions means that they are the most popular, if not the most effective, type of activity. Civil servants are the focus of much of the attention, and these organizations view them as the most effective means of contact. Perhaps the most interesting results in table 8.1 are the comparatively high use of parliamentary lobbying and the low use and effectiveness ranking of committees.

In a parliamentary system the legislature is not expected to play an important role in policy-making. Nelson Polsby has distinguished among the policy-making powers of national legislatures, through the use of a continuum running from "arena" legislatures to "transformative" legisla-

Table 8.1.   Business Associations, Unions, and Types of Political Activity: Percentage Frequency of Use and Effectiveness Rankings

"Under a Conservative government, how often does your organisation use the following types of activity to influence government policy? Under a Conservative government, which of the following types of activity does your organisation find most effective in influencing government policy?"

	Often	Sometimes	Rarely	Never	Most Effective
Committees	7	23	33	38	0
Meeting ministers	27	46	23	4	22
Meeting civil servants	55	22	22	1	34
Written submissions	61	32	6	1	5
Lobbying	44	44	9	4	18
PR campaign	30	30	34	6	21
Protests/strikes	7	27	19	47	8

tures, those that have an independent capacity to make policy. The House of Commons is at the arena end of the scale, put there principally by the dominant position of a disciplined political party controlling a majority of the seats. Compared to the U.S. Congress, its powers may not be very impressive, but the data indicate that British economic interests treat the House of Commons as a serious stage in the policy process.

The limited role of committees indicated in the survey is consistent with responses on two other items. In 1988, respondents were asked to assess the importance ("very important, important, or unimportant") of the NEDC. Prime Minister Harold Macmillan's government set up the NEDC to provide a regular, institutionalized forum for business, unions, and government to meet at the highest levels on economic issues. About 82 percent rated the NEDC as unimportant in 1988 (it was abolished under John Major). Respondents were also asked to compare bipartite meetings with tripartite meetings in effectiveness —76 percent thought one-on-one meetings most effective. It is very likely that the anticorporatist ethic contained within Thatcherism reduced the reliance on committees, even Royal Commissions. But even under the last Labour government—some very important committees like the Health and Safety Commission notwithstanding—committees were generally not the focus of economic interest representation.

The results presented so far provide a simplified general overview. To add further complexity to the discussion, the survey elicited some supplementary comments on the question of the types of activity used to influence government. The point made most consistently was the importance of the substance of the issue influencing the choice of approach to government: "the most effective way of influencing Government on a detailed issue without wide political implications would usually be by meeting the relevant civil servants: whereas on some other issues a public relations campaign and parliamentary lobbying are more appropriate."

While some groups may have the discretion to choose between methods, other groups may always be on the "outside," with recourse only to lobbying, campaigns, and protests. Thus far the assumption, consistent with pluralist theory, has been that all economic interests approach the policy process with more or less the same set of tools of influence. Others have, however, distinguished between "insiders" and "outsiders," arguing that privileged access is accorded some groups, whereas others are left on the outside to campaign and protest. Business interests are the consummate insiders.

Thus if one distinguishes between trade unions and business groups by types of activity and assessments of effectiveness, two different patterns will emerge. Business, with its privileged position, will interact with government more frequently, at a higher level, and more "effectively." For support for this expectation see table 8.2, which shows the percentage of business groups and unions in the "most often used" and "most effective" categories for each type of political activity. It seems that the weighting of contacts in favor of the executive that emerged from the overall picture (table 8.1) is more attributable to employer groups. The two sides of economic representation make very different use of the types of political activity. For the labor side, protest activity is more frequent than meetings with ministers, and public relations campaigns are more frequent than meetings with civil servants. One union respondent wrote, rather poignantly, that representatives of his organization "had not been asked to meet a minister since 1979." It seems reasonable that unions use lobbying less frequently than business groups given the size of the government's parliamentary majority at the time of the survey. The relatively high union effectiveness rating for lobbying probably reflects their desperate situation with respect to the executive, rather than any notable successes in the House of Commons. Union respondents sometimes annotated the item on effectiveness with statements that no type of activity "seems effective at present," or "N/A—no influence." These patterns will confirm the likely impressions of any observer of British politics over the last fifteen years or so. However, our theories have, at best, elided the advantageous position business interests possess in the political system and ill-prepare us for this British evidence.

As unions rely less on their own activity and more on the TUC for representation, the specific reception of the labor-side peak organization in government circles becomes more important. Analysis of TUC activity alone produces results, including the importance of protest activity, consistent with those reported here (Marsh 1992; Mitchell 1987). The contrasts in table 8.2 are not contrasts in tactics, for that term implies an ele-

Table 8.2. Types of Political Activity: Percentage Frequency of Use and Effectiveness for Business Associations and Unions

	Most Often Used		Most Effective	
	Associations	Unions	Associations	Unions
Committees	7	6	0	0
Meeting ministers	47	6	27	17
Meeting civil servants	86	21	58	10
Written submissions	78	43	6	3
Lobbying	57	29	10	24
PR campaign	21	38	3	38
Protests/strikes	0	14	0	13

ment of choice. Choices are being made by the government rather than the groups. Protests and public relations are the resort of interests denied access elsewhere in the political system.

The political party that controls government affects economic interest representation. Respondents were asked to distinguish between parties of government in some of their responses. Table 8.3 shows the way respondents compare the policy benefits of Conservative and Labour governments (see chapter 4 for an analysis of firm responses alone). Firms, business associations, and trades unions differentiate between the political parties in terms of policy benefits in the predictable directions. The unions are more solid and cohesive in their evaluations of parties than are employer groups or firms. In evaluating the policy benefits of a Conservative government, the unions are united in negativity. They remember, however, generally beneficial policies from Labour governments. The unions perceive the gap between the political parties as widest in policy terms. While revealing a preference for a Conservative government, firms and employer groups, even under a Labour government, more often than not choose a positive or "neutral" response rather than a negative one.

Introducing the activity of countervailing interests directly into the analysis reinforces the asymmetrical picture of economic representation. Moving from assessments of their own activities to business and labor assessments of their political position in relation to each other as opposing interests produces a perhaps surprising union and business consensus on the relative strength of the two sides. Among business associations, some 47 percent perceive their access to government as advantageously weighted in their favor, with the rest, perhaps more cautiously, rating their access as no worse than equal. Without wishing to overinterpret the modal "equal"

Table 8.3. Political Parties and Policy Benefits (by percentages)

"Indicate whether you agree/disagree with the following statement: Under a Labour or Conservative government, government policy directly concerning my organisation is usually beneficial to my organisation."

	Conservative Government			Labour Government		
	Firms	Assoc.	Unions	Firms	Assoc.	Unions
Strongly agree	9	3	0	0	3	16
Agree	34	50	0	9	15	61
Neutral	55	39	0	58	39	24
Disagree	2	8	21	30	39	0
Strongly disagree	0	0	79	2	3	0
Total	100	100	100	99	99	101
	($N=44$)	($N=36$)	($N=38$)	($N=43$)	($N=33$)	($N=38$)

response for business groups in table 8.4, when the rules are working in one's favor there is some self-interest in declaring them fair, or in this case "equal," for everybody. Among unions, 97 percent agree that access to government is weighted in the opposing groups' favor. While access does not automatically mean influence, lack of it translates easily into lack of influence. The groups themselves are quite aware of how much access depends on the type, business or nonbusiness, of interest involved.

Scholars have constructed a similar picture of an unbalanced representation system in the United States. Kay Schlozman and John Tierney, in an analysis of organizations that have representation in Washington D.C., found that in 1980, 72 percent of all interest-representing organizations represent business. Of these business organizations, 52 percent of the total are corporations, and 20 percent are trade and other business associations (Schlozman and Tierney 1986, 77). "Taken as a whole," they say, "the pressure community is heavily weighted in favor of business organizations. . . . The over representation of business interests takes place at the expense of two other kinds of organizations: groups representing broad public interests and groups representing the less advantaged"(Schlozman and Tierney 1986, 68). John Kingdon discovers a comparable pattern in his research on the transportation and health policy agendas in the late 1970s. On the basis of interviews with congressional staff, civil servants, and lobbyists, he finds that business interests are the most important of interest groups, with organized labor "involved less frequently," and consumer and environmentalist groups "sometimes" affecting policy agendas. Organized labor "were important in the emergence of issues in only 5 of the 23 case studies, with no marked differences between health and transportation," he says. With health policy, professional groups representing doctors and hospitals are the most important (Kingdon 1984, 50–51).

Table 8.4.   Comparative Access Assessments (by percentages)

"Under a Conservative government, how would you describe your organisation's access to government in comparison with organisations with opposing interests?"

	Associations	Unions
Highly advantageous	15	0
Advantageous	32	0
Equal	53	3
Disadvantageous	0	28
Highly disadvantageous	0	69
Total	100	100
	($N = 34$)	($N = 36$)

Approaching the issue with survey data on the policy process from the groups themselves, or with an assessment of how well groups are placed for interest representation, or with interviews of government officials provides consistent evidence concerning the comparative advantage of business interests in the policy process.

In the United States interest group activity focuses on the legislature rather than the executive. As a presidential system, with a clearer separation of powers and ill-disciplined political parties, the U.S. Congress more nearly approaches a transformative style legislature, in Polsby's terms. In a parliamentary system the "fusion" of powers between executive and legislature, except in extraordinary circumstances, results in the legislature largely ratifying decisions made by the executive. This type of system requires "disciplined" political parties; that is, members of the same party vote together in the legislature. Without this discipline the executive, dependent as it is on controlling a voting majority in the legislature, would find its existence in perpetual doubt. In contrast, in presidential systems the electorate chooses the executive independently of the legislature. Consequently, different parties may control these institutions. For this system to work "ill-disciplined" parties are a requirement. With discipline, even less would get done. Confronted with a Republican Congress, Democratic presidents hope they can rely on ad hoc cross-party coalitions to advance their legislative programs item by item. Therefore it is reasonable that, in contrast to the United Kingdom, the legislature in the United States, toward the transformative end of Polsby's continuum, should be the focus of interest group attention. Not only do legislatures provide more points of access for interest groups in presidential systems, their importance to the policy process makes such access worthwhile.

Interest organizations are well aware of these implications of institutional design. In Schlozman and Tierney's survey of interest organizations, 89 percent rated Congress as a "very important focus of activity." Executive agencies came second with 65 percent considering them very important, followed by the White House with 55 percent, and the courts with 22 percent. All types of organizations, corporations, trade associations, unions, and citizens' groups, rated Congress as the most important of American political institutions. The most significant differences among organizations emerged over the importance of the White House, with unions and citizens' groups regarding it as less important than corporations and trade associations (Schlozman and Tierney 1986, 272–73). These data reflect the situation with the Reagan White House and are supported by other studies. In an analysis of presidential meetings with interest organizations, Orman shows that between 1981 and 1983, President Reagan met with small business six times, corporate leaders forty-two times, business groups ten times, and professional associations six times. Among them these representatives of business had White House audiences on sixty-four occasions, or 35 percent of the total meetings held. President Reagan met with unions eighteen times and never met with public interest groups. In contrast, President Carter met with unions thirty-five times and business representatives (small business, bankers, professional associations, corporate leaders, national business groups) on thirty-nine occasions between 1977 and 1979, or 24 percent of the total meetings held (see Orman 1987, 63). Consistent with the British evidence, policymakers' agendas, most crudely distinguished by political party, have a distinct impact on the nature, in this case the frequency, of group-government interaction in the United States.

The national arena is not the only policy arena in which we should assess relative power positions. We can think about other aspects of the problem of countervailing powers in the way that we have been thinking about union movements in a national political context, and, as argued in the last chapter, we can add the consequences of the global economy to the other adverse economic trends unions face. With the addition of national differences, the global economy compounds the problem of coordination for unions. In circumstances where opponents might check business interests at the national level, business interests increasingly have the capacity, facilitated by the development of international organizations and regimes, to use the threat of exit and their international mobility to advantage. American firms, and foreign firms investing in America, manipulate federalism and interstate economic rivalry to achieve a more favorable investment environment in terms of local taxes, worker compensation laws, or even incorporation costs. The nimble multinational will treat nations no differently, wringing concessions not just from unions but from national governments as well.

The temptation for unions is to negotiate individually, to "defect" and to give up rights and wage demands to gain advantages over unions in other countries. So in 1993 the Amalgamated Engineering and Electricians' Union made a variety of concessions to persuade Hoover to switch investment from France to Scotland. The lesson, presumably, is not lost on the hundreds of unemployed French workers. While there may be an abstract awareness that unions would be better off if they cooperated on common standards in determining their bargaining position with multinationals, if left to themselves they will engage instead in competitive self-destruction. Cross-national cooperation is the counter strategy of the countervailing powers, a strategy that is at once more difficult and ultimately more rewarding than self-reliance and defection.

European integration is a business project. Labor's original ambivalence or hostility, notably from the TUC, was appropriate and to be expected because integration represented an uncontrolled expansion of the labor market. NAFTA represents a similar threat to U.S. unions. With integration accomplished to a significant degree, French, Scottish, German, or Belgian union members and social democrats must begin to think of themselves as Europeans, and, improbable it may sound, U.S. union members must begin to think of themselves as North-Central Americans. As Paulette Kurzer writes, "if social democratic parties and their allies miss this critical opportunity, they will fail to counter the influence of capital at the European level and will fail to inject a progressive element into the supranational European regulatory space" (Kurzer 1993, 253). To have a chance at countervailing the bargaining power of multinationals, unions and their political supporters have to organize and reach agreements on an international level. Such international cooperation for unions is very difficult to achieve and enforce.

In the European context it would be most efficient from a union perspective if EU institutions could establish and monitor cooperation, without permitting national defectors (the United Kingdom's "opt out" of the social chapter of the Maastricht Treaty). International relations theory suggests that the establishment of cooperation requires a dominant actor (a hegemon), one that has enough at stake to be willing to pay the price to establish a "regime" (see Keohane 1984). Germany is the only possible contender for this position, and the strength of its own union movement gives it an interest in such cooperative arrangements, hence its support of the social chapter. However, with generally high unemployment levels throughout Europe, the immediate prospects for improved international coordination among unions look bleak. One positive development for EU trade unionists is that the new members, Sweden, Austria, and Finland, are countries with strong union movements, both in density and in concentration.

Existing arrangements for coordinating union activity on a European level are weak. Currently the representation system in Brussels looks much like that in Washington or London. One study found approximately 72 percent of European interest groups to be industry and commerce groups. These groups tend to have better resources and have a "dense network of personal contacts and channels of information. Organizations representing social interests are fewer in number and younger. Promotional or cause groups are a very recent phenomenon" (Kohler-Koch 1994, 169–70). The European Trade Union Confederation, while supported financially and politically by the EU, remains understaffed and organizationally weakened by the rivalries that the national confederations carry with them. It does not include some important national centers, notably the French CGT. An alternative is for national unions to develop cooperative strategies on a more limited industry or firm basis. A possible forum for these strategies is the European Works Councils established by some European multinationals with French and German companies leading the way, or longer term there may be pressure to internalize the costs of these sorts of transactions by forming multinational unions.

In Europe, labor was at its strongest industrially and politically in the 1970s, the moment that corporatist theory froze. As labor's position improved in national institutions at this time, the improving mobility of business increasingly shifted issues of importance to labor to international institutions. As long as labor is unorganized at this level, business failures are even less likely. Clearly, national institutions can still do good or harm and strike better or worse bargains with nimble business. The problem for labor is that the expanded and internally divided labor market has created more options for business interests and national political incentives for governments, whether controlled by the right or the left, to trade domestic social priorities and arrangements for domestic or foreign investment. Commentators on European integration are fond of analogies to the birth of the United States, and the transition from independence, to the Articles of Confederation and to the federal system. It is fair to say that one dimension of the United States of Europe has been achieved, and Europeans are now experiencing the beggar-my-brother rivalry that federal systems can create in labor movements.

The ingredients of national union strength, density and concentration, remain important in this new "federal" economy. At this level, as at the national level, unions must aim to maximize membership and minimize organizational rivalry, which are accomplished most easily by reducing the number of unions organizing the work force. In some ways, the environmental movement, grounded more purely on commitment and long sensitive to the supranational nature of many environmental problems, promises the more "internationalist" of approaches. There are instances of union-environmentalist international cooperation. But firms move much more easily in the international economy that they have fashioned.

In part 3, I have examined the issue of countervailing powers, arguing that business divisions do not represent an effective check, and that unions vary cross-nationally in their capacity to resist business interests. In general, unions are in decline as national institutions, in part as a result of government design. Yet, as Polanyi points out, since the age of steam they have performed a vitally important civilizing function in interfering and encouraging governments to interfere in the labor market. What changes, moving from the Jet Age to the Net Age, is the size of the market, not the need to interfere with it.

PART 4

Business Failure

CHAPTER 9

Why Business Loses

Business interests are not routinely countervailed in the policy process. Their political resources and incentives to participate (large stakes/few interests) are usually greater than other interests. The further development of the international economy only adds to the privileged position. In identifying these advantages, it is explicitly recognized that business may still fail in the policy struggle; that is where the policy carries despite business political opposition to the policy. Such failures are treated as theoretically significant events, not as reason enough to dismiss the political advantages of business interests.

If policymakers' preferences are controlled, if there is such a thing as "structural" power rather than just a business confidence factor, if financial resources are known and convert through a frictionless process into political influence, with this information the policy outcome is simply predicted. In reality, captains of industry, well-armed though they are, engage in policy *struggles,* characterized by sometimes unreliable, perhaps heroic, politicians, a shifting set of adversaries, and volatile public preferences. The theoretical challenge lies in this uncertainty.

The argument begins with the simplifying assumption that policymakers seek to turn their ideas into policy, for which they will also seek political support. Policymakers choose among the policy positions of rival interests on the basis of the degree of congruence of those positions with their own ideas and on the basis of the capability of the interest to contribute to or detract from their public support. Their superior resources, their strong incentives to participate relative to citizens generally, and the structure of policymakers' goals and incentives generally favor business interests in the policy struggle. I develop this theoretical argument in four parts, briefly looking at the goals of policymakers, the characteristics of policies, the political resources of groups, and in some detail at the conditions under which business is in danger of losing in the policy struggle.

Taking the goals of policymakers seriously distinguishes this approach from pluralism or from any theory that assumes policymakers shift their positions more or less opportunistically to the interests of the most powerful groups or classes. Where do the goals of policymakers come from? A part of the answer lies with the policymakers themselves. Both elected and appointed policymakers will seek the rewards associated with their careers. Negatively, they would rather not lose their jobs, and positively they aspire to higher office. Politicians, however, are also members of political parties, and the assumption that political parties are just vehicles for careers in politics oversimplifies their influence on policy (see Budge and Keman 1990).[1] Political parties originate in the social, political, ideological, and religious divisions that characterize a society and collect around common beliefs about how society and government fit together. "Party is organized opinion," said Benjamin Disraeli. We now refer to organized opinion as ideology, from which political parties derive policy agendas. Parties attract individuals committed to a core constituency and to beliefs, in addition to their own careers. While treated with a good deal of public cynicism, party manifestos or platforms document the different policy agendas.

In understanding the policy struggle, the goals of public officials are the obvious place to start, but the pursuit and modification of these goals take place in a political context structured by the characteristics of the policy and the resources of affected interests. The characteristics of the particular policy will influence the degree of resistance or support policymakers meet when pursuing their policy agendas. Policy theory is helpful in pointing to the variation in incentives to participate politically. The size and distribution of expected costs and benefits for the affected interests will suggest how much effort those interests will be willing to expend to influence policy. If the costs or benefits of a policy are high and the affected group is small, then, as Stigler argues, they will have sufficient stake to try to influence the outcome. Generally policies concerning business are likely to be ones where the benefit is particular and tangible for the business interests and the costs are dispersed across everybody else as taxpayers or consumers, or where the costs are particular and tangible for business and the benefits are widely distributed. In either category, what

---

1. This approach is consistent with Ian Budge and Hans Keman's 1990 treatment of political parties and coalition formation. In their analysis they argue that politicians who are members of democratic parties seek government office in order to pursue policy agendas. The primary goal Budge and Keman identify is to "counter threats to the democratic system." The successful politicians will first want to maintain and defend the system through which they achieved their success. Threats to the political system increase the autonomy of policymakers from domestic interests and justify policy measures, perhaps public ownership or control over investment and product decisions, that in normal circumstances would not be considered. If there are no threats, the normal situation, then, as Budge and Keman argue, the ideologically specific agendas, within the context of getting reelected, guide policy-making.

James Q. Wilson termed client politics or entrepreneurial politics (1980), the incentives to be politically active favor business interests. The antibusiness position suffers from the difficulties involved in generating interest in an issue that affects large numbers of individuals only a little, within a political system characterized by relatively high information costs and infrequent political participation. The more concentrated these costs or benefits are on a small number of affected organizations then, the lower the temptation to free ride in the policy struggle. The more dispersed the costs or benefits, the higher the temptation to free ride.

What policy theorists tend to neglect is that the resources that actors can bring to bear, as well as the incentives actors have to be active, structure the policymakers' pursuit of goals, goals that are more complicated than simple office-seeking. The common resources of groups, possessed in varying amounts, include financial resources, the provision of information and expertise, the numbers and status of members, access to policymakers and the media, and the capacity to influence public preferences. If resources are in place, if there is a Washington office and a mechanism and budget for making financial contributions to politicians, for example, it is likely that the group will become politically active at a lower incentive level than a group that does not have these resources in place. On broader, industrywide or businesswide issues, the diminished incentive for any particular firm to be politically active, that is, the increased temptation to free ride, likely will be offset by the heightened activity of industry and businesswide associations. These are exactly the issues on which members expect the associations to play an important role and on which associations feel they can safely take a position and an activist stance. So the structure of business interest representation encourages a strong political presence on both narrow and broad issues of concern to business.

Business interests usually perform strongly on these resource dimensions. So much so that even if one restricts one's discussion of business power to these resources alone, the conventional resources of politics, it is questionable to claim that business is just a more important interest group or organization. As a claim it is analogous to the statement that "superpowers" or "hegemons" are just more important nation states. Yet to these conventional political resources business adds, and uniquely, its influence over investment, employment, income, and personal aspirations, which can translate into political influence through the importance of these factors to election outcomes. How business interests join the nuclear club, so to speak, is that public policymakers in a private economy are highly sensitive to the consequences of their decisions on business confidence, anticipating its effect on the indicators of economic performance and ultimately on public confidence in government. Some have referred to this dimension of business power as "structural dependence."

As already argued, structural dependence is better referred to as the business confidence factor, since the former may imply an invariable attention to business demands by government, whatever the policy agenda and ideology of government officials and whatever the direct political effort of business through electoral and interest group activity. The term *structural dependence* is misleading insofar as it connotes an automatic, constant, and inarticulate quality to this aspect of the relationship between business and government. The requirements for business confidence need to be identified to policymakers, policymakers must decide to act or not, and business interests have a strategic political interest in broadening the economic implications of a policy choice to others in the electorate—in other words, in creating a business confidence issue. One can think of the business confidence factor as an aspect of coalition building, although the other partners to the coalition are silent and yet to be mobilized.

Policymakers' willingness to make concessions to business will depend on how they assess the policy problem (see Anderson 1975), as well as what sort of economic and policy conditions business interests indicate are necessary. Public policymakers' assessment of the reasons for economic performance, and the policy justifications they can offer for their policies, will depend on the historical and intellectual context—the defunct economist of the day. It is not just the rise and fall of the economy but how they understand the economic cycle that determine how sensitive policymakers will be to business demands. This special dimension of business power, reinforced by the exhaustion of socialism and the prevailing conservative currents of analysis, serves to gear the more reform-minded politicians to business demands.

Focusing on the analysis, on the policy preferences derived from economic theory, as well as the actuality, is a more complicated approach to understanding policy-making, and more narrowly instances of business policy failure. Economists have developed useful indicators of cyclical patterns of business behavior, creating a temptation to apply these in our search for more certain knowledge of the policy-making process. There are no comparable measures of the situation of business in the short and long cycles of political-economic discourse. And while political scientists, economists, and sociologists have made progress in measuring business groups and organizations' capabilities in terms of the conventional resources of politics, they have not gotten very far with the work required to measure the business confidence factor in political decision making. It is a much more difficult task to measure policymakers' sensitivity to the effect their decisions will have on business investment plans than to examine the financial contributions to election candidates or lobbying efforts. It is not enough to examine policy outcomes and attribute business successes to the business confidence factor. Given the superior electoral and lobbying resources of business, they alone could account for the successes (see Quinn and Shapiro 1991 for this sort of argument). We should conceive business confidence as an incentive, not an imperative, for politicians to conform to business interests, operating in conjunction with the interest group dimension of business political power. While conservative parties will generally find this incentive reinforcing their natural inclinations, social democrats, in the absence of an economic theory that rescues them from the dilemma, will perpetually struggle with the trade-off between votes and principles.

How, then, can business interests lose in the policy struggle? In office, conservative or probusiness parties openly and actively pursue their declared conceptions of what will improve national business performance. And we are accustomed to socialist or social-democratic parties, laboring under quite orthodox analyses of the economy and aware of the political importance of keeping appropriate macroeconomic indicators and election cycles in harmony, consistently surrendering to the temptation to trim their reforms. Where public policymakers do not already want what business wants, business has to resort to its formidable lobbying resources. At the same time the general characteristics of policy mean that business interests are often the most highly motivated participants in the decision-making process, whereas their opposition often suffers from the high costs of becoming informed and organized for political participation.

Some argue that because divisions exist within the business community, business political power effectively countervails itself. There is something in this argument, but not perhaps as much as one might think. The empirical evidence, discussed in chapter 7, suggests that business interests are more often in alliance, or indifferent, than in opposition. Most importantly, on the normative level, democrats should be no more satisfied with the argument that because business interests disagree, say telephone and cable television companies, the viewers' interest is therefore represented than they are with the argument that because male legislators, say Senator Kennedy and Senator Specter, disagree, therefore women's interests are necessarily represented. Yet division may increase nonbusiness interests' bargaining power. A tactical goal of policymakers who wish to defy business will be to divide business interests.

If significant business interests emerge on both sides of a policy issue, as in the United States with the 1986 Tax Reform Act, the situation cannot really be described as a business policy failure and is theoretically less interesting from the perspective I present in this book. Cathy J. Martin provides a detailed account of the significant split between service-oriented industries and manufacturing and real estate industries in the struggle over American tax reform in 1986 (1991). Here the interesting cases are where business loses to nonbusiness interests, that is, where the raw power of business interests does not prevail. Part of the analytical challenge, as we shall see, is establishing that there are such cases where business loses. The temptation for business dominance theorists is to define away these losses by identifying splits, latent or actual, in the business community. Part of the problem is that the business world is not so particular about who belongs, and it will always have its share of mavericks, even socialists: Robert Owen to Bernard Tapie. Consequently, on any issue it may be possible to find some trace of division, although that division is not decisive in the policy outcome. In chapter 10, I return to this issue in the case analyses of business policy losses.

So in the absence of significant business division on a policy issue how can business lose? One possibility is that policymakers are indifferent to the superior resources and the consequences for their political support: the public policymaker with a policy agenda in conflict with business interests, who refuses to compromise with the imperatives of encouraging business investment and electoral short-termism, refuses to bend to financial and lobbying pressure, and heroically raises his or her risk of losing public confidence and possibly office in order to act according to principle. Individuals may behave in this way, and in some cases individuals alone may be able to make policy, but it would seem unlikely that legislative majorities would find such resolve. Instead of an explanation based solely on "two-o'clock-in-the-morning" heroism, let us think about the circumstances under which ordinary politicians might recalculate the risks of going against business interests.

Returning to the discussion of the goals of policymakers, in extreme circumstances such as war the threat to the system that gave the policymakers power will take precedence over all other considerations (see Budge and Keman 1990). For business, the likelihood of policy losses increases when business interests are opposed to a policy designed as a response to a threat to the political system. Although not often made explicit, this statement is straightforward, unlikely to be controversial, and given the rarity of these sorts of circumstances of limited explanatory interest. Absent these extreme circumstances, how is it that policymakers can at times be led to see their interests in opposition to business interests?

At the heart of politics is the exercise of power. Getting someone to do what you want, one way or another, is exercising power. Power rests on having the means to coerce, to induce, and on the opinion that the exercise of power is justified—in short, that it is legitimate, is consonant with wider values, or has political support: "Scholars often equate political legitimacy and political support, and we have found it useful to do so as well" (Caldeira and Gibson 1995, 357). Even authoritarian systems cannot rely on force alone, as David Hume long ago pointed out:

> It is, therefore, on opinion only that government is founded, and this maxim extends to the most despotic and most military governments as well as to the most free and most popular. The soldan of Egypt or the emperor of Rome might drive his harmless subjects like brute beasts against their sentiments and inclination. But he must, at least, have led his mamalukes or praetorian bands, like men, by their opinion. (1948, 307)

In using the concept legitimacy, the interest here is in the perception, not whether some practice or action is or is not legitimate.

Business risks losing in the policy struggle when business's policy position lacks legitimacy or policymakers expect the business position to lack legitimacy. In the discussion of the first pillar of business power, legitimacy was described as public support for economic, social, or political practices. This support depends on the perceived consonance of the practice with the wider set of values that a community shares. Legitimacy problems increase in severity as the number of individuals that perceive the exercise of power is unjustified rises, as the groups and organizations to which these individuals belong diversify, and as the scope of criticism moves from very specific issues (say Richard Nixon or Roger Smith of GM) to institutional or systemwide issues (say the presidency or capitalism). Legitimacy problems impair business interests' capability of delivering public support to politicians. Business vulnerability on policy positions results from legitimacy problems redefining, at least temporarily, the self-interest of politicians. Elected officials, when faced with a choice between business confidence and public confidence, so to speak, are likely to choose the latter.

Policy theory helps us isolate the political problem for antibusiness interests. To overcome their relative disadvantages in resources and in the usually unfavorable policy cost and benefit calculus, antibusiness interests must aim to raise the stake that the public has in an issue, reduce information costs, and create an incentive for citizens to become politically active. They can do this by raising or leveraging a business legitimacy problem. For policymakers the more widely distributed the awareness of a policy and its possible consequences, the more significant a factor it will be to their decision making. In other words, the public attention an issue is receiving and the distribution of opinion on the issue are important components of the decision (see Lindblom 1984). If the corporation conspicuously does the wrong thing, the politician can afford to be virtuous, and the likelihood of a business policy loss increases.

The policy opportunity presented is more likely to be seized by reformist or social-democratic parties. This statement seems commonplace. But the existing theories, from pluralism to policy theory, give political parties a minimal role. The "organized opinion" and constituencies of these types of parties will make the policy debate more open and competitive. When the legitimacy of business is questioned, social democrats do not have to choose between their beliefs and their support. Policymakers from these parties will be more accessible to the adversaries of business, and they will welcome the liberating effect on their policy agenda. In short, when the legitimacy of business is questioned, the axioms of legislating ideas and of generating support are in harmony, not conflict.

Legitimacy is a useful concept, linking as it does the power of business to the circumstances under which we might expect policymakers, particularly reformers, to detach themselves from business interests. Legitimacy problems, when they arise, compensate for the characteristics of the political process, noted by policy theorists, that favor business interests, the ill-informed, and infrequent political participation of citizens. Political scientists know the important role of political events in destabilizing opinion and shifting public support on an issue and the importance of the activities of talented and dedicated individuals and organizations in capitalizing on the event to mobilize the public on an issue. Yet it ought to be possible to be more specific about the sorts of issues most likely to be awkward or problematic for business interests.

Four dimensions to business legitimacy problems can be identified: the legal dimension, the ethical dimension, the economic or efficiency dimension, and the traditional loyalty dimension. Depending on the case, business may lose legitimacy on one or more of these dimensions. The legal dimension refers to cases where the business interest visibly breaks the law, perhaps caught sabotaging a competitor's products, and the consequent pressure on the government to take action. The broader ethical dimension involves business practices that may be within the law but are perceived as unfair or irresponsible, varying from instances of conspicuous consumption and lapses of taste (CEOs accepting large compensation packages while downsizing) to life-threatening business decisions concerning employees or products. The economic dimension refers to cases where the business interest is operating inefficiently but continues in business, cases of market failure. The traditional loyalty dimension is where business practices are in conflict with some national or cultural object of uncritical admiration, the British pub, American baseball, or French cheese.

Legitimacy is broader than legality. But legality is an important component. Most obviously business interests visibly breaking the law are vulnerable to sanctions by government. Instances of bribery, violating safety or hiring regulations, insider trading, or other forms of business illegality demand a response from government. Government officials themselves risk the accusation of double standards and a loss of public confidence if they do not pursue the business interests involved.

The prosecution of savings and loan officials in the United States would fit this dimension, but there is no shortage of other examples that have had political repercussions at the highest levels. In Japan, the sensational affair of illegal donations to a leading politician in the Liberal Democratic party, Shin Kanemaru, involved a firm connected to organized crime, the Sagawa Kyubin delivery company. This affair contributed to the defeat of Prime Minister Miyazawa and the Liberal Democratic party and presaged a lengthy period of at least surface political instability in Japan. One rather ironic case is the Matrix Churchill affair in the United Kingdom. Customs and Excise took Matrix Churchill to court for breaking a government prohibition on selling equipment with military uses to Iraq. It only became clear in court that Matrix Churchill executives had actually received the permission of several government ministers to break the government prohibition. Apparently the ministers were willing to see these executives imprisoned rather than have their own role exposed. In response to this embarrassment, Prime Minister Major set up Sir Richard Scott's independent inquiry, which reported that ministers had misled the House of Commons and raised constitutional questions concerning ministerial responsibility.

Legitimacy questions for business interests may arise over ethical issues, commonly connected to concerns about selfishness or power. In asking "what is there specifically about business that troubles the American people," Lipset and Schneider say that "first of all, there is the fact that business is perceived to be motivated exclusively by considerations of self-interest. . . . The second factor is more properly associated with big business . . . namely, the concentration of an enormous amount of power . . ." (1987, 359). A corporation's actions may be within the law. Nevertheless others may consider their actions fundamentally unfair or irresponsible. One result may be new law. Ethical issues can arise over the product or commodity, over the internal operation of the business, and over the relationship the business has with the local community or the government. With the growth of the railroad corporations in the United States in the late nineteenth century, some questioned the fairness of the subsidies these corporations received in the form of public land grants. This issue was the focus of a popular movement of midwestern and western farmers, known as the Granger revolt. Their political impact was sufficient to persuade both the Democrats and the Republicans in the 1872 election to condemn further grants of land to these corporations. Ethical issues also arise over the internal operation of a business. In the nineteenth century slave labor, child labor, and the length of the working day excited the public conscience. In the twentieth century the right to bargain collectively or racial or gender discrimination are more commonly the issues around which questions of legitimacy, first as an ethical issue and then as a legal issue, might arise. In terms of the uncertainty and the magnitude of effects, the ethical dimension of business legitimacy is the most serious for business interests and the most interesting for analysis.

The ethical responsibility of automobile manufacturers for their product was at issue when Congress passed the National Traffic and Motor Vehicle Safety Act in 1966, which set mandatory safety standards and required manufacturers to notify customers and the government of defects. With this act, "the giant, fearsome, incredibly wealthy automobile industry—and politicians are prepared to stand in awe of industrial giants . . . turned out to be a paper hippopotamus" (Drew 1966, 96). Congress had shown some interest in the subject of auto safety, not least because the number of traffic deaths rose sharply in the 1960s. From 1950 to 1960, fatalities increased by 10 percent to 38,091. In 1965, the number of fatalities was 49,000, an increase of 29 percent in five years (*Congressional Quarterly Almanac* 1966, 267). In November of that year Ralph Nader published *Unsafe at Any Speed: The Designed-In Dangers of the American Automobile.* The book described how General Motors' rear-engined Corvair, model years 1960–1963, had a suspension system that gave it alarming cornering characteristics. Nader charged that the company was deliberately producing an unsafe product. The company responded by investigating Nader's personal characteristics. A detective agency, through surveillance, interviews, and some more creative techniques gathered information on Nader's political and sexual tastes. This tactic, when it became public, further embarrassed the company. When Elizabeth Drew asked a senator what happened, he replied, "it was that Nader thing. Everybody was so outraged that a great corporation was out to clobber a guy because he wrote critically about them" (1966, 99). GM President James M. Roche apologized to Nader and agreed with Senator Ribicoff that it "was most unworthy of American business" (Sobel 1976, 26). Industry executives proposed exemption from antitrust and the setting up of their own industry safety board, and Henry Ford II warned Congress not to "do something that is irrational" or it might "upset the economy of this country very rapidly" (Sobel 1976, 28–29), but without success. As Drew put it, "politicians discovered that, beyond the merits of the issue, automobile safety was good politics" (Drew 1966, 95). The scandal and public attention provided a general incentive, yet "a group of liberal senators were central in strengthening the bill" (Nadel 1971, 142). Public support and policymakers' ideas combined in a way dangerous for even the most powerful of business interests.

Business interests generally prevail because of the weaker incentives of others to participate and because of politicians' respect for their resources and desire to maintain business confidence. These general factors did not hold with auto safety. Surprisingly, the industry was weakly organized for politics in Washington in the mid-1960s (Drew 1966, 99). Public interest rather than disinterest characterized this subject, and though Henry Ford used the business confidence card, it was trumped by the legitimacy issue and played into the hands of the "liberal group." Nadel's analysis of media coverage (1971, 35) and the Opinion Research Corporation's data on company favorability ratings (Lipset and Schneider 1987, 39) indicate that the industry and GM in particular were doing poorly in terms of public opinion at this time (1965–1967). Those policymakers most supportive of consumer protection legislation were most likely to be "liberals." Policy ideas and a shift in public support both contributed to the defeat of the industry position. Social scientists refer to the individuals who generate or capitalize on public attention as "entrepreneurs." The term is a poor one in suggesting an exclusively careerist, opportunistic, incentive on their part, and in not recognizing their ideological and policy commitments. To refer to them as "heroes" may overcorrect in the opposite direction, although the distinction between spontaneous and calculated heroism is a useful one in this context.

Currently, the tobacco industry faces considerable public criticism of its product. Since the 1950s an accumulation of scientific evidence connects smoking to a variety of unhealthy consequences that significantly increase the chance of death. The conventional liberal position is that if smoking is considered an activity that only affects the smoker, the smoker should be able to make up his or her own mind about whether to take up this risky habit, so long as the risks are known (Goodin 1989, 119; Fritschler 1983). The initial policy question was whether the smoker had the information to make a rational decision. The tobacco companies had not been forthcoming with what they knew of the health risks. In the 1960s, governments took measures to legally obligate these companies to warn smokers that smoking carried health risks and to restrict the ways in which they advertised their products. Complicating the issue from an ethical standpoint are the addictive properties of nicotine and that many smokers become addicted as children. It becomes controversial whether smokers are voluntarily weighing risks against benefits and deciding to smoke, or whether they are hooked. Aware of these arguments the trade association, The Tobacco Institute, under the heading of public service, draws attention to its "youth initiatives" to discourage young people from smoking and claims to have supported new state laws that make eighteen the minimum age to buy cigarettes (n.d.). A related complication is whether it is fair to have health risks imposed on us by involuntarily breathing other people's smoke. With public concern about these issues, government has targeted the tobacco industry, illustrated by the taxes levied on its products and the restrictions placed on advertising and consuming these products.

Despite these general concerns, even tobacco has not been an easy target for government, and the government's attention has not been completely negative from an industry point of view. Since the 1960s regulation in the tobacco industry has grown only incrementally, from publishing warnings on cigarette packets to banning smoking on airlines. The publicity on smoking's downside, from successive U.S. Surgeon Generals to the American Cancer Society, has had an impact on domestic demand. Manufacturers must look abroad for new consumers, which raises the additional fairness issue of what we owe citizens of other countries and the policy issue of whether to control what and how we export. Even the health warning on the product has the legal advantage for the tobacco companies of providing them with a defense against smokers or surviving relatives of deceased smokers' legal actions against them.

Throughout this period cigarette manufacturers have fought a determined and expensive rear-guard action in Washington, again stressing the importance of the industry to overall economic well-being. This action has been surprisingly successful when one considers the unremitting accumulation of negative evidence on the product. Table 9.1 shows two important dimensions of the political activities of the three leading tobacco companies and their trade association, The Tobacco Institute. The sales of these three firms make up about 80 percent of U.S. cigarette sales. Lobbying refers, in this table, to the number of Washington representatives, counsels, and consultants employed by the organization in 1988 and 1990.[2] PAC dollars is the amount the organizations contributed to federal election campaigns, through their political action committees, in the 1987–88 and the 1989–90 election cycles. Tobacco interests made direct contributions to candidates totaling over $1 million each cycle. To make these figures more meaningful, consider how much these tobacco companies spent in comparison to the average corporate PAC's contribution of

---

2. The total for Philip Morris includes the listings for Philip Morris Companies, Philip Morris International, Philip Morris Management Corporation, and Philip Morris USA.

$30,922 in 1988 and $32,415 in 1990. Philip Morris adds to its already formidable political effort significant sums of "soft money" contributions to the political parties—$134,650 in 1989–90. RJ Reynolds is a subsidiary of RJR Nabisco, and the latter contributed $201,755 in soft money in 1989–90 (Makinson 1992, 17). The Tobacco Institute is a trade association for twelve tobacco companies. It coordinates an industrywide approach to the political problems that face the manufacturers of cigarettes and other tobacco products. The drop in lobbying between 1988 and 1990 reflects a cut in the number of outside counsels retained by the institute, not in the size of its Washington office. The Tobacco Institute's PAC spending for these years was about four times higher than the average trade association's PAC spending.

Effective participation in the policy struggle depends on marshaling arguments, as well as disposing resources. The tobacco industry's case rests more positively on economic grounds than on the difficult ethical terrain of the right to make oneself and other people ill. Its advocates can shift attention from the illness of individuals to the industry's salutary contribution to overall economic well-being, from the fatal effects of consuming tobacco, to the vital economic activity of producing and packaging it. The Tobacco Institute says "the aim of the institute is to increase awareness of the historic role of tobacco and its place in the national economy, and to foster understanding of issues relating to tobacco" (n.d.). Describing the 1965 Cigarette Labeling and Advertising Act as a victory for cigarette manufacturers, a way of avoiding the much more severe regulations proposed by the Federal Trade Commission, Lee Fritschler points to the superior political resources of the tobacco industry and the effective arguments made by industry representatives in the congressional hearings.

Table 9.1.   Tobacco Industry Electoral and Lobbying Activity, 1988–90

		Lobbying		PAC ($)	
Organization	% Mkt. Share	1988	1990	1988	1990
Philip Morris	39	28	25	558,530	573,410
R.J. Reynolds	32	13	11	260,675	720,500
Brown & Williamson	10	2	2	103,650	58,100
Tobacco Institute		24	13	195,057	204,525
Total				1,117,912	1,556,535
Average corporate PAC				30,922	32,415
Average association PAC				52,434	57,347

Source: Washington Representatives 1992; Washington Representatives 1994; Almanac of Federal PACs: 1990, (1990); Almanac of Federal PACs: (1994/1994); Eagleton 1991, 60.

Bowman Gray, chair of RJ Reynolds, claimed that "unwise legislation in this field could produce repercussions which would be felt throughout the country's economy" including on the balance payments (Fritschler 1983, 126). Currently about two million people depend on the tobacco and associated industries in the United States (Eagleton 1991, 49). The tobacco case nicely illustrates the resources business can bring to politics directly and through efforts to influence public opinion, and the way it can appeal for friendly policy to support business confidence, as it tries to compensate for its political vulnerability over the increasingly questionable characteristics of its product.

Business must avoid the perception of pursuing economically harmful or inefficient practices, the third dimension of business legitimacy. Policymakers commonly take the competitive market as the guarantor of efficiency. Where economists argue that there is a case of "market failure," for example, then the business position is vulnerable. An obvious case is a situation of monopoly or oligopoly. While direct interference in a laissez-faire age, the Sherman Act was in keeping with the economic ideal of competition. Congress passed this act in 1890, haunted, according to Donald Dewey, by various specters: "the spread of cartels, the plight, real or imagined, of western farmers, shipper grievances over railroad rates, so-called destructive competition, the size of eastern banks, and, above all, the activities of the Standard Oil Company" (1990, 4). Dewey's argument is that the popularity of antitrust lay more in its effort to disperse power than in the ideas of economists. To avoid hostile policy in this situation businesses can argue the advantages of large-scale production, claim that prices are fair, and that they are using their power in a "socially responsible," not predatory, manner. In as much as antitrust was about "robber barons," as about the efficiency of perfect competition, it represented an ethical evaluation as much as an "efficiency" evaluation and illustrates how an issue can raise more than one type of legitimacy problem.

With the judicial application of this policy in the breakup of AT&T, assurances of social responsibility were to no avail. How did business lose in this case? Almost from its beginning the telephone company and the government had been coming to terms with each other. During this century, the Department of Justice has brought three antitrust suits against the company. AT&T weathered the Progressive era and the New Deal quite well. With the sacrifice of its Western Union stock in 1913 in response to the first suit, the company maintained its telephone service monopoly. The New Deal brought reduced demand, a company policy to spread work in order to maintain employment and which AT&T claimed prevented the layoff of 42,000 people (AT&T 1933, 6), and increased political pressure, culminating in the Communications Act of 1934 that created the Federal Communications Commission (FCC). Congress instructed the FCC to investigate AT&T's relationship with its subsidiary Western Electric and the telephone equipment market. The FCC had investigated by 1939, but World War II delayed government action. Ten years later, the Department of Justice, on the basis of the New Deal FCC investigation, filed suit against AT&T (Temin 1987, 13–15). The Department of Defense, however, "recalled Bell's service in the Second World War and valued Western Electic's management of the Atomic Energy Commission's Sandia Laboratories" (Temin 1987, 15), and the country elected General Eisenhower president. In the 1956 consent decree, the government gave up its action with minimal negative consequences for the company.

A competitor, not Congress, contributed to the pressure for fresh FCC investigations and a third Department of Justice antitrust suit against the company in November 1974. MCI, in March of that year, had lodged its antitrust complaint against AT&T. MCI's case led to the award of damages, and the Justice Department's case led to AT&T's break-up, with the separation of the local operating companies from AT&T's long lines as of January 1, 1984. We can reduce this story to these two key decisions: to file in 1974 and to settle in 1982.

Attorney General Saxbe took the first decision. Although serving a Republican president, Saxbe headed a department wracked by scandal. John Mitchell and Elliot Richardson had come and gone as attorney generals. Watergate was drawing public attention to the darker side of business-government relations, one legislative outcome of which was the 1974 campaign finance reform legislation. Saxbe decided on his own, despite strong opposition from the secretary of the treasury to file the antitrust complaint against AT&T, while President Ford was in Japan (Temin 1987, 110). "Saxbe, it's been reported, wanted to clean up the image of Justice. . . . What better way than don the white hat . . . [and] go ahead against AT&T" (Kraus and Duerig 1988, 96). A lone policymaker with his own agenda, Saxbe's decision nevertheless achieved some resonance with public opinion. AT&T experienced a sharp drop in public "favorability" ("I'd like to know how favorable or unfavorable your opinion or impressions are of AT&T") ratings between 1965 and 1975. From Lipset and Schneider's discussion, it would seem that of all the companies individually identified, including chemical, oil, and motor vehicle companies, AT&T experienced the largest decline in support over this period (1987, 38–39). Peter Temin, in his account of the antitrust suit, describes the legitimacy problem in the following way:

> In fact, from a political point of view, AT&T was too big. It had grown rapidly in the 1960s and 1970s and appeared to have over-

whelming power, equal almost to that of the federal government. . . .
Although no one in power ever said so, the United States found it
difficult to tolerate any company quite as large and omnipresent as
the old AT&T. (1987, 342)

To make matters worse, shortly before Saxbe's decision, the CEO of
AT&T, John deButts, had "belligerently proclaimed that the government
. . . should adhere to the established traditions of the regulated monopoly.
With great verve and determination he had steered AT&T close to the
rocks of public conflict. In 1974 the telephone company ran aground"
(Temin 1987, 112). AT&T's vulnerability coincided with Saxbe's effort to
validate the Department of Justice.

Assistant Attorney General William Baxter took the second decision.
He made the agreement with AT&T, known as the Modification of Final
Judgment, or in Temin's phrase "the microeconomic adventure" (1987,
337), that divested the twenty-two operating companies and left AT&T
with Western Electric and Bell Labs. In February 1981, the Reagan administration appointed Baxter, a Stanford law professor, with an ideology that
"blended two parts of neoclassical economics with one part of law," and
"committed to implementing that ideology as only a true believer can be"
(Temin 1987, 217). Baxter, as a result of the recusals of his superiors in this
case, took the opportunity to act independently and withstood pressure
from Defense Secretary Casper Weinberger and Commerce Secretary Mal-
colm Baldridge, who wanted him to drop the case against AT&T. The
recent decisions by juries against AT&T in the MCI and Litton Systems
antitrust suits encouraged the company's compliance.

The low points of this company's relationship with the government,
the three Department of Justice suits against AT&T, marked the three
great waves of antibusiness sentiment in America in this century, the Progressive era, the New Deal (the genesis of the 1949 suit), and the counter-
culture of the 1960s and early 1970s. The Justice Department's last
antitrust suit against AT&T is interesting on a variety of levels. Business
can lose in the policy struggle under probusiness administrations. Legitimacy, the preferences of the policymaker, and competing business interests were the critical factors. In the judicial policy arena the substantial
time lag in policy-making (1974–1982) means that the public legitimacy
problem might well be resolved before the policy decision. In 1956, the set-
tlement of the second antitrust suit, this lag worked in the company's
favor. In 1982, in addition to opposition from competing business interests, AT&T was unfortunate to encounter an unaccountable policymaker,
unaccountable either to his superiors or to the electorate, singularly committed to a vision of economic legitimacy and what is good for the business

system, if not for actual business institutions. Baxter illustrates that neoclassicists with political power, supportive of business as a system rather than business as an interest, can be as dangerous to business interests as social democrats.

The economic and fairness dimensions of legitimacy intersect in the pharmaceutical industry's relationship with the Clinton administration. Committed to reforming health care in the United States, President Clinton singled out drug companies and their pricing policies. Specifically pointing to a misallocation of resources, he argued that these companies put profit over the public interest. The drug companies, with no illusions about the great significance of government decisions to their business, recognized the importance of maintaining legitimacy in order to harness elected representatives to their interests in the policy struggle. In an extraordinary appeal "to the American people from the people who work in pharmaceutical companies," the Pharmaceutical Manufacturers Association took a full page advertisement in the *New York Times* to argue that their prices were fair, reflecting the cost of research and Americans' ability to pay, and that drug prices were not a major cause of the rapidly increasing cost of health care in the United States (March 2, 1993). Fortunately, for the industry, the hope of a substantial reform of health policy foundered on the determined and effective opposition of other business interests (and Harry and Louise) concerned either about the effect of reform on their business (insurance) or about who would carry the cost of reform (employer mandates), and on divisions within the Democratic party. Then hope sank with Republican control of Congress. The policy was off course from the start, with the critical attention given the special process devised for formulating health policy eroding the widespread public support for substantive reform.

An earlier president was more successful in his equally public confrontation with the steel industry. This confrontation provides another example of how a particular understanding of the economic problem, a commitment to a particular economic strategy, braced a policymaker to defy a powerful business interest. Rather than a response to an already mobilized public, President Kennedy's heroic defiance of U.S. Steel's actions was based on his view that these actions could not be justified with his wider economic strategy and the calculation that the public would perceive the company's actions as illegitimate.

The tension of this three-day crisis in mid-April 1962 does not compare to the thirteen day crisis in October of that year, but it had its moments. It began with a visit to the White House by Roger M. Blough, chair of United States Steel Corporation. The purpose of his visit on Tuesday, April 10, was to deliver to the president the news that his company was going to raise the price of steel by 3.5 percent. What made this presidential business, the essence of this decision, was that it violated a wage-price agreement forged by the Kennedy administration to curb inflation, and Kennedy already had the unions on board. In the Kennedy administration's view, the steel industry was critical to the general success of their economic policy. Kennedy himself said, in September 1961, that steel was "a bellwether" (Schlesinger 1965, 634). When Blough arrived that Tuesday evening, the president invited Secretary of Labor Arthur Goldberg to join them. According to the *New York Times,* Goldberg said that the price increase

> would jeopardize the Government's entire economic policy. . . . it would undercut responsible collective bargaining . . . and that the decision could be viewed only as a double-cross of the President because the company had given no hint of its intentions while the Administration was urging the United Steelworkers of America to moderate its wage demands. (Carroll 1962)

Blough left, undeterred. The president met immediately with his Council of Economic Advisers, Walter Heller, Kermit Gordon, and James Tobin, to enlist their help in the "effort to prove that the price increase was unjustified," in other words, illegitimate. He is quoted as saying: "my father always told me that all business men were sons-of-bitches, but I never believed it till now." Afterward, in conversation with Adlai Stevenson and Arthur Schlesinger, President Kennedy quite directly raised the issue of the legitimacy of the steel executives, in saying of them: "They are a bunch of bastards—and I'm saying this on my own now, not just because my father told it to me" (Schlesinger 1965, 636). Meanwhile the president called the attorney general, the secretary of defense, the secretary of the treasury, Senator Estes Kefauver, chair of the Senate's Antitrust Subcommittee, and a press conference for the next day. He did not underestimate the gravity of his decision to resist U.S. Steel.

Next morning President Kennedy learned that the second largest steel producer, Bethlehem Steel, and four other companies, had followed U.S. Steel's lead and increased their prices. At the press conference Kennedy stated that the

> actions of U.S. Steel and other leading corporations . . . constitute a wholly unjustifiable and irresponsible defiance of the public interest.
> . . . the American people will find it hard, as I do, to accept a situation in which a tiny handful of steel executives whose pursuit of pri-

vate power and profit exceeds their public responsibility can show such utter contempt for the interests of 185 million Americans.

. . . the Department of Justice and the Federal Trade Commission are examining the significance of this action in a free, competitive economy. The Department of Defense and other agencies are reviewing its impact on their policies of procurement.

. . . Sometime ago I asked each American to consider what he would do for his country, and I asked the steel companies. In the last twenty-four hours we had their answer. (Chase and Lerman 1965, 223–24)

President Kennedy's first priority was to make the legitimacy of the business interest the issue. He did so by emphasizing the self-interested nature of the action, precisely the point of vulnerability identified in the analysis of the first pillar of business power in chapter 3. At the same time Kennedy alerted the steel companies to the coercive measures, including antitrust and procurement policies, at his disposal. He actually enlisted the FBI to interview a journalist about comments made by Bethlehem Steel executives concerning that company's decision to raise its price. Finally, he managed to divide the steel industry by persuading a small group of steel producers, most notably Inland Steel, to not raise prices. His economic advisers estimated that this group, representing 14 percent of industry capacity, would put considerable competitive pressure on U.S. Steel and the others. The Defense Department, on April 13, awarded a contract to a steel producer that had not raised prices (Carroll 1962; Schlesinger 1965, 637). That afternoon Bethlehem Steel rescinded its increase, and that evening Blough blinked. President Kennedy's confrontation with Roger Blough of U.S. Steel provides a vivid illustration of the way in which business can lose in the policy struggle.

Of President Kennedy, Schlesinger said, "the steel fight showed once again his cool understanding of the uses of power. . . . he mobilized every fragment of quasi-authority he could find and, by a bravura public performance, converted weakness into strength" (Schlesinger 1965, 639). By late April, according to the *New York Times* Kennedy was at the "peak of his popularity," having "gained in the public mind by his strong measures that reversed the recent steel price increases" (Kihss 1962). While the business interest failed in this case, the extraordinary political effort required to secure that outcome is once again testimony to the advantages business possesses in the routine of politics. President Kennedy's behavior during the steel crisis comes close to two-o'clock-in-the-morning courage. Deciding to defend his economic strategy, he reacted vigorously to U.S. Steel's action, and gambled that public opinion and support would follow, if he could successfully question the company's legitimacy. His reward was increased public confidence in his presidency. This was a case of the hero creating the legitimacy problem, rather than the legitimacy problem creating the hero—more spontaneous than calculated heroism.

Finally, legitimacy questions may arise over traditional loyalties. Traditional loyalty perhaps runs the danger of becoming a residual category into which all else falls, yet there is an analytically separable dimension that does not fit on the legality, ethical, or economic dimensions and makes business interests vulnerable in the policy struggle. Business must fear situations where one can argue that its position is in conflict with some symbol of the national heritage. Sometimes it may be possible for business interests to use these symbols to achieve success in the policy struggle—the brewing industry, the Conservative government, and the pub, for example. But that is not always the case. While Japanese business investment in the United States is substantial, the Japanese right to do business in America's national parks or to invest in baseball teams attracts widespread and hostile public attention—not on the grounds of efficiency but of nationality. The French attachment to the *monde rurale* that led the Mitterrand government to jeopardize an economically far more important GATT round for the sake of maintaining high subsidies to inefficient French farmers and their innumerable cheeses is an example of the importance of these traditional loyalties. Another illustration is the nationalization of the motor vehicle firm Renault by the Liberation government. Louis Renault's factories had manufactured vehicles for the German war machine. On October 4, 1944, the government ordered the confiscation of the Renault factories, without compensation, as they "had been a tool in the hands of the enemy" (*L'Année Politique, 1944–45* 1946, 79–80). The collaborator was arrested, dying before his trial (Rioux 1987, 70). In these sorts of cases it may be, however, that foreign businesses are generally more likely to come in conflict with traditional loyalties and are therefore more vulnerable.

In raising the question of the legitimacy of the business position, the opponents of business are likely to be most effective in harnessing the aims and purposes of policymakers to their cause if, as discussed in chapter 3, they can draw on expert and scientific opinion. Scientific research is generally thought a respectable basis for policymakers to defend their actions to the public despite pressure from business interests.

In 1991, the U.S. Department of Agriculture decided to replace the four food groups with the Food Guide Pyramid to teach children about nutrition. Because their products appeared near the point of the pyramid, tucked below fat, sweets, and oils, indicating that they should be used "sparingly," the meat and dairy industries pressured Edward Madigan, the Agriculture Secretary, to delay publication of the pyramid. After nutritionists' defense of the pyramid, and $1 million of research to stiffen Madigan's resolve, the pyramid was adopted a year later. According to the *New York Times* a spokesperson for the Center for Science in the Public Interest commented, "I'm appalled they wasted almost $1 million of taxpayer money to prove what earlier research had already shown" (*New York Times* April 28, 1992). It may have been squandered money in a biological sense. Politically, it was the cost to insulate the policymaker from industry pressure.

To summarize the critical elements of the argument, the policy ideas of policymakers, generally constrained by the anticipated impact on public support in the context of the political activities of relevant interests, determine public policy decisions. In the absence of significant business division in the policy struggle, a business policy loss is likely when business fails to harness policymakers' goals to its own interests in policy. Such a failure is a result of a superseding priority (threat to the political system), indifference to public support, referred to as two-o'clock-in-the-morning heroism (quite rare), or actual or expected low public support for the business position. Low public support can be considered a breakdown in business control of public and policymakers' preferences, probably precipitated by an opinion-destabilizing event, and attributable to the effective mobilization of opinion by antibusiness organizations. Such mobilization is most likely to be effective with certain categories of issues.

For policies affecting business, the public preferences that constitute the legitimacy of business positions are grounded in definitions of legality, fairness, efficiency, or traditional loyalty and considered an artifact of the activities of organizations supporting and opposing business interests. Politicians' susceptibility to financial and electoral incentives varies according to the type and visibility of the particular issue in the policy struggle. Some issues, particularly those where their consciences are on display, carry politicians out of the reach of business influence. In addition to the incentive contained in the shift in public preferences, these opposing organizations offer reasoned policy proposals and justification for policymakers to deviate from business interests. Under these circumstances, even ordinary politicians might recalculate the risks of going against business interests. The likelihood of a failure increases if the government officials are members of reformist or social democratic parties.

While the discussion has focused on this simplified structure of elements and relationships, the arguments and evidence in this and earlier chapters suggest additional factors that will contribute to policy decisions. First, the definition of policy is too simple. The focus has been, for the most part, on policy formulation. Noting that the implementation stage of policy is critical, this approach suggests the importance of clarifying the goals of appointed officials and their degree of accountability to elected officials, within the context of the ways that business interests can influence the structure of incentives that they face. Despite President Carter's dedicated chair, Michael Pertschuk, who had the support of consumer groups and who took the Federal Trade Commission's consumer mandate seriously, this agency was unable to vigorously pursue various regulatory policies because of opposition from broadcasters (over the issue of television advertising directed at children), tobacco companies (which had been an early target of the commission in 1964), funeral firms, and used car dealers. Corporate opposition led Congress, in 1980, to temporarily stop funding the agency in order to bring it back in line (see Tolchin and Tolchin 1983, chap. 5). While the agency had the authority to make rules for industries, by 1980 legislators could no longer afford the virtue they had demonstrated in the 1960s and early 1970s, calculating that the various business interests, notably the broadcasters, had the greatest capability to influence public support.

Second, even if the economic performance of business is not the policy problem, it can plausibly be thought to influence the policy struggle. The influence is complicated, however. There is the dynamic that interests David Vogel (1989): the perception of poor economic performance encourages the political position that business cannot afford the imposition of further costs. But we know that poor performance on macroeconomic indicators decreases public confidence in business leaders and political leaders. A better way of formulating the relationship between economic performance and the likelihood of business losing in the policy struggle is to suppose that when economic performance deteriorates, political leaders fearful of losing political support (1) will be more willing to consider measures affecting business interests—that is, more active in the area of economic policy; and (2) depending on their analysis of the specific policy problem, they will be willing to consider measures both favorable to and opposed by business interests.

It is also likely that some relationships described in the simple model are reciprocal. The legitimacy of business interests will also affect the political organization and activities of business and antibusiness interests. There is a relationship between the political activities of business and of antibusiness. Increased antibusiness organization for political activity will stimulate increased business organization for political activity. The policymaker influences, as well as responds to, shifts in political support and legitimacy, as the Kennedy case demonstrates.

It remains to be seen how this sketch of the factors and relationships, in particular the role of business legitimacy, fills out in the more detailed analysis of policy cases. Opinion poll data provide direct evidence of political support and are the easiest way of exploring the relationships between the exercise of political and economic power and values. But it may be possible to tap other symbols of public acceptance or hostility in examining in greater detail cases where, despite its "big battalions," business has lost in the policy struggle.

CHAPTER 10

Heroic Policy: The Environment, Labor, and the Slave Trade

With the advantageous balance of political resources and the mechanisms that favor business interests in the policy struggle, one might expect them to win consistently. But they do not. Chapter 9 offered an explanation of how losses happen. Business interests have much at stake and are generally better equipped for the policy struggle. But they can still lose collectively made decisions when the policymakers' assessment is that the likely contribution of business opponents to public support, through mobilization around questions of business legitimacy, outweighs the business interests' contribution—calculated heroism. Spontaneous heroism, indifference to a decision's consequences for public support, is more likely in situations where an individual alone has decision-making authority. In this chapter, I elaborate the theoretical argument with a more detailed treatment of cases where business interests have lost collectively made decisions.

It is difficult to find cases where scholars, in repeated examination of a policy, identify the interests of business in the same way and arrive at the same assessment as to the winners and losers in the policy struggle. Of course, not just students of politics have this difficulty. Even with other more physical struggles, we may be left with only a foggy appreciation of the outcome. On that autumn day in 1812, the victor of Borodino may have seemed clear. The battlefield was in Napoleon's possession and the route to the capital lay open. Yet just weeks later, and without another major engagement, he and his Grand Army were in full flight.

For our purposes a business loss in the policy struggle is where the issue is placed on the agenda by nonbusiness interests, no significant division of business interests exists on the issue for the reasons discussed earlier, and the policy carries despite business political opposition. This is a political, not economic, definition of losing. It may be that business interests lose on some issues that they raise, for example, requesting a reduction in regulation or taxation. But it is easier to dismiss this sort of loss as just another instance of business demanding a great deal and perhaps not expecting to get all they want. When nonbusiness groups raise the issue, say auto safety, then it is less easy to doubt the seriousness of business interests' commitment to the policy struggle. It may be, particularly with some policies producing broad-based costs that affect all firms in the industry, that these firms will eventually pass the costs on to consumers, but at the time business interests committed resources to opposing the policy. The loss is defined by the policy struggle, not by longer term profitability.

The underlying assumption is that business people are well enough informed to know what is in their own interest and take political positions consistent with that interest. This is a tenable position, but not one taken lightly. It is most vulnerable to the criticisms that there may well be a distinction between short-term and long-term interests and a differentiation between what is good or bad for a particular business interest, known by business people, and what is good or bad for the business system, perhaps known by politicians. By emphasizing the importance to business of controlling cost-push inflation, one could reinterpret as stark a confrontation as that between U.S. Steel and the president as a long-term victory for business as a system. These complications are addressed as they arise in the discussion of the particular cases. In general, the choice has been to run the risk of oversimplifying rather than following these sorts of distinctions to the absurd conclusion that business never loses in the policy struggle.

Choosing policy cases from different policy sectors, institutional systems, and historical periods strengthens the claim that any common findings from the analysis of these cases represent more general types of interaction between business and government. Here the focus is on pieces of environmental, labor, and trade policy. These cases all illustrate the ethical dimension of business legitimacy. The ethical dimension has analytical priority because of the degree of uncertainty and the magnitude of the consequences for the affected interests.

The environment has been a sensitive policy area for business interests in the postwar period. In this chapter I examine an important piece of legislation that has attracted little scholarly attention, the Emergency Planning and Community Right to Know Act of 1986. On the other hand, labor policy, and in particular the Wagner Act, is a favorite topic of social scientists. The content of the legislation and the politics surrounding it have led social scientists to "see the Wagner Act as a telling test case for any theory of modern U.S. politics" (Skocpol and Finegold 1990, 1298), and it will provide the second case for analysis. Perhaps most interesting is the third case, the British decision to unilaterally abolish the slave trade. Both environmental and labor policies are relatively familiar terrain for political scientists, and the undemocratic institutional structure that shaped the struggle over the slave trade, the geopolitical pressures on

British policymakers occupied by defeat in America and the rise of revolutionary France, as well as the international market in the transport of
slaves, should have insulated this policy area from reform. British policymakers had difficulty defending it even as efficient policy, because they
could not control the replacement of British traders and ports by foreign
traders and ports. Beyond the nature of the international trade, the decision rested on persuading a majority of legislators, not an individual, in a
political system where one would not expect a high value to be placed on
public support. To put it another way, from a resource-based, incentive-
based, or state autonomy-based analysis of the policy process it is a "least
likely case" (see Eckstein 1975). The policy position of the opponents of
business rested on nothing but virtue. But let us begin on the more familiar terrain.

In the post–World War II period, business interests have been very
active in the struggle over environmental policy. Whether seeking total victory, or settling for partisan sniping and well-lodged amendments, business opposition typifies environmental policy-making. At the earliest
stages, in the fight for public attention and priority on the policy agenda,
the task of environmental advocates is to steady the public nerve in the
face of dire predictions of the economic consequences of their proposals.

According to environmentalists, the Emergency Planning and Community Right to Know Act of 1986 is one of the most important in the last
twenty years.[1] This legislation requires manufacturers that use any of 300
chemicals to report to the Environmental Protection Agency (EPA) and to
states, toxic substances that they release into the environment. Reports are
required for each chemical. The EPA maintains and publishes a toxic
chemical inventory. Since 1991, manufacturers also have had to describe
measures taken to reduce the amount of toxic waste. Citizens can sue businesses that do not comply with the Community Right to Know requirements and can sue federal or state officials for failure to carry out its provisions. The possibility of citizen legal action makes it more difficult for
business interests affected by the legislation to "capture" the relevant
agencies and officials.

It is not so much individual citizens but environmental and public
interest groups that are using the EPA's inventory to draw attention to the
polluters. According to the *New York Times,* once equipped with such
toxic release information, the Louisiana Environmental Action Network
named American Cyanamid its "polluter of the month." Predictably, the
company claimed that many jobs would be affected if the company could

1. Environmental Defense Fund interview with the author. Much of what follows is
drawn from U.S. General Accounting Office 1991.

not continue releasing its toxic wastes, though its spokesperson also claimed, in response to increased public pressure, that it was reducing the amounts released (Schneider 1991). This policy can carry a quite particularized cost for business interests.

For policymakers at the federal and state level the data on toxic emissions are very useful. The EPA used the inventory data as evidence for the 1990 Clean Air Act. About thirty states say they use the data to monitor toxic emissions and for enforcement purposes. As a result of efforts by concerned interest groups, Oregon and Massachusetts have passed legislation requiring reductions in the use of toxic chemicals (U.S. General Accounting Office 1991, 22–23) . Although there are questions about the reliability and completeness of the data as a consequence of the EPA's limited capability to verify the reports, the Community Right to Know Act has redressed the information imbalance between business interests and environmental and public interest groups in this policy area.

The Community Right to Know Act passed, according to the *New York Times,* "despite a desperate lobbying campaign by manufacturers, opposition by the White House, and public denouncements by the most powerful lawmakers in Congress, who thought the bill would prove to be too much of an onus on industry" (Schneider 1991). Business continues to oppose the act by trying to remove certain toxic substances from the list of those that they must report. From 1987 until 1991 industry petitioned the EPA forty-five times to delete substances from the list—no industry petitions were made to add substances. The Chemical Manufacturers Association, and large corporations like Dow, Monsanto, Amoco, and American Cyanamid, submitted these petitions. Twelve were granted (*Working Notes on Community Right-to-Know* 1991, 2).

Public availability of this toxic release data, powerful information for the community, makes specific business interests more vulnerable to antibusiness group activity and unwanted public attention. How did environmentalists and the community prevail over business, especially at a time when economic competitiveness, market forces, and the *individual* rather than the *community* seemed to be the dominant policy values of the day? In the analysis of the successful passage of environmental policy in the United States and elsewhere, a common theme is a critical initiating event that gives rise to public concern and impetus to environmental political organizations. In 1953, London's "killer smog" was reported to have claimed up to 4,700 lives. The attention given these deaths, in conjunction with the work of the Smoke Abatement Society, created a new item on the political agenda. The British Clean Air Act of 1956 was the Conservative government's legislative response (Enloe 1975, 21–25). Similarly, the Santa Barbara oil spill preceded the passage of the American Water Quality

Improvement Act of 1970. A series of environmental disasters in the 1960s stimulated Japanese environmental policy. These events assisted political mobilization that "made a critical difference in the incentives created for national elites" (Reich 1984, 387). Public concern about the environment in 1970 was sufficient to persuade the Diet to pass fourteen bills on the environment (Reich 1984, 394), even in the business-dominated politics of Japan.

Crises or scandals focus public attention—they put polluters in the position of defending an exposed and sometimes morally awkward position and make it easier for policymakers to defy the counterpressures created by polluters. The event, through its impact on public confidence, rearranges the incentives facing policymakers, making one choice more likely than another. This relationship between an event that creates the opportunity to mobilize the public and public policy is not mechanical. It is difficult to predict what sort of an event will capture public attention and stimulate policy. In American politics, as an illustration, any number of events might suggest the urgent need for an effective gun control policy, from shooting the president or the White House to the publication of statistics enumerating the thousands of Americans, in contrast to Japanese or Europeans, who die from gunshots. But there is no such policy. It is difficult to imagine how horrible the event would have to be to shift the policy agenda and who would step forward, Nader-like, to mobilize the public on this issue.

It is plausible to argue that the thousands of Indian and Soviet citizens who lost their lives at Bhopal in 1984 and at Chernobyl in 1986 have counted for more with American policymakers than the thousands of American victims of the government's nondecision on gun control. Of course there was some national connection to the Bhopal disaster, since it was an American company, Union Carbide, that was responsible. As Representative Gerry Sikorski said "Just 1 year ago, 1 year ago and 2 weeks, the worst chemical disaster in history left over 2,000 people dead and over 200,000 people injured. . . . That was in India, but an American company was operating that facility, a replica of an American facility" (U.S. Congress 1986, 3). The Bhopal disaster made it easier for Congress to establish the right of communities to know the dangerous chemicals in their neighborhood and to require local and state planning on how to respond to emergencies. Sikorski justified the policy on the principle that "Millions of Americans in thousands of neighborhoods exposed to toxic chemicals have a simple, a fundamental right to know about what chemicals, toxic chemicals, are being released into their environment hour after hour . . ." (U.S. Congress 1986, 3). Despite the difficulty of being against a "right to know" in a representative democracy, there was opposition from manufacturers and from the White House. The Synthetic Manufacturers Chemical Association, the Independent Lubricant Manufacturers Association, and the Chemical Manufacturers Association argued that the proposed legislation would impose unnecessary burdens on business. Representatives from environmental groups such as the National Resources Defense Council and Environmental Action supported the legislation (U.S. Senate 1985). Despite the specific costs the policy entailed, the far less tangible and far more dispersed "community" interest prevailed. In *Congressional Quarterly's* assessment, "Congress in 1986 accomplished as much significant environmental legislation as it had in any year since the environmental decade of the 1970s." It notes the "two catastrophes that loomed over Congress" and the fact that "the public was inundated with media coverage" of Bhopal and Chernobyl (1986, 109). Media coverage represents "focused public opinion" (see Erfle, McMillan, and Grofman 1990) and creates an incentive for policymakers to move on an issue. Public opinion itself shifted on the environment in the mid-1980s. Asked if we are "spending too much, too little, about right on improving and protecting the environment," in March 1980 48 percent said too little, in 1982 the figure was 50 percent, in 1984 59 percent, in 1986 59 percent, and in March 1987 it increased to 65 percent (Niemi, Muller, and Smith 1989, 79). The Chernobyl accident happened in April 1986 and so its effect would only show up in the 1987 figure.

Scandal as well as catastrophe marked environmental politics at this time. The shameful, at times farcical, behavior of officials entrusted with environmental responsibilities had put the administration in a difficult position by the mid-1980s. Anne Gorsuch Burford's leadership of the EPA, Rita Lavelle's management of the "superfund" clean-up, her appearance before Congress and imprisonment, and James Watt's abbreviated tenure at the Department of the Interior publicly embarrassed the opposition to further environmental legislation. This record, combined with the terrible accidents and a committed Minnesota Democrat, contributed to a morally awkward position for business interests. The business position on the right to know could not be seen as contributing to public support for policymakers facing midterm elections and permitted this reformist measure under a probusiness administration.

Even when business interests are defeated over environmental policy, some of the most perceptive public policy analysts have doubted the durability of such legislation, noting its dependence on the public mood and questioning the quality of leadership in the environmental movement. George Stigler, speaking of Ralph Nader "and his graduate and prep school students" said that "the self-appointed savior and his colleagues and legislative allies may get an occasional law. But they will not, year in and year out, attend the appropriation hearings, and the unending sequence of hearings on new appointments, which in the long run determine the direction and personnel of the regulatory agency" (Stigler 1975, 188). Anthony Downs points to public boredom with the issue and young people's "short-lived staying power." He says that it is likely that the environment as an issue "will also suffer the gradual loss of public attention characteristic of the later stages of the issue-attention cycle" (Downs 1972, 50). Stigler's and Downs' positions are similar. Either the leaders or the public will lose stamina before those who have to bear the costs of environmental regulation.

In contrast to expectations, pressure for environmental protection endures. Where there is no environmental political party, "environmentalists have been able to institutionalize their goals in the form of government regulations and agencies, scientific research endeavors, university curricula, and media positions (e.g., environmental reporters)" (Dunlap 1989, 133). In his analysis of the politics of air pollution control in Chicago in the 1970s, Paul Sabatier credits a local association with maintaining over a period of years a supportive local constituency for pollution control (Sabatier 1975). Some argue that Stigler's and Downs' environmental mood swing of the 1960s and 1970s is part of a more fundamental shift in political culture, from materialism to postmaterialism, visible in industrial society generally (see Inglehart 1990). Further, there is a developing environmental business lobby (producers of pollution control equipment), what Downs himself referred to as "the environmental-industrial complex" (1972, 49).

Environmental policy-making provides interesting material for thinking about the conditions under which business interests are likely to lose in the struggle over policy. At the same time, with any concentration on one policy area come the concerns about the limitations of evidence. Does business lose in a similar way over other issues? It is possible that the environment represents an isolated policy area, supporting quite exotic political structures. Environmental politics may produce issues peculiarly suited to political mobilization and on which business interests are particularly vulnerable. For a broader understanding of business policy failure, it is necessary to move away from an exclusive focus on this policy area and beyond a purely contemporary setting.

Business interests were on the losing side in 1935 when Congress passed, and a disinterested president signed, the National Labor Relations Act. Senator Robert Wagner's Act provided American labor unions with legal recourse to facilitate union activities and growth. Even with this result, there is an interesting controversy about how to explain this legislative victory over business interests and over how genuine was the business opposition. Irving Bernstein claims that for many senators their support was contingent on the expectation that the Supreme Court would rule the Wagner Act unconstitutional (1970, 341). There may be an element of fortune, as well as "virtue" in business failures. The labor victory was not decisive, and unions subsequently experienced legislative reversals in the Taft-Hartley and Landrum-Griffin acts that hindered organizing and limited strike action and union political activities. This series of legislation illustrated for unions the importance of influence on national politics and policy in the United States.

Prior to 1935, these organizations had experienced the severe negative consequences of public policy that originated principally in the courts. The courts applied conspiracy doctrines to unions and prevented strikes by issuing injunctions. They turned the Sherman Act of 1890 upside down and interpreted union activities as restraints on interstate commerce in a number of cases over a period of three decades—even after the Clayton Act of 1914, which unions understood as freeing them from the antitrust legislation but which the courts did not. Unions, outside the railroad industry, had to wait until the last year of the Hoover administration for some beneficial legislation.

The Norris-LaGuardia Act restricted the use of injunctions against unions. It also undermined the "yellow-dog contract," a device to make an individual's employment conditional on a promise not to join unions. In defense of this act, Wagner claimed, "simple justice commands that we unfetter the worker in his effort to achieve his goal" (Huthmacher 1968, 66). Yet the system-changing legislation was the New York senator's own act. This act protected workers' right to organize and bargain collectively, prohibited "unfair labor practices," and set up the administrative machinery necessary to implement the legislation. A union became recognized as the exclusive representative if a majority of eligible employees voted for it. Employers had a duty to bargain with the union and could be charged with unfair labor practices if they interfered with union members or potential union members through some form of yellow-dog contract or the setting up of a company union. At the same time the Wagner Act permitted the closed shop. The members of the National Labor Relations Board, appointed by the president and confirmed by the Senate for five-year terms, would supervise elections and decide on unfair practice.

Senator Wagner emphasized the fairness issue in the struggle for union rights. He argued that "only a well-organized labor group can equal the forces of cooperating businessmen and bring about justice and security for everyone" (Huthmacher 1968, 159). He also tried to incorporate an "efficiency dimension" to the argument by claiming that unionization would improve wages and domestic demand and create more harmonious labor relations. These arguments appealed to the president, but business interests were not persuaded. The secretary of the Employers Association of New Jersey said that "we believe it to be inequitable, economically unsound, pregnant with class antagonism, and therefore contrary to sound public policy. . . . We feel its enactment would assure an unprecedented volume of labor disturbance" (National Labor Relations Board 1985, 512–13; hereafter NLRB 1985). William S. Elliot of International Harvester commented that "the proponents of this bill . . . assure you that this bill will reduce industrial strife and therefore expedite recovery. On the other hand, the vast amount of testimony put in against the bill by people who know business . . . seems to me overwhelmingly to indicate that this bill will create strife in 10 places where there was 1 before, and it will delay recovery" (NLRB 1985, 953). For Wagner, labor peace was not worth any price. "A tranquil relationship between employer and employee . . . is not a sole desideratum. It all depends upon the basis of tranquillity. The slave system of the Old South was as tranquil as a summer's day, but that is no reason for perpetuating in modern industry any of the aspects of a master-servant relationship" (Huthmacher 1968, 167). In the public struggle to justify the policy, the ethical dimension was more important than efficiency for Wagner.

Government, through this act, compensated for the unbalanced power of employers over their employees and the legal advantages given employers by earlier policymakers. According to Bernstein, "the opposition comprised the business community in virtually solid phalanx, company unions, an academician, and the Communists" (1970, 330–31). There are, however, accounts that portray business as divided on this policy issue, depending on whether they belong to a labor-intensive or capital-intensive industry (Ferguson 1995) or whether they preferred industrial unions to craft unions or subscribed to the view that union-induced wage increases would increase demand and promote recovery (Gordon 1994). But there is no very convincing evidence of significant business division over the Wagner Act that could be defined in any general investment or industry type.[2] Arthur H. Young of U.S. Steel pointed out to the Senate committee, "the significant fact that not a single witness before your com-

---

2. Some of the evidence appears contradictory. Ferguson says "if the chairman of the General Electric Company was actively aiding New York Senator Robert Wagner in preparing the National Labor Relations Act . . ." (1995, p. 41), and Gordon says "firms such as GE were among the firmest opponents of the act and the first to challenge its authority after 1935" (1994, 215). As David Plotke says, "Efforts to demonstrate substantial business support for the Wagner Act have been unsuccessful" (1989, 113). Plotke is convincing in his claim that "the Wagner Act was passed by Progressive liberals . . . in alliance with a mass labor movement" (1989, 105).

mittee as a proponent of this bill appeared as an employer" (NLRB 1985, 758).[3] Only if you bundle the Wagner Act with other contemporary legislation and make the research problem explaining the New Deal as a whole, is it plausible to claim that significant business division existed on this policy effort.

Examining the legislative history of the act, 99 percent of the business interests testifying in the Senate hearings or submitting petitions opposed the legislation. Representatives of two tobacco companies, the Axton-Fisher Tobacco Company and Brown and Williamson, appeared (after Young) in support of the legislation. Wood Axton, president of Axton Fisher and a man well ahead of his time, stated that on "April 1, 1889, I requested the secretary of the Tobacco Workers International to come to Owensboro and organize the employees in my plant." He argued that labor is not a "commodity" and "heartily endorsed" the American Federation of Labor (NLRB 1985, 1595–96). In addition, William Davies, representative of the Twentieth Century Fund, appeared in support.[4] In 1934 and 1935 approximately 160 representatives of business interests, including the National Association of Manufacturers, the Full Fashioned Hosiery Association, the U.S. Chamber of Commerce, the National Association of Furniture Manufacturers, the Wire Machinery Builders Association, the American Transit Association, the National Automobile Chamber of Commerce, the United States Steel Corporation, the American Rolling Mill Company, the American Mining Congress, the American Petroleum Institute, the National Council of American Shipbuilders, the Institute of American Meat Packers, the National Erectors Association, the Goodyear Tire and Rubber Company, the National Machine Tool Association, Caterpillar Tractor, the Association of Creamery Buttery Manufacturers, the Association of General Contractors of America, the General Cigar Company, the Kennecott Copper Corporation, the Linoleum and Felt Base Manufacturing Industry, the National Association of Finishers of Textile Fabrics, the National Electrical Manufacturers Association, Indianapolis Employers, the Grocery Manufacturers of America, the Automobile Parts and Equipment Manufacturers, as well as the dean of the Harvard Business School, went to the effort of stating their opposition to the legislation.

Wallace B. Donham, the dean, said that "too much power placed in

---

3. Senator Walsh responded that "Mr. Dennison . . . appeared before the committee . . . and indicated with an amendment . . . he would favor it," and Young replied that Dennison "appeared before you as a member of the industrial advisory groups" (NLRB 1985, 759).

4. Outside the legislative history, there were some scattered instances of business support. Huthmacher states that "industrialists like Ernest G. Draper, who endorsed the bill, and Charles Edison, who scorned the narrowness of businessmen . . . were hard to find" (1968, 164).

the hands of the labor group without slow educational processes which fit it to exercise these responsibilities, subjects the country to the dangers of tyranny. . . . It is a step in the direction of making revolution easy. . . . Corruption would thrive" (NLRB 1985, 641). Guy Harrington of the National Publishers Association said that "It is a misconception and fallacious to assume that an increase in the wages of labor in itself, would increase the country's buying power" (NLRB 1985, 500). Roy Hall of the National Lock Company said, "I regard this bill of Senator Wagner's as a primer from Moscow, and I think that this committee and the Senate, which they represent, should turn their backs on it, pick up the American flag, and walk in the other direction" (NLRB 1985, 596). And William Bell, president of American Cyanimid and representing the Manufacturing Chemists Association said that "if we cannot run our plants in a proper state of efficiency, we will blow you gentlemen clear out of the country, we will poison you . . ." (NLRB 1985, 552). The senators recessed for lunch.

Theda Skocpol and Kenneth Finegold argue that the National Labor Relations Act is an example of how the state can develop policy autonomously, uninstructed by social movements and interest groups. They focus on past policy, the economic and political elite, political parties, and institutional capacities. In contrast, reasserting the importance of society, Michael Goldfield uses this same policy "to suggest the importance of the past and potential effects of broad social movements in affecting U.S. politics" (Goldfield 1989, 1258). The Wagner Act in his account is the bittersweet fruit of working-class wrath. Without question widespread social and economic unrest characterized the early to mid-1930s. In 1934, says Irving Bernstein, "labor erupted," with "1,856 work stoppages involving 1,470,000 workers, by far the highest count in both categories in many years" (Bernstein 1970, 217). If the cumulative affect of these work stoppages moved the labor question higher on the political agenda, so did some spectacular individual strikes. The Battle of Toledo placed Auto-Lite, a supplier of ignition systems and lighting to a variety of car producers including Chrysler, and eventually the Ohio National Guard in conflict with an AFL local, which was in alliance with an organization of the unemployed, and resulted in street violence, bayonet charges, and the National Guard killing two people. The alliance between the AFL and the unemployed indicated that business's "industrial reserve army" was behaving in an unreliable way, a development deeply worrying to business people and mentioned by Roy W. Howard of Scripps-Howard newspapers in a letter to Louis Howe in the White House:

> "it is nothing new to see organized unemployed appear on the streets, fight police, and raise hell in general. But usually they do this for their own ends . . . At Toledo [they helped] striking employees win a strike,

tho you would expect their interest would lie the other way—that is, in going in and getting the jobs the other men had laid down. (Bernstein 1970, 221)

Under the mediation of Charles Taft, son of the former president, management settled the strike with a wage increase, recognition of the union, and an agreement to hire the strikers (Bernstein 1970, 226).

Bernstein argues that Wagner's "bill was presented at the most favorable possible moment politically, for 1935 was the apogee of the New Deal as a domestic reform movement. The influence of labor was at its height . . ." (Bernstein 1970, 341). Along with labor, the unemployed, farmers, the Communist party, and the followers of Father Coughlin and Huey Long were all on the move, and the Democratic party achieved a great victory in the 1934 congressional elections, giving impetus to Democratic policymakers. But for Michael Goldfield, the government designed their response to these social movements "with primary concern for preserving social stability and assuring the continued electoral success of the Roosevelt-led Democratic party" (Goldfield 1989, 1269). While produced by unrest and group or class activity, the act, then, was not such a clear defeat for business. It represented a containment effort that attempted to benefit the more moderate AFL, at the expense of the more militant industrial unions.

Business customarily wants a variety of things from government and, along with subsidies and restrictions on market entry, these certainly might include a favorable industrial relations environment. But business people specifically did not expect Wagner's policy to produce this result. Historically, and parenthetically, the National Labor Relations Act seems to have had the effect that business people at the time anticipated and the reverse effect of a mechanism designed to control labor. Statistical analysis confirms the important positive effect of the act on union growth and in increased strike activity. The Taft-Hartley Act was important in reversing these trends (Wallace, Rubin, and Smith 1988). Business opposition to the act is a problem for the social-control interpretation and the idea that the Wagner Act was passed with a view to the long-term interests of capitalists. One could argue that business does not always know what is in its own best interest and consider business opposition to the act in that context. Yet even if one does so, and one finds a way to reconcile the impact on union growth with business interests, the National Labor Relations Act remains a defeat for the expressed interests of business: presumably one no less keenly felt, no less hard fought, than if it were a "real" defeat. The "unreal defeat," illustrating the possibility of a real defeat, was the result of reformist policymakers confronting business interests on an issue of fairness and able to capitalize on mass support.

Regulations or prohibitions on trade have been a more direct threat to business interests for far longer than have labor or environmental regulations. It is now over 200 years since the slave trade became a national issue in British politics. The analytical value of this remote episode lies, in part, in its remoteness. It is useful to examine how business relates to government in the context of capitalist democracy in its infancy, in unreformed British politics when Manchester bathed in the industrial sunrise. In this way one can separate what holds more generally from what is qualified by time and institutional development. Fortunately these have not been idle years for historians, and there is a rich seam of scholarship to explore and a wealth of information on which to draw.

William Wilberforce, James Stephen, and Thomas Clarkson are the heroes of British abolition. These "Saints," are the central actors in the traditional explanation of the decision to abolish the slave trade, as Ralph Nader and his prep school students are central to understanding American consumer protection and environmental legislation. The successful parliamentary vote against the trade in March 1807 was the culmination of years of hard work marshaling evidence and argument by this extraordinary group of individuals. Reginald Coupland describes the "Saints" in the following way: "For it was their selfless devotion to high causes, their lack of all personal ambition, their scrupulous honesty and candour, their frank appeal to conscience and Christianity, that gave that little group a power in the House of Commons out of all proportion to its numbers or its parliamentary gifts" (Coupland 1964, 80). The Enlightenment, as well as the Saints, secured passage of abolition. Roger Anstey concludes:

> one is so conditioned to expect interest to masquerade as altruism that one may miss altruism when concealed beneath the cloak of interest—the mass of independent members of Parliament were ready, against all the evidence of the West Indies importance to the nation, to act as the children of the later eighteenth century, with its manifest antislavery convictions, that they really were. (Anstey 1975, 408)

To tie up these themes, the opponents of the slave trade made the argument for public policy with a religiously couched extension of national standards of conduct to all humanity, murder was murder. A decisive legislative victory rewarded virtuous men with a virtuous aim.

Peter Jupp describes the calculations of Lord Grenville, the new prime minister who "was in no position to make abolition a government measure because of the fear of arousing the King's opposition and that of Sidmouth and the other gradualists in the Cabinet," but, "he could feel reasonably sure that the election would increase his political authority and enable him to push through a nongovernment measure" (Jupp 1985, 389). With a history of concern for the issue going back to the 1780s, Grenville decided to introduce the abolition bill in November 1806, even before knowing the outcome of the autumn election and relying, as Jupp puts it, "on the moral case" (1985, 390–91). It was sufficient to achieve parliamentary approval.

The Saints were up against the West Indian Interest, which could claim some seventy-five members of Parliament connected in some way with West Indian plantations or with the trade with the islands (Thorne 1986, 325). A Committee of West India Planters and Merchants was formed in 1778. One sugar planter viewed the abolitionists, in company with the borer-worm, as a threat to West Indian property, and the reason, in 1788, that "precluded him from advancing some money for a correspondent . . ." (Pares 1968, 114). In the House of Commons debate in 1791 it had been pointed out that "the property of the West Indians is at stake; and though men may be generous with their own property, they should not be so with the property of others" (Warner 1963, 61). Property was a powerful political symbol, the centerpiece of Locke's political theory, at issue in the American revolution, integral to definitions of citizenship, and now subject to the coeval threat of grubs and abolitionists.

The virtuous were also up against great commercial centers like Liverpool. That city owed its development to the trade and added its political and business leaders to the opposition to abolition. While the Elizabethan pioneer of the trade, John Hawkins, had sailed from Plymouth, by the last half of the eighteenth century, that is when the trade was at its apex, Liverpool was the most important British port engaged in the slave trade, more important than Bristol or London. To get an idea of the dimensions of the trade, between 1783 and 1793, 878 slave ships set out from Liverpool to transport 303,737 slaves worth £15,186,850 (Williams 1897, 685). Williams' data (1897, 681–84) indicate that over fifty different owners each invested in at least one slave voyage originating in Liverpool in the single year 1798.

It was in these great ports that Thomas Clarkson, providing an early example of the importance of expert opinion in policy-making, carried out his research on the trade. At Cambridge he had written a prize-winning essay on "Is It Right to Make Men Slaves Against their Will?" The essay had been set by the Master of Magdalene, Dr. Pickard, an opponent of slavery (Warner 1963, 44). Clarkson took risks in his research, at one point in imminent danger of being pushed off a Liverpool pier by agitated defenders of the trade. Wilberforce, the principal parliamentary foe of the trade, was the target of threats from the slave trader John Kimber, whom he had accused of murdering a slave girl (Pollock 1977, 116). Wilberforce took his policy position not from the interests of his Yorkshire constituents but from a religious rebirth in the mid-1780s and discussions with the former slaver John Newton, Clarkson, and others, and wrote that "God Almighty . . . has set before me two great objects, the suppression of the slave trade and the reformation of manners" (Ehrman 1969, 391). But he, like Clarkson, realized the triumph of the spiritual position depended on carefully gathered evidence on the conditions of slaves and of sailors engaged in the trade.

They were up against war heroes like Admiral Nelson and Admiral Rodney, and the view that since British merchant shipping was where the Royal Navy recruited its sailors, damage to the trade would damage recruiting and Britain's military capabilities. Lord Rodney, who knew the West Indies, said that he had not heard "of a Negro being cruelly treated" and wished that "the English labourer might be half as happy" (Warner 1963, 53). His views were, likely, conditioned by his own harsh profession. Rodney's Royal Navy knew something of cruelty's depths. In 1789, the year that Wilberforce stood in the Commons to declare "I mean not to accuse anyone but to take the shame upon myself, in common indeed with the whole Parliament of Great Britain, for having suffered this horrid trade to be carried on under their authority. We are all guilty . . ." (Pollock 1977, 89), Captain Bligh was set adrift in *Bounty's* launch. The *Bounty* had been dispatched to Tahiti by the government in order to transport breadfruit to the West Indies to solve the problem of feeding slaves (Humble 1976, 55–56)—not one of the more well-conceived or better-implemented public subsidies of a business (although Bligh did get the breadfruit to their destination, somewhat behind schedule).

Charitably, it might be supposed that Rodney was manipulated by the planters. They felt they had much at stake, and deception was the least of their offenses. On March 20, 1800, John Pinney, a Nevis planter, who had an alleged abolitionist as a guest, wrote to his manager:

> Do not suffer a negro to be corrected in his presence, or so near him to hear the whip . . . point out the comforts the negroes enjoy . . . show him the property they possess in goats, hogs, and poultry. . . . By this means he will leave the island possessed with favourable sentiments. (Pares 1968, 122)

The inhumanity of this business practice, even by the standards of the day, was recognized by both sides as the critical policy issue. Supporters of the trade downplayed or hid the suffering, and opponents sought to expose it.

The other service depended on the trade even more directly than the navy. According to James Rawley, regiments of the British army, short of men to serve in the West Indies, bought slaves, including 1,000 in the final year of the trade (Rawley 1981, 169).

Abolishing the trade raised other strategic and foreign policy issues. There was the problem that Granville Sharp had brought to Wilberforce's attention: "if Parliament enacted Abolition a strong movement might arise in the West Indian colonial assemblies to declare independence and to federate with the United States" (Pollock 1977, 88). In 1791, a planter's agent in the West Indies wrote "surely the Enthusiastic rage of Mr. Wilberforce and friends can never prevail in a matter of such consequence to the Colonies and the Mother Country" (Pollock 1977, 105). Defeat in America and revolution in France created an uncertain geopolitical context for British policymakers, and the anticipated consequences of abolishing the trade added to this uncertainty. Further, the abolitionists had to explain why British interests should be made to bear the costs of abolition, when the trade would continue under other flags, notably the French. Clarkson actually visited revolutionary France, where he was called an English spy by French slavers, and confronted with the argument that "if France gave up the Trade before England, would not England reap the profit?" (Warner 1963, 62). In this context, abolition was a suboptimal choice for unsaintly policymakers in a single nation. They would be agreeing to sacrifice Liverpool for Bordeaux. For the sacrifice to be meaningful, they would also have to agree to a policy of enforcing abolition on their own nationals and, sharply increasing the potential costs of the policy, on others. Therefore the selfish interests of the planters and the traders could be recast as national and strategic interests and autonomous reasons for state support of the trade.

There were efforts to argue the trade on other grounds. In 1788, a Rev. Raymond Harris wrote a pamphlet, for which he received £100 from Liverpool Corporation, entitled "Scriptural Researches on the Licitness of the Slave Trade, showing its Conformity with the Principles of Natural and Revealed Religion, delineated in the sacred writings of the Word of God" (Williams 1897, 573–74). This pamphlet was quickly refuted by abolitionists, returning the defenders to the economic and national interest arguments.

I own I am shocked at the purchase of slaves,
And fear those who buy then and sell them, are knaves;

What I hear of their hardships, their tortures, and groans,
Is almost enough to draw pity from stones.
I pity them greatly, but I must be mum,
For how could we do without sugar and rum?[5]

National interest and concerns of efficient policy seemed on the side
of the slave trade, and the most obvious beneficiaries were a people distant
in miles, in custom, and in appearance from the British people, and with
whom most never ever came in contact. The "political realist" of the time
would have argued against abolition, and the political analyst would not
have been optimistic for its chances in the policy struggle. If the analyst's
approach is to compare the incentives to political participation of those
bearing the costs and those benefiting from policy (policy theory), victory
goes to the slavers. If the approach is to compare the resources of the interests involved (group theory), victory goes to the slavers. If the approach is
to examine the autonomous interest of state officials (state theory), commonly defined in geopolitical or strategic terms, the slave traders sail on.
But they did not.

The Saints could quote Adam Smith about the comparative advantages of wage labor over slave labor but without convincing the planters
involved, who opted for coercion over incentives in managing the murder-
ous work of the plantations. Where Wilberforce relied on appeals to self-
interest, it was as likely to be of a more ethereal kind: "And, Sir, when we
think of eternity, and of the future consequences of all human conduct,
what is there in this life which should make any man contradict the principles of his own conscience, the principles of justice, the laws of religion,
and of God?" (Pollock 1977, 90). Material interests and efficient policy
considerations favored the slave traders. Flags of convenience and other
countries' involvement in the trade made British abolition appear an
empty but expensive gesture paid for by domestic business interests.

The most direct challenge to the "heroic" interpretation offers a
Marxist analysis of the abolition decision. The argument is that despite
appearances, the continuance of the slave trade was contrary to capitalist
interests, and the decision to abolish is attributable to the demands of this
dominant economic group. With this argument the slave trade decision
becomes a nice example of the difficulty of finding unequivocal cases of
business losing. Eric Williams, in *Capitalism and Slavery,* explains:
"Whereas before, in the eighteenth century, every competent vested interest in England was lined up on the side of monopoly and the colonial system; after 1783, one by one, every one of those interests came out against

---

5. William Cowper (1731–1800), quoted in Williams 1897, 594.

monopoly and the West Indian slave system" (1961, 154). In this view William Wilberforce becomes a peripheral figure of somewhat doubtful integrity: "Wilberforce was familiar with all that went on in the hold of a slave ship but ignored what went on at the bottom of a mineshaft" (Williams 1961, 182). Williams' analytical focus is on interests rather than individuals. So, for Williams, the relationship between slavery and capitalism changed over time. By the turn of the nineteenth century the slave trade was in decline and a drag on the further development of British capitalism.

One difficulty with this explanation is a lack of evidence of business group opposition to the slave trade. No business groups submitted abolitionist petitions to Parliament, and the parliamentary debates provide "little evidence of proabolitionist commercial interests" (Drescher 1977, 178). There is, however, evidence of anti-abolitionist business group activity by the West Indian Planters and Merchants, by the merchants of Liverpool, and by the trustees of Liverpool dock (Anstey 1975, 395). The Committee of the Liverpool African Merchants sent some of their number to London to lobby for the trade, and in 1788 these individuals received "the freedom of the borough" on their return to Liverpool. For his support of the trade, the corporation recognized Lord Liverpool, prime minister from 1812 to 1827, in a similar way and in 1796 invited him "to quarter the arms of Liverpool with his own" (Williams 1897, 611). In 1804, the Liverpool merchants petitioned Parliament with nineteen pages of signatures, saying:

> that your petitioners, observing that a Bill is now depending in Parliament for a total abolition of the African Slave Trade, . . . beg leave to express, with greatest respect, that many of your petitioners, having, under the protection of the Legislature embarked a considerable part of their property in that Trade, will be very materially injured if the said Bill should pass into a Law . . ." (Mackenzie-Grieve 1968)

Here the merchants were pointing out explicitly that they had made their decisions to risk their capital in the trade on the basis of current government policy.

In addition to the lack of business group activity in opposition to the slave trade, several recent historians of the period have shown that the trade was still profitable at the time of abolition, not unprofitable as Williams maintained. Up to abolition, British interests dominated the slave trade, with British ships directly responsible for approximately half the trade, as well as substantial British financing of foreign ships. Seymour Drescher concludes, "In terms of both capital value and overseas trade, the slave system was expanding, not declining, at the turn of the nineteenth century" (1977, 24). David Eltis says that if the British were primarily concerned with economic self-interest they should have been encouraging the slave trade at this time: "Such a policy would have been highly effective in achieving national goals as laid down by the amalgam of London merchants and landed gentry who dominated the British government at this time" and the "material aims of manufacturers and wage earners alike" (1987, 6). Thus the trade was still viable, and British involvement was substantial at the very moment Parliament abolished it. The absence of an economic reason for campaigning against the slave trade fits with the absence of evidence of such business political activity. Whether one approaches the policy process from the perspective of identifying the groups involved or whether one examines the interests affected by a policy decision, one has to leap well beyond the evidence to conclude that business interests were responsible for its end.

Despite Britain's dominant role in the trade, it did not end with the unilateral decision for abolition. The business continued from foreign ports, just as opponents of abolition had argued that it would. In fact, the trade was sufficiently vital to carry on for another half a century, despite an active policy of suppression by the Royal Navy. While the navy could search and seize British slavers, it had no authority to do the same to the foreign ships involved. Effective suppression required the agreement of other countries either to police the seas themselves or to concede to the Royal Navy the right to search ships flying their flag. For the next half a century British governments tried diplomatic and financial persuasion on the governments of Spain, Portugal, the United States, and Brazil and resorted to illegal methods to achieve an end to the slave trade. They bribed the Portuguese and Spanish governments (£300,000 and £400,000, respectively) in the effort to get them to agree to abolition (Woodward 1938, 354). In 1838, Palmerston ordered the navy to seize Portuguese slavers and blustered: "We cannot class Portugal among [the] powers with which England is on terms of friendly alliance. We consider Portugal as morally at war with us and if she does not take good care and look well ahead she will be physically at war with us also" (Bethell 1970, 155). The French stationed ships off Africa in the 1840s, while continuing to refuse the right of search to the British. British naval officers said that the French squadron was of little help, being in harbor most of the time (Ward 1970, 49). In 1845, the U.S. representative in Rio said: "We are a byword among nations—the only people who can now fetch and carry any and everything for the slave trade, without fear of English cruisers" (Bethell 1970, 193). With Lincoln's presidency the United States conceded the right of search in the Washington Treaty of 1862.

Pursued unilaterally by one nation, one might expect that the suppression policy would have negligible impact on the slave trade. However, implementing the policy for forty-five years, the Royal Navy caught 1,500 slave ships and freed 160,000 slaves (Leveen 1977, 2). The suppression policies also had a deterrent effect and increased operating costs for the slavers. Philip Leveen, in his interesting work, concludes that over 800,000 slaves would have been shipped from Africa but for the suppression policy. This benefit is balanced against the tangible costs of the policy. The policy of suppression cost Britain financially, diplomatically, and strategically, and approximately 5,000 British sailors died suppressing the slave trade. Leveen estimates that the public and private cost of suppression was £33.3 million, as opposed to a private benefit of £5 million. Strategically, naval ships now had an additional mission to that of maintaining British national security. Not only did costs heavily outweigh benefits, Leveen says "that almost no private group had much at stake in suppression until a long time [twenty years] after the policies were initiated" (78–81). As historians have pointed out, public policy guided by public and private economic calculation would have reestablished the trade, not tried to suppress it. The abolition and suppression of the slave trade, given the remote benefits for those called upon to take that political action and its inefficiencies, would belong in George Stigler's unilluminating category of "temporary accident." Yet there is no evidence of a running out of "stamina," or the "issue cycle" in the suppression policy.

Although we find neither business pressure nor the objective interests of business at work in the abolition decision, or the subsequent policy of suppression, we cannot yet dismiss an economic explanation. Once again a distinction can be made in terms of short-term and long-term economic interests, and abolition and suppression can be held to be consistent with the long-term interests of the capitalist class. Williams, at times, advances this sort of explanation.

> The decisive forces in the period of history we have discussed are the developing economic forces. These economic changes are gradual, imperceptible, but they have an irresistible cumulative effect. Men, pursuing their interests, are rarely aware of the ultimate results of their activity. The commercial capitalism of the eighteenth century developed the wealth of Europe by means of slavery and monopoly. But in so doing it helped to create the industrial capitalism in the nineteenth century, which turned round and destroyed the power of commercial capitalism, slavery, and all its works. (Williams 1961, 210)

While independent of capitalist interests, the success of the antislavery movement should be viewed in the context of the large economic forces at work in Britain at the time. Specifically, its success is an expression of the triumph of industrial capital over commercial capital and necessary to long-term economic progress. A problem inherent in the use of *long term* is the nonspecificity of the term itself. The trade remained profitable for decades after the decision to abolish. Without specifying the long term, we do not know what the evidence is that would falsify a hypothesis that refers to the long term. Further, to seriously recommend such a hypothesis for investigation requires explaining why the relevant actors are interested in the long term, after all, "what will posterity do for them"?

At this higher level of abstraction, one can turn to Nicos Poulantzas as a proponent of this type of explanation for political action (1969). He recognizes "fractions" within the capitalist class and argues that classes and the state are "objective structures" related as "an objective system of regular connections" in which people act as "the bearers of objective instances," while claiming that their actual motivations have no explanatory value.

Whatever the gain by recognizing "the relative autonomy of the state," by refusing to frame explanations in terms of motivations, and by not specifying the mechanisms by which objective structures or economic necessities are translated into public policy, the question of how business can lose is replaced by the mystery of how a policy is arrived at that is in the long-term interests of capitalism but contrary to the expressed interests of capitalists. As for the autonomous interests of the state, the most easily identifiable are international and strategic interests, and these would not have led to the abolition and suppression decisions. One might argue that at times political leaders are particularly prescient, more in tune with the needs of business than business people, yet in doing so actors and their motivations, rather than structures, return to the core of the explanation.

If business interests cannot account for the decision to abolish the slave trade, and we remain suspicious of heroic policy, where do we go for an explanation? Pressure on Parliament from British public opinion is Seymour Drescher's argument. Given the centrality of elections in the contemporary analysis of how public opinion translates into policy, Drescher's explanation may seem somewhat improbable in the context of the slavery issue and unreformed British politics. Clearly the immediate beneficiaries of abolishing the trade were unlikely to be able to repay the benefit at the polls. Frank O'Gorman provides a detailed account of an election system characterized by limited male suffrage, more uncontested constituencies than contested constituencies, and the custom of buying votes in elections. The buying and selling of seats did not become illegal until 1809. Voters in some electoral districts formed cartels to sell their votes at high prices: the Malt House club voters at Arundel got £30 each in the 1780 election (O'Gorman 1989, 31). Under this system, it seems odd that the political opinions of their fellow citizens would concern members of Parliament.

The pecuniary side of what modern political scientists call "home-style" did not, however, squeeze out all other considerations from voters' decisions. In the eighteenth century all politics was not local. According to O'Gorman, "the widespread reprinting of parliamentary news in the London press ensured that a national political community existed even by the middle of the eighteenth century" (1989, 288). National issues, as well as more "pocketbook" local considerations, influenced unreformed voting: "as the general elections of 1784 and 1807 demonstrated in many constituencies, and as particular, long-term issues, such as the war in America, Catholic emancipation, slavery, the Corn Laws, and parliamentary reform demonstrated constantly. To offend the voters by ignoring their sensitivities was no way to hold on to a seat" (O'Gorman 1989, 53). Charles Tilly puts it this way:

> The British experience between the 1750s and the 1830s will stand as a major example of durable transition from relatively parochial to substantially national popular political life. . . . Although nothing like popular sovereignty had arisen in land- and capital-dominated nineteenth-century Great Britain, even landlords and capitalists had to consider the relations between their own interests and the claims organized workers, Irish Catholics, or un-enfranchised opponents of slavery were making on the state.
>
>   To put it differently, Great Britain had created citizenship . . . (Tilly 1995, 383)

Or as E. L. Woodward has said: "There was considerable truth to the view . . . that parliament was subject to real democratic pressure. This pressure showed itself in the number of petitions to the House of Commons, in the interest taken by the country as a whole in parliamentary debates, and in the increasing number of organs of public opinion" (1938, 28). Such consistent testimony to the more open nature of unreformed British politics from other social scientists and historians pursuing different research programs is important. It makes Seymour Drescher's connection of the abolition decision to public opinion, measured by mass petitions, seem a less radical analytical step.

It is more difficult to identify a critical initiating event, comparable to Bhopal in the policy history of the Community Right to Know. The slave uprising in the French colony of St. Domingue in 1791 heightened the attention of the British public to the issue. While Wilberforce felt that the bloody turmoil from which Haiti eventually emerged could be turned to the abolitionists' advantage, subsequent British military intervention and defeat in the larger context of Britain's relations with France complicated the interpretation of the uprising (see Geggus 1982).

Ten years before the St. Domingue uprising began, there occurred a graphic demonstration of the violent economics of the trade. This demonstration was the mass murder by drowning of slaves, part of the cargo of the *Zong*. In the autumn of 1781 this ship, owned by the Liverpool firm of Gregson, sailed for Jamaica with 400 African slaves (some Liverpool ships of this era carried up to 700 slaves). Many of the *Zong's* slaves were sick, about 60 had died. The owners insured the slaves for £30 each against death necessitated by the safety of the ship, though not against "natural death" caused by sickness or suicide. To shift the loss from the owners to the insurers, the *Zong's* captain, Luke Collingwood, ordered 133 sick slaves thrown overboard, claiming a freshwater shortage. One of these survived after managing to climb back into the ship (see Anstey 1975; Ehrman 1969; Rawley 1981; Shyllon 1974; Williams 1897). Other ships' captains made Collingwood's calculation. In 1819, the French captain of Le Rodeur threw overboard 39 slaves blinded by opthalmia, "expecting to recover his losses from the underwriters" (Rawley 1981, 293). In this way the insurance industry structured the payoff to encourage further inhumanity in this trade.

The courts did not decide the legal issues raised by the *Zong* until 1783. It was an insurance case, with the insurers disputing the owners' claim of the necessity of killing the slaves. The *Zong's* owners won the case. This case drew the attention of the newspapers and of Granville Sharp, who had won the freedom of slaves in Britain in the James Somerset case in 1772. Sharp agitated for a murder case, yet, despite letters to the prime minister, was unsuccessful (Shyllon 1974). The more immediate legislative response to the actions of the *Zong's* captain was the Dolben Act of 1788, which attempted to reduce sickness and mortality by regulating the number of slaves carried in a ship, limiting the insuring of slaves, differentially rewarding captains (£50–100) and surgeons (£25–50) for a slave mortality rate of under 3 percent, and requiring slave ships to carry a surgeon. According to Anstey, the Dolben Act achieved a significant drop in the mortality rate (Anstey 1975, 31; Rawley 1981, 304), but it also resulted in the increasing use of "flags of convenience" by British owners (Kay 1967, 93). The act also included a restriction on the command of slave ships to those who had already served as officers on such ships—an effort to restrict entry to the trade and a palliative to the traders (Kay 1967, 93). Politically the story of the *Zong* had a galvanizing effect on public opinion, and Wilberforce and his colleagues managed to keep abolition of the slave trade on the political agenda, crowded as it was with revolution in France and then war with France. They contrived the public support for abolition and provided the incentive for Lord Grenville and the parliamentary majority to act heroically.

In 1787, 11,000 Mancunians signed a petition for abolition. Manchester was significant as it indicated the extensive support for abolition in a "hard-nosed manufacturing town," which had "perhaps a larger share than any other inland city in Britain" invested in the trade. Popular support, like elite support, rested on the ethical case. The petition "based demands for action on the offensiveness of such a traffic to humanity, justice, and national honour" (Drescher 1987, 71–73). From this beginning developed "a social movement that expanded in size and articulation for over 50 years" and achieved abolition of the slave trade in 1807 and emancipation in the colonies in 1833. It grew from 100 petitions in 1788, to 500 in 1792, to 5,000 petitions in 1833 (93). In addition to petitioning, abolitionists attempted consumer boycotts of "slave sugar." Late eighteenth century dealers sold "free sugar" in many areas of Britain. Drescher credits this tactic with "some peripheral successes" (79). John Pinney, the Nevis planter, took the tactic seriously. He claimed that "the combinations entered into by a set of enthusiasts in this country to leave off the use of sugar, in order, as they say, to destroy the slave trade, by slow but certain means, have had . . . a great effect on the consumption . . ." and said, solipsistically, "the poor planters will be the sufferers" (Pares 1968, 199). We tend to consider this a tactic of contemporary consumer capitalism, a way of making tuna dolphin-safe.

Drescher's criticisms of the economic explanation of abolition in his book *Econocide* now seem generally accepted, yet critics have questioned the balance he strikes between popular pressure and the actions of the intellectual and political elite in his more positive efforts to advance an alternative explanation (Davis 1988). There is, of course, no reason to consider these explanations as exclusive and in fact considerable explanatory benefit to considering them in conjunction with each other. One can even find traces of such an approach in the work of Reginald Coupland: "The British Slave Trade may be said to have been doomed when Sharp, Clarkson, Wilberforce, and their little band of propagandists opened their countrymen's eyes to the actual brutalities it involved (1964, 111). Such a synthesis of the traditional explanation with the "social movement" explanation would seem to promise a more satisfactory account of the decision to abolish the slave trade, and it fits with what we know about the nature of public opinion and the "first pillar of business power." This policy case provides evidence to support John Zaller's arguments that the "flow of information in elite discourse determines which considerations are salient," and how "political leaders are seldom the passive instruments of majority opinion" (1992, 36, 96). On January 25, 1788, "Wilberforce told Lord Stanhope that Pitt and he were both urgent that "petitions for the abolition of the trade in flesh and blood should flow in from every quarter of the kingdom" (Pollock 1977, 76). The leaders of the abolition movement understood the pressures at work on legislators and designed a campaign that showed a measurable shift in public support for their antibusiness position. This trade became vulnerable to hostile public policy not because it was in decline, but because it became conspicuously bad. In 1789, Edmund Burke asked members "were they not prepared to pay the price of virtue?" (Warner 1963, 58). A sense of outrage among the political elite found an echo in public opinion sufficiently strong to ultimately convince ordinary policymakers that virtue was affordable.

From Williams on, scholars have questioned why, if reform was on the agenda, did not other reform issues develop in the way that antislavery did. Parliament passed a Mines Act in 1842. Prohibiting the employment of women and children underground, this act passed despite the centrality of mining to the nineteenth century British economy and despite the harm it did to business interests with strong representation in Parliament. As with the slave trade issue, although "many of the beneficiaries had no votes," public support, focused by riots in 1842, outweighed the arguments put by business interests. In this case, and more like the Wagner Act, legislators' actions in voting for the Mines Act have been interpreted either as "generosity or as social control" (McLean 1990, 279–81). In that same year, the British made war to maintain the opium trade with China. No reform movement can right all wrongs, and we must seek the reason that some issues receive a higher priority than others in the goals of policymakers, in the legitimacy of the interests involved, and in the activities of intellectuals, experts, government figures, and others in fastening public attention to a particular cause. In Victorian liberal discourse, from John Stuart Mill to Sherlock Holmes, opiates were more defensible than slavery.

Connecting these public policies, separated by political system, subject matter, and years, are various common threads. One notes, particularly with the abolition of the slave trade and the National Labor Relations Act, the argument over deciding who won and lost. As abolishing the slave trade was ridding capitalism of a bygone work relationship, social control is the way "long-term" capitalists make their presence felt in the analysis of the Wagner Act. Somewhat surprising for analysts, at least in the slave trade and environmental cases, is the longevity of the antibusiness policy. The effort to suppress the trade was not, as a hostile cabinet minister described the Dolben Act, "a five days fit of philanthropy"

(Warner 1963, 53). In general, environmental regulation in the United States has not steadily expanded, but neither has it "cycled." In the union case, the antibusiness policy was more clearly temporary. If the role of public attention and legitimacy is as important as suggested, then it should be the case that the Taft-Hartley reversal for unions was in the context of an anti-union shift in attitudes— the mood in *On the Waterfront* rather than *The Grapes of Wrath*. Without exploring the data, there is a superficial fit with the beginnings of the cold war, with a strike wave that may have alienated the public, and with a post-Wagner perception of unions having too much power.

The case evidence is collected in table 10.1 for the heroic policy model. In accounting for business policy failures, priority is given to the preferences of policymakers, group resources, and the characteristics of the policy issue, in particular how a policy position can be justified and how it contributes to or detracts from public support. Excepting significant business divisions on a policy issue, the theoretical argument identifies two categories of policy failure. The first category is where policymakers are indifferent to the consequences of their actions on political support—two-o'clock-in-the-morning courage. While Wilberforce or Wagner no doubt possessed this courage, the decision they wanted taken was not theirs alone. The second category is where a shift in public support disengages a policymaker from business interests. All three policy cases fall into the second category, where the opponents of the business position could effectively raise the question of fairness, to the community, to labor, or to other human beings. The role of individuals and their organizations was to draw attention to the legitimacy of the activity, whether slaving,

Table 10.1. Case Evidence for Heroic Policy

	Slave Trade	Wagner	Right to Know
Party/Belief	Whig/ Lord Grenville and the Ministry of All Talents	Democrat	Democrat (Sikorski)
Public Support	Petitions	Unrest/strikes	Media coverage Public opinion data
Business	West India Interests/ city of Liverpool	NAM/business community	Chemical manufacturers
Antibusiness	Saints/Quakers/Anti-Slave Trade Abolition Society	Senator Wagner/ unions	Congressman Sikorski Environmental orgs.
Event	*Zong*	Battle of Toledo	Bhopal

polluting, or union-busting. The petitions of those opposed to the slave trade were replaced by unrest and strikes as the expression of popular feeling on the labor question. This interaction between committed political leadership and popular movements, over business practices that are at odds with community standards, seems critical and most dangerous for business interests in the political arena. It is stretching to make a "Saint" of Senator Robert Wagner, a New York Democrat with Tammany Hall connections. Yet early exposure to New York politics impelled him to reform rather than corruption (Huthmacher 1968). He served on the commission that investigated the deaths of over 100 employees of the Triangle Shirtwaist Company in the hellish fire of 1911. He supported the suffragettes, and he sponsored antilynching legislation, in addition to his concern for wage laborers.

Wagner, like Wilberforce and his colleagues, or Nader and his students, displayed an independent, enduring interest in deepening popular concern and connecting this concern to political action. What makes their work so memorable is that it interrupted politics as usual. By using public support to balance the political resources of business interests, they allowed elected officials to calculate a "fit of heroism."

CHAPTER 11

Conclusion

The heroic deed of an early nineteenth century Parliament, when analyzed within the structure of incentives facing policymakers, becomes more ordinary. In the political world, as in Napoleon's world, it seems spontaneous heroism is rare. The remarkable achievement becomes the efforts of the individuals and organizations to manufacture support for abolition from an, at best, detached public in an age of slavery, sufficient to allow legislators their moment of virtue.

Taking as axiomatic the importance of policy ideas and public support to actors in a political system, I have explored specifically how these axioms apply to business in the policy struggle. In the book I have developed a general explanation that isolates the conditions under which success or failure in the policy struggle is likely and that can be fitted to particular instances and actors in the policy struggle. Policymakers assess the policy positions of affected interests through their own policy agendas and through the capacity of the interest to contribute to their public support. An interest's capacity to contribute to public support depends on its political resources and on the perceived legitimacy of the particular policy position. Legitimacy issues can be disaggregated along the four dimensions of legality, fairness, efficiency, or traditional loyalty. Public policymakers are not always on the side of the big battalions when the policy position is difficult to justify and when the opposition takes careful aim at public support.

Despite their generally superior resources, and in the absence of significant business divisions, business interests may lose in the policy struggle for two reasons: (1) when policymakers are indifferent to superior resources and the likely consequences for their political support—two-o'clock-in-the-morning heroism; or (2) when policymakers assess that the business position detracts from rather than contributes to public support—calculated heroism. Calculated heroism is more common than spontaneous heroism, particularly for legislatures as opposed to individual policymakers.

This argument recognizes business advantages in the policy process, while accounting for the possibility of business failure and so compensates for the deficiencies of existing theories. Significantly, even the critics of business dominance models, when advocating a pluralist or multi-interest theory of the policy process, at times state that business is the most important of the interests. This statement should be explicitly recognized in the general conception of the process. Business interests, whose principal activity is of general importance to public confidence in politicians, devote more attention and time to policy issues of concern to them, hire more lobbyists, commit more money in support of their political activities and goals, and have more mobility than other organized interests. Business dominance theorists, on the other hand, have missed or dismissed the significance of business losses in the policy struggle—business asks for more than it wants, it was a temporary accident, or it was in the long-term interest of the business system—and in so doing have oversimplified the relationship between business interests and politicians in the policy struggle. The conspicuous corporation, while deploying formidable resources, also creates political opportunities for its opponents in the policy struggle.

In developing the argument, I have examined the dimensions of business power and political success, beyond which opened up the analytical prospect of business failure. Empirically, the approach has been to draw on different forms of evidence, including survey data, data from published sources, and case evidence. The strategy has been to anchor the argument to multiple lines of social scientific inquiry, including analyses of voting behavior, political parties, the media, and collective action, the idea being to increase confidence in the theoretical argument by showing how the argument and evidence presented intersect with findings in related research areas.

How does the argument translate into lessons for business and for democrats? Investigating nonmarket threats to business is an aspect of what is sometimes referred to as political risk analysis. Political risk analysis includes both conventional threats emerging from within the political system and unconventional threats that challenge both business and the political system. Here the focus is restricted to threats that emerge within the political system and may result in public policy. To put the argument in terms of anticipating rather than explaining events, what might be called the high-risk factors for business failure are: divisions among business interests; oligopoly or monopoly—where business is perceived as having power and therefore responsibility; foreign ownership; the presence of organized and vocal antibusiness interests; business practices that are inconsistent with widely held values; restrictions on business access to elected and appointed government officials; the election of a social democratic party of government; civil servants insulated from external incentives; and, early in the electoral term, giving the policymakers time to recoup if they miscalculate public support for an issue.

Business practices will not be equally acceptable or unacceptable in all communities. The legitimacy of a product or method of production will vary according to local cultural norms and values. Child labor is more acceptable in the surface coal mines of Colombia, or in nineteenth century Britain, than in twentieth century Britain. Industrial degradation of the environment was more acceptable in East Germany than West Germany. Or to draw, once again, on the tobacco industry, while cigarettes, wherever they are lit, do harm to lungs and hearts, start fires, and cause burns, there is cross-national as well as cross-temporal variation in how acceptable they are. When asked if they would favor or oppose a ban on all forms of direct advertising of tobacco products, Europeans generally favored such a ban. Yet there were some marked differences among respondents in the different countries. In Portugal, 88 percent of those surveyed were in favor of a ban on cigarette advertising, whereas public support in Denmark for such a policy declines to 53 percent (*Eurobarometer* 1991).

A common dynamic is at work from political system to political system, from predemocratic Britain to a presidential democracy like the United States. But there is no uniform picture of the exercise of business power, as a result of variations in the institutional overlay and in the strength of countervailing forces. Systems with stronger countervailing forces—historically, socialist parties and unions—provide a more competitive market of political ideas and a wider spectrum of policy choices for their citizens. Consequently, business legitimacy is more fragile in these political systems, and business faces a more sustained political challenge. Yet these systems are now themselves challenged, victims of the general crisis of socialism that marked the late 1980s.

For democrats, the lesson is to increase the risks for business by thinking about ways to shield policymakers in political systems based on the assumption of equality, from the influence of economic inequality. James Tobin poses the problem in this way:

> I said earlier that we cannot expect to eliminate economic inequality. If it is true that political procedural democracy requires the abolition of economic inequality, then we are not going to have procedural democracy. Therefore, I hope it is not true. That is why I want to ask this of Bob [Dahl] and the other political scientists here. Have you given up on ways to insulate the democratic process from the consequences of disparities in wealth and income? I hope not. (1988, 165)

If we do not give up, the place to begin is to think about what happens when economic inequality does not convert into political inequality, that is, when business fails in the policy process. It provides one with a sobering appreciation of Tobin's challenge.

The problem becomes institutionalizing heroism, without severe economic and investment penalties. Any effort to insulate the political system raises the "exit," "voice," and "loyalty" options for business (Hirschman 1970). Business can leave, protest, or accept. Federalism made U.S. firms past masters at leveraging influence from mobility and exit. Exit is an increasingly available option for large firms operating beyond national markets. While union opposition at the inception of international arrangements that improve the mobility of capital is quite understandable, that struggle is over. Now their interest, and the interest of any organization likely to find itself in opposition to business interests, is to embrace and politically deepen supranational organizations in the way that earlier generations fashioned national institutions and regulations in the wake of a national economy. In the 1960s and 1970s it appeared, in the form of the welfare state and the formal inclusion of labor in policy-making, that national institutions had caught up, and political theorists captured that moment, not the century as it turned out, in the concept of neocorporatism. But the arena shifted. Where much public policy of interest to business is concerned, nations are already part of an international policy dynamic.

Surveys of British Firms, Employer Organizations, and Trade Unions

Two surveys were administered to collect information on the lines of communication between economic interests and government in the United Kingdom. This appendix describes survey procedures and the samples of respondents. The first survey was mailed to forty-seven major employer and business groups, fifty-nine trade unions with more than 5,000 members, and to the top 100 (*Times 1000 1987–1988*), addressed appropriately to directors, general secretaries, and chairmen. It was administered in three waves of mailings during January and February 1988. The overall response rate was 59 percent. About 77 percent of the business groups, 64 percent of the trade unions, and 48 percent of the large firms returned completed questionnaires. For mail surveys a response rate of between 20 and 40 percent is typical (Nachmias and Nachmias 1981, 183). Business groups that identified themselves as representing both small and large businesses were the largest category of business respondents. The manufacturing sector had the most respondents, followed by the service sector, with the financial sector having the fewest respondents. Both white-collar and manual unions were about equally represented among the responding unions. The firms that responded were distributed across the range of the top 100 by size (sales) and by industrial category. All the major industrial classifications represented in the top 100 were also represented in the survey. The lowest response rate was the single firm in the "finance, insurance, business services" class.

Among the nonrespondents, the business groups were the most likely to write to explain why they were not going to participate. Some described themselves as "nonpolitical" organizations and therefore did not wish to participate, others cited a lack of the resources necessary to respond. Firms that did not respond generally stated that it was against company policy to do so. Nonresponding trades unions were unlikely to write to explain why—the most informative of the letters received was from a union that claimed to be "too busy." From these letters, and from notes that often accompanied the returned questionnaire, the questionnaire was usually completed or otherwise responded to by directors, deputy directors, general secretaries, research officers, senior managers, or "parliamentary liaison officers." The relatively good response rate, the overall distribution of responses, and the positions of the respondents suggest that the survey findings provide a useful basis from which to examine the lines of communication between economic interests and government in the United Kingdom.

While alternative sources of data should be used to supplement the survey information, no source could substitute for survey data given the aims of this research. The chief drawback of a single survey is that the information is qualified by the general circumstances of the time the survey was administered.

For the second survey, survey instruments were mailed successfully to 192 of the top 225 British firms (*Financial Times* January 13, 1992) in three waves of mailings in November and December 1992, after John Major's general election victory in June 1992. The *Financial Times* list was used to improve the representation of banks and other financial institutions. Some 64 firms (33.3 percent) completed and returned the instrument. A further 34 firms wrote to explain why they were not participating in the survey. Of these the most common explanation was that they receive too many such invitations to participate, one manager claimed to receive twenty surveys a week, and others used terms like "inundated," "deluged," and "bombarded" to describe the volume of contacts from curious social scientists. In the personal interviews that preceded and accompanied the mail survey, it was suggested that the recent growth of business schools in the United Kingdom and MBA students "searching for dissertation topics" was the problem. Whatever the source, social scientists interested in business are in this case participating in, rather than just observing, a "tragedy of the commons" problem. Left to our own devices, we are overfishing this valuable source of information. An obvious solution is for some central sorting house, known to business, to give or deny, even by lot if necessary, a stamp of approval to proposed questionnaires. Given the present situation, the response rate of 33.3 percent is respectable.

Of the most salient market characteristics, the sample is quite representative. Looking at size, fourteen respondents are ranked in the top 50, twenty-one are ranked between 51 and 100, ten between 101 and 150, and eighteen have a rank over 150. These firms represent a total of thirty-three different sectors, including banks, insurance companies, utilities, brewers and food processors, newspapers and the broadcast media, retail, machinery manufacturers, building and construction companies, chemical companies, and the extractive industry.

References

Alexander, Herbert E., and Monica Bauer. 1991. *Financing the 1988 Election.* Boulder, Colo.: Westview Press.

Almanac of Federal PACs: 1990. 1990. Washington, D.C.: Amward Publications.

Almanac of Federal PACs: 1994. 1994. Washington, D.C.: Amward Publications.

Almond, Gabriel. 1988. "The Return to the State." *American Political Science Review* 82:853–74.

Alston, Chuck. 1991. "Lobbyists Storm Capitol Hill, Clash over Banking Bill." *Congressional Quarterly Weekly Report,* August 24.

Amenta, Edwin, and Theda Skocpol. 1989. "Taking Exception: Explaining the Distinctiveness of American Public Policies in the Last Century." In *The Comparative History of Public Policy,* ed. Francis G. Castles. Cambridge, Mass.: Polity Press.

American Telephone and Telegraph. 1933. *Annual Report of the Directors of American Telephone and Telegraph Company to the Stockholders.*

Anderson, Charles W. 1975. "System and Strategy in Comparative Policy Analysis." In *Perspectives on Public Policy Making,* ed. W. B. Gwyn and G. C. Edwards. New Orleans: Tulane University Press.

Anderson, Charles W. 1978. "The Logic of Public Problems: Evaluation in Comparative Policy Research." In *Comparing Public Policies,* ed. Douglas Ashford. Beverly Hills, Calif.: Sage.

Andres, Gary. 1985. "Business Involvement in Campaign Finance: Factors Influencing the Decision to Form a Corporate PAC." *PS* 18:213–20.

Anstey, Roger. 1975. *The Atlantic Slave Trade and British Abolition, 1760–1810.* London: Macmillan.

Arnold, Thurman. 1937. *The Folklore of Capitalism.* New Haven: Yale University Press.

Bachrach, Peter. 1967. *Theory of Democratic Elitism: A Critique.* Boston: Little, Brown.

Bachrach, Peter, and Morton S. Baratz. 1963. "Decisions and Nondecisions: An Analytical Framework." *American Political Science Review* 57:632–42.

Bain, George Sayers, and Robert Price. 1980. *Profiles of Union Growth: A Comparative Statistical Portrait of Eight Countries.* Oxford: Basil Blackwell.

Ball, Alan R., and Frances Millard. 1987. *Pressure Politics in Industrial Societies: A Comparative Introduction.* Atlantic Highlands, N.J.: Humanities Press International.

Barry, Brian. 1970. *Sociologists, Economists, and Democracy.* London: Macmillan.

Bauer, Michel, and Benedicte Bertin-Mourot. 1995. Centre National de la Recherche Scientifique. Report cited in *Economist,* May 6.

Beard, Charles A. 1957. *The Economic Basis of Politics.* New York: Vintage Books.

Becker, Gary S. 1985. "Public Policies, Pressure Groups, and Dead Weight Costs." *Journal of Public Economics* 28:329–47.

Bentley, Arthur. [1908] 1966. *The Process of Government.* Reprint, Cambridge, Mass.: Belknap Press.

Bernstein, Irving. 1970. *Turbulent Years.* Boston: Houghton Mifflin.

Berry, Jeffrey M. 1989. "Subgovernments, Issue Networks, and Political Conflict." In *Remaking American Politics,* ed. Richard Harris and Sidney M. Milkis. Boulder, Colo.: Westview Press.

Bethell, Leslie. 1970. *The Abolition of the Brazilian Slave Trade.* Cambridge: Cambridge University Press.

Block, Fred. 1987. *Revising State Theory: Essays in Politics and Postindustrialism.* Philadelphia: Temple University Press.

Boies, John L. 1989. "Money, Business, and the State: Material Interests, Fortune 500 Corporations, and the Size of Political Action Committees." *American Sociological Review* 54:821–33.

Bryce, James. 1908. *The American Commonwealth.* Vol. 2. New York: Macmillan.

Budge, Ian, and Hans Keman. 1990. *Parties and Democracy.* Oxford: Oxford University Press.

Bunn, Ronald F. 1984. "Employers Associations in the Federal Republic of Germany." In *Employers Associations and Industrial Relations: A Comparative Study,* ed. John P. Windmuller and Alan Gladstone. Oxford: Clarendon Press.

Burris, Val. 1987. "The Political Partisanship of American Business: A Study of Corporate Political Action Committees." *American Sociological Review* 52:732–44.

Butler, David, and Dennis Kavanagh. 1984. *The British General Election of 1983.* London: Macmillan.

Butler, David, and Dennis Kavanagh. 1992. *The British General Election of 1992.* London: Macmillan.

Caldeira, Gregory A., and James L. Gibson. 1995. "The Legitimacy of the Court of Justice in the European Union: Models of Institutional Support." *American Political Science Review* 89:356–76.

Cameron, David R. 1984. "Social Democracy, Corporatism, Labour Quiescence and the Representation of Economic Interests in Advanced Capitalist Society." In *Order and Conflict in Contemporary Capitalism,* ed. John Goldthorpe. Oxford: Oxford University Press.

Campbell, Joan. 1992. *European Labor Unions.* Westport, Conn.: Greenwood Press.

Carnegie, Andrew. [1887] 1962. *The Gospel of Wealth and Other Timely Essays.* Reprint, Cambridge, Mass.: Harvard University Press.

Carroll, Wallace. 1962. "Steel: A 72-Hour Drama With an All-Star Cast." *New York Times,* April 23.

Cawson, Alan. 1986. *Corporatism and Political Theory.* Oxford: Basil Blackwell.

Chang, Clara, and Constance Sorrentino. 1991. "Union Membership Statistics in 12 Countries." *Monthly Labor Review* 114:46–51.

Chase, Harold W., and Allen H. Lerman, eds. 1965. *Kennedy and the Press: The News Conferences.* New York: Thomas Y. Crowell.

Choate, Pat. 1990. *Agents of Influence: How Japan's Lobbyists in the United States Manipulate America's Political and Economic System.* New York: Alfred A. Knopf.

Clawson, Dan, and Alan Neustadtl. 1989. "Interlocks, PACs, and Corporate Conservatism." *American Journal of Sociology* 94:749–73.

Cockett, Richard. 1994. *Thinking the Unthinkable: Think-Tanks and the Economic Counter- Revolution, 1931–1983.* London: Harper Collins.

Cohen, Joseph. 1921. *Insurance against Unemployment.* New York: P. S. King and Son.

Coleman, William, and Wyn Grant. 1988. "The Organizational Cohesion and Political Access of Business: A Study of Comprehensive Associations." *European Journal of Political Research* 16:467:87.

Confederation of British Industry. 1995. "Firms Value Check-off Arrangements but Predict Further Falls in Union Membership." London: Confederation of British Industry. January.

Congressional Quarterly. 1987. *Almanac, 99th Congress, 2nd Session, 1986.* Washington, D.C.

Conradt, David P. 1993. *The German Polity.* New York: Longman.

Coupland, Reginald. 1964. *The British Antislavery Movement.* New York: Barnes and Noble.

Crenson, Matthew. 1971. *The Unpolitics of Air Pollution: A Study of Non-Decisionmaking in American Cities.* Baltimore, Md.: Johns Hopkins University Press.

Crewe, Ivor. 1993. "The Thatcher Legacy." In *Britain at the Polls: 1992,* ed. Anthony King. Chatham, N.J.: Chatham House.

Crewe, Ivor, and Donald D. Searing. 1988. "Ideological Change in the British Conservative Party." *American Political Science Review* 82:361–84.

Crouch, Colin. 1979. *The Politics of Industrial Relations.* Manchester: Manchester University Press.

Crouch, Colin. 1982. *Trade Unions and the Logic of Collective Action.* Glasgow: Fontana.

Dahl, Robert A. 1961. *Who Governs?* New Haven: Yale University Press.

Dahl, Robert A. 1982. *Dilemmas of Pluralist Democracy.* New Haven: Yale University Press.

Dalton, Russell J. 1993. *Politics in Germany.* New York: Harper Collins.

Davis, David Brion. 1988. "The Benefit of Slavery." *New York Review of Books,* March 31.

de Leon, Peter. 1993. *Thinking about Political Corruption.* New York: M. E. Sharpe.

de Sola Pool, Ithiel. 1981. "How Powerful Is Business?" In *Does Big Business Rule America?* ed. Robert Hessen. Washington, D.C.: Ethics and Public Policy Center.

Dewey, Donald. 1990. *The Antitrust Experiment in America.* New York: Columbia University Press.

Downs, Anthony. 1967. *Inside Bureaucracy.* Boston: Little, Brown.

Downs, Anthony. 1972. "Up and Down with Ecology—The Issue-Attention Cycle." *The Public Interest* 28:38–50.

Drescher, Seymour. 1977. *Econocide: British Slavery in the Era of Abolition.* Pittsburgh: University of Pittsburgh Press.

Drescher, Seymour. 1987. *Capitalism and Antislavery: British Mobilization in Comparative Perspective.* New York: Oxford University Press.

Drew, Elizabeth. 1966. "The Politics of Auto Safety." *The Atlantic Monthly,* October.

Drew, Elizabeth. 1983. *Politics and Money: The New Road to Corruption.* New York: Macmillan.

Dunlap, Riley E. 1989. "Public Opinion and Environmental Policy." In *Environmental Politics and Policy: Theories and Evidence,* ed. James Lester. Durham, N.C.: Duke University Press.

Eagleton, Thomas F. 1991. *Issues in Business and Government.* Englewood Cliffs, N.J.: Prentice Hall.

Eckstein, Harry. 1975. "Case Study and Theory in Political Science." In *Handbook of Political Science.* Vol. 7, *Strategies of Inquiry,* ed. Fred L. Greenstein and Nelson W. Polsby. Reading, Mass.: Addison Wesley.

Edelman, Murray. 1964. *The Symbolic Uses of Politics.* Urbana: University of Illinois Press.

Ehrman, John. 1969. *The Younger Pitt.* New York: E. P. Dutton.

Ehrmann, Henry W., and Martin A. Schain. 1992. *Politics in France.* New York: Harper Collins.

Eltis, David. 1987. *Economic Growth and the Ending of the Transatlantic Slave Trade.* New York: Oxford University Press.

Enloe, Cynthia H. 1975. *The Politics of Pollution in Comparative Perspective.* New York: David McKay.

Erfle, Stephen, Henry McMillan , and Bernard Grofman. 1990. "Regulation via Threats: Politics, Media Coverage, and Oil Pricing Decisions." *Public Opinion Quarterly* 54:48–63.

Esping-Andersen, Gosta. 1990. *The Three Worlds of Welfare Capitalism.* Cambridge, Mass.: Polity Press.

Eurobarometer, December 1991.

Europa Yearbook. 1992. London: Europa Publications.

Evans, Diana. 1988. "Oil PACs and Aggressive Contribution Strategies." *Journal of Politics* 50:1047–56.

Evans, Peter B., Dietrich Rueschemeyer, and Theda Skocpol. 1985. *Bringing the State Back In.* New York: Cambridge University Press.

Fallows, James. 1996. "Why Americans Hate the Media." *The Atlantic Monthly,* February.

Federal Election Commission. 1989. *Reports on Financial Activity, 1987–88, III.* Washington, D.C.: U.S. Government Printing Office.

Ferguson, Thomas. 1995. *The Golden Rule: The Investment Theory of Party Com-*

petition and the Logic of Money-Driven Political Systems. Chicago: University of Chicago Press.

Finley, M. I. 1977. *The World of Odysseus.* London: Chatto and Windus.

Fraser, George Macdonald. 1986. *Flashman at the Charge.* New York: Penguin Books.

Freedom House. 1995. *Freedom in the World: The Annual Survey of Political Rights and Civil Liberties.* New York: Freedom House.

Freeman, Richard, and Jeffrey Pelletier. 1990. "The Impact of Industrial Relations Legislation on British Union Density." *British Journal of Industrial Relations* 28:141–64.

Frendreis, John, and Richard Waterman. 1985. "PAC Contributions and Legislative Behavior: Senate Voting on Trucking Deregulation." *Social Science Quarterly* 66:401–12.

Fritschler, A. Lee. 1983. *Smoking and Politics: Policymaking and the Federal Bureaucracy.* Englewood Cliffs, N.J.: Prentice Hall.

Galbraith, John K. 1954. "Countervailing Power." *American Economic Review* 44:1–6.

Gallup, George, Jr. 1991. *The Gallup Poll Public Opinion, 1990.* Wilmington, Del.: Scholarly Resources.

Gallup, George, Jr. 1994. *The Gallup Poll Public Opinion, 1993.* Wilmington, Del.: Scholarly Resources.

Gans, Herbert J. 1979. *Deciding What's News: A Study of CBS Evening News, NBC Nightly News, Newsweek, and Time.* New York: Pantheon Books.

Garcia Marquez, Gabriel. 1989. *Love in the Time of Cholera.* Harmondsworth, England: Penguin Books.

Geggus, David. 1982. "British Opinion and the Emergence of Haiti, 1791–1805." In *Slavery and British Society 1776–1846,* ed. James Walvin. London: Macmillan.

Gilbert, Bentley. 1966. *The Evolution of National Insurance in Great Britain.* London: Michael Joseph.

Gilson, Mary. 1931. *Unemployment Insurance in Great Britain.* New York: Industrial Relations Counsellors.

Glasgow University Media Group. 1980. *More Bad News.* London: Routlege and Kegan Paul.

Golden, Miriam. 1993. "Unions and Economic Performance." *American Political Science Review* 87:439–54.

Goldfield, Michael. 1987. *The Decline of Organized Labor in the United States.* Chicago: Chicago University Press.

Goldfield, Michael. 1989. "Worker Insurgency, Radical Organization, and New Deal Labor Legislation." *American Political Science Review* 83:1257–82.

Goldfield, Michael. 1990. "Explaining New Deal Labor Policy." *American Political Science Review* 84:1304–13.

Goldthorpe, John H., ed. 1984. *Order and Conflict in Contemporary Capitalism.* Oxford: Clarendon Press.

Goodhart, David, and Lisa Wood. 1992. "Necessity Forces Consorting with the Old Enemy." *Financial Times,* September 8.

Goodin, Robert E. 1989. *No Smoking: The Ethical Issues.* Chicago: University of Chicago Press.

Gopoian, J. D. 1984. "What Makes PACs Tick? An Analysis of the Allocation Patterns of Economic Interest Groups." *American Journal of Political Science* 28:259–81.

Gordon, Colin. 1994. *New Deals: Business, Labor, and Politics in America, 1920–1935.* New York: Cambridge University Press.

Grant, Wyn. 1993. *Business and Politics in Britain.* Basingstoke, England: Macmillan.

Grantham, Cliff, and Colin Seymour Ure. 1990. "Political Consultants." In *Parliament and Pressure Politics,* ed. Michael Rush. Oxford: Clarendon Press.

Gray,Virginia, and David Lowery. 1988. "Interest Group Politics and Economic Growth in the U.S." *American Political Science Review* 82:109–31.

Grenzke, Janet M. 1989. "PAC's and the Congressional Supermarket: The Currency Is Complex." *American Journal of Political Science* 33:1–24.

Grier, Kevin B., Michael C. Munger, and Brian E. Roberts. 1994. "The Determinants of Industrial Political Activity, 1978–1986." *American Political Science Review* 88:911–26.

Hall, Peter A. 1987. "The Evolution of Economic Policy under Mitterrand." In *The Mitterrand Experiment: Continuity and Change in Modern France,* ed. George Ross, Stanley Hoffmann, and Sylvia Malzacher. Cambridge, Mass.: Polity Press.

Hall, Richard L., and Frank W. Wayman. 1990. "Buying Time: Moneyed Interests and the Mobilization of Bias in Congressional Committees." *American Political Science Review* 84:797–820.

Harris, Richard A. 1989. "Politicized Management: The Changing Face of Business in American Politics." In *Remaking American Politics,* ed. Richard Harris and Sidney M. Milkis. Boulder, Colo.: Westview Press.

Heclo, Hugh. 1974. *Modern Social Politics in Britain and Sweden: From Relief to Income Maintenance.* New Haven: Yale University Press.

Heinz, John P., Edward O. Laumann, Robert L. Nelson, and Robert H. Salisbury. 1993. *The Hollow Core: Private Interests in National Policy Making.* Cambridge, Mass.: Harvard University Press.

Hessen, Robert, ed. 1981. *Does Big Business Rule America?* Washington, D.C.: Ethics and Public Policy Center.

Hirschman, Albert O. 1970. *Exit, Voice, and Loyalty.* Cambridge, Mass.: Harvard University Press.

House of Commons. 1982. *Parliamentary Debates,* vol. 17.

House of Commons. 1990. *Parliamentary Debates,* vol. 166.

House of Commons Select Committee on Members' Interests. 1991. *Parliamentary Lobbying,* Third Report, Session 1990–1991, H.C. 586. London: HMSO.

Humble, Richard. 1976. *Captain Bligh.* London: Arthur Barker.

Hume, David. 1948. "Of the First Principles of Government." In *Humes's Moral and Political Philosophy,* ed. Henry D. Aiken. New York: Hafner Press.

Humphries, Craig. 1991. "Corporations, PACs, and the Strategic Link between

Contributions and Lobbying Activities." *Western Political Quarterly* 44: 353–72.

Huthmacher, J. Joseph. 1968. *Senator Robert F. Wagner and the Rise of Urban Liberalism.* New York: Atheneum.

Index to International Public Opinion, 1991–1992. 1993. Westport, Conn.: Greenwood Press.

Inglehart, Ronald. 1990. *Culture Shift.* Princeton: Princeton University Press.

International Monetary Fund. 1989. *Direction of Trade Statistics Yearbook.* Washington, D.C.: International Monetary Fund.

Iyengar, Shanto, and Donald R. Kinder. 1987. *News That Matters.* Chicago: University of Chicago Press.

Jackman, Robert W. 1987. "The Politics of Economic Growth in the Industrial Democracies, 1974–1980: Leftist Strength or North Sea Oil?" *Journal of Politics* 49:242–56.

Jaeger, Hans. 1980. "Business and Government in Imperial Germany, 1871–1918." In *Government and Business,* ed. Keichiro Nakagawa. Tokyo: University of Tokyo Press.

Jefkin, Frank. 1993. *Planned Press and Public Relations.* London: Blackie Academic and Professional.

Jordan, A. G., and J. J. Richardson. 1987. *Government and Pressure Groups in Britain.* Oxford: Clarendon Press.

Jordan, Grant, and Klaus Schubert. 1992. "A Preliminary Ordering of Policy Network Labels." *European Journal of Political Research* 21:7–27.

Jupp, Peter. 1985. *Lord Grenville, 1759–1834.* Oxford: Clarendon Press.

Katzenstein, Peter. 1984. *Corporatism and Change; Austria, Switzerland, and the Politics of Industry.* Ithaca, N.Y.: Cornell University Press.

Kay, F. George. 1967. *The Shameful Trade.* London: White Lion.

Keeler, John T. S. 1985. "Situating France on the Pluralism-Corporatism Continuum: A Critique of and Alternative to the Wilson Perspective." *Comparative Political Studies* 17:229–49.

Keohane, Robert. 1984. *After Hegemony: Cooperation and Discord in the World Political Economy.* Princeton: Princeton University Press.

Keynes, John Maynard. [1936] 1964. *The General Theory of Employment, Interest and Money.* Reprint, London: Macmillan.

Kihss, Peter. 1962. "Publishers Find Kennedy at Peak of His Popularity." *New York Times,* April 23.

Kingdon, John W. 1984. *Agendas, Alternatives, and Public Policies.* Boston: Little, Brown.

Koh, B. C. 1989. *Japan's Administrative Elite.* Berkeley and Los Angeles: University of California Press.

Kohler-Koch, Beate. 1994. "Changing Patterns of Interest Intermediation in the European Union." *Government and Opposition* 29:166–80.

Krasner, Stephen D. 1978. *Defending the National Interest: Raw Materials Investments and U.S. Foreign Policy.* Princeton: Princeton University Press.

Krasner, Stephen D. 1984. "Approaches to the State: Alternative Conceptions and Historical Dynamics." *Comparative Politics* 16:223–46.

Kraus, Constantine Raymond, and Alfred W. Duerig. 1988. *The Rape of Ma Bell: The Criminal Wrecking of the Best Telephone System in the World.* New York: Lyle Stuart.

Kurzer, Paulette. 1993. *Business and Banking: Political Change and Economic Integration in Western Europe.* Ithaca, N.Y.: Cornell University Press.

Labaton, Stephen. 1994. "Big Business Is Sharply Shifting Its 1994 Campaign Donations to Democrats." *New York Times,* October 21.

Labour Party Research Department. 1980. "Company Donations to the Tory Party and Other Political Organisations." *Information Paper No. 11.*

Labour Research. London: LRD Publications Ltd.

Lane, Robert E. 1991. *The Market Experience.* Cambridge: Cambridge University Press.

Lange, Peter, and Geoffrey Garrett. 1985. "The Politics of Growth: Strategic Interaction and Economic Performance in the Advanced Industrial Democracies, 1974–1980." *Journal of Politics* 47:792–827.

L'Annee Politique, 1944–45. 1946. Paris: Le Grand Siecle.

Lehmbruch, Gerhard, and Philippe Schmitter, eds. 1982. *Patterns of Corporatist Policy Making.* London: Sage.

Lehne, Richard. 1993. *Industry and Politics: United States in Comparative Perspective.* Englewood Cliffs, N.J.: Prentice Hall.

Leveen, E. Philip. 1977. *British Slave Trade Suppression Policies, 1821–1865.* New York: Arno Press.

Lewis-Beck, Michael S. 1988. *Economics and Elections: The Major Western Democracies.* Ann Arbor: University of Michigan Press.

Lijphart, Arend, and Markus Crepaz. 1991. "Corporatism and Consensus Democracy in Eighteen Countries: Conceptual and Empirical Linkages." *British Journal of Political Science* 21:235–56.

Lindblom, Charles. 1977. *Politics and Markets.* New York: Basic Books.

Lindblom, Charles. 1984. "Comment." In *The Impact of the Modern Corporation,* ed. Betty Bock, Harvey J. Goldschmid, Ira Millstein, and F. M. Scherer. New York: Columbia University Press.

Lipset, Seymour Martin, and William Schneider. 1987. *The Confidence Gap: Business Labor and Government in the Public Mind.* Baltimore, Md.: Johns Hopkins University Press.

Mackenzie-Grieve, Averil. 1968. *The Last Years of the English Slave Trade: Liverpool 1750–1807.* London: Frank Cass.

Macmillan, Harold. 1938. *The Middle Way.* London: Macmillan.

Makinson, Larry. 1992. *Open Secrets: The Encyclopedia of Congressional Money and Politics.* Washington, D.C.: Congressional Quarterly.

Maloney, William A., Grant Jordan, and Andrew M. McLaughlin. 1994. "Interest Groups and Public Policy: The Insider/Outsider Model Revisited." *Journal of Public Policy* 14:17–38.

Marsh, David. 1992. *The New Politics of British Trade Unions: Union Power and the Thatcher Legacy.* Ithaca, N.Y.: ILR Press.

Marsh, David, and Gareth Locksley. 1981. "Trade Union Power in Britain: The Recent Debate." *West European Politics* 4:19–37.

Martin, Cathie J. 1991. *Shifting the Burden: The Struggle over Growth and Corporate Taxation.* Chicago: University of Chicago Press.

Martinelli, Alberto, and Tiziano Treu. 1984. "Employers Associations in Italy." In *Employers Associations and Industrial Relations: A Comparative Study,* ed. John P. Windmuller and Alan Gladstone. Oxford: Clarendon Press.

Marwell, Gerald, and Ruth E. Ames. 1981. "Economists Free Ride, Does Anyone Else?" *Journal of Public Economics* 15:295–310.

Marx, Karl. [1852] 1968. "The Eighteenth Brumaire of Louis Bonaparte." In *Marx Engels Selected Works.* Reprint, London: Lawrence and Wishart.

Masters, Marick F., and Gerald D. Keim. 1985. "Determinants of PAC Participation among Large Corporations." *Journal of Politics* 47:1158–73.

Mazey, Sonia, and Jeremy Richardson. 1993. *Lobbying in the European Community.* Oxford: Oxford University Press.

McCloskey, Herbert, and John Zaller. 1984. *The American Ethos: Public Attitudes toward Capitalism and Democracy.* Cambridge, Mass: Harvard University Press.

McConnell, Grant. 1966. *Private Power and American Democracy.* New York: Alfred A. Knopf.

McFarland, Andrew S. 1991. "Interest Groups and Political Time: Cycles in America." *British Journal of Political Science* 21:257–84.

McLean, Iain. 1990. "The Politics of Corn Law Repeal: A Comment," *British Journal of Political Science* 20:279–81.

Meier, Kenneth J. 1988. *The Political Economy of Regulation: The Case of Insurance.* Albany: State University of New York Press.

Mitchell, Neil J. 1987. "Changing Pressure-Group Politics: The Case of the Trades Union Congress, 1976–84." *British Journal of Political Science* 17:509–17.

Mitchell, Neil J. 1989. *The Generous Corporation: A Political Analysis of Economic Power.* New Haven: Yale University Press.

Mitchell, Neil J. 1995. "The Global Polity: Foreign Firms' Political Activity in the United States." *Polity* 27:447–63.

Mitchell, Neil J. 1996. "Theoretical and Empirical Issues in the Measurement of Union Power and Corporatism," *British Journal of Political Science* 26:419–28.

Mitchell, Neil J., and John G. Bretting. 1993. "Business and Political Finance in the United Kingdom." *Comparative Political Studies* 26:229–45.

Mitchell, Neil J., Wendy Hansen, and Eric Jepsen. 1996. "The Determinants of Corporate Political Activity." Presented at the annual meeting of the Western Political Science Association, San Francisco.

Mizruchi, Mark. 1992. *The Structure of Corporate Political Action: Interfirm Relations and Their Consequences.* Cambridge, Mass.: Harvard University Press.

Moe, Terry M. 1989. "The Politics of Bureaucratic Structure." In *Can the Government Govern?* ed. John E. Chubb and Paul E Peterson. Washington, D.C.: Brookings Institution.

Moe, Terry M. 1990. "The Politics of Structural Choice: Toward a Theory of Public Bureaucracy." In *Organization Theory: From Chester Barnard to the Present,* ed. Oliver E. Williamson. Oxford: Oxford University Press.

Mucciaroni, Gary. 1995. *Reversals of Fortune: Public Policy and Private Interests.* Washington, D.C.: Brookings Institution.

Nadel, Mark V. 1971. *The Politics of Consumer Protection.* Indianapolis, Ind.: Bobbs-Merrill.

National Industrial Conference Board. 1932. *Unemployment in Theory and Practice.* New York: National Industrial Conference Board.

National Labor Relations Board. 1985. *Legislative History of the National Labor Relations Act, 1935.* 2 vols. Washington, D.C.: U.S. Government Printing Office.

Nay, Catherine. 1987. *The Black and the Red.* San Diego, Calif.: Harcourt Brace Jovanovich.

Niemi, Richard, John Mueller, and Tom W. Smith. 1989. *Trends in Public Opinion: A Compendium of Survey Data.* New York: Greenwood Press.

Nordlinger, Eric. 1981. *On the Autonomy of the Democratic State.* Cambridge, Mass: Harvard University Press.

Nordlinger, Eric. 1988. "The Return to the State: Critiques." *American Political Science Review* 82:875–85.

Norpoth, Helmut. 1992. *Confidence Regained.* Ann Arbor: University of Michigan Press.

O'Gorman, Frank. 1989. *Voters, Patrons and Parties: The Unreformed Electoral System of Hanovarian England, 1734–1832.* Oxford: Clarendon Press.

Olson, Mancur. 1971. *The Logic of Collective Action.* Cambridge, Mass.: Harvard University Press.

Olson, Mancur. 1982. *The Rise and Decline of Nations.* New Haven: Yale University Press.

Olson, Mancur. 1983. "The Political Economy of Comparative Growth Rates." In *The Political Economy of Growth,* ed. Dennis C. Mueller. New Haven: Yale University Press.

Orloff, Ann, and Theda Skocpol. 1984. "Why Not Equal Protection? Explaining the Politics of Public Social Spending in Britain, 1900–1911, and the United States, 1880's–1920." *American Sociological Review* 49:726–50.

Orman, John. 1987. *Carter, Reagan, and the Macho Presidential Style.* New York: Greenwood Press.

Ostrom, Elinor. 1990. *Governing the Commons: The Evolution of Institutions for Collective Action.* New York: Cambridge University Press.

Page, Benjamin I., Robert Y. Shapiro, and Glenn Dempsey. 1987. "What Moves Public Opinion?" *American Political Science Review* 81:23–43.

Parenti, Michael. 1992. *Make-Believe Media: The Politics of Entertainment.* New York: St. Martin's Press.

Pares, Richard. 1968. *A West-India Fortune.* New York: Archon Books.

Peltzman, Sam. 1976. "Toward a More General Theory of Regulation." *Journal of Law and Economics* 19:211–40.

Pempel, T. J. 1979. "Corporatism Without Labor? The Japanese Anomaly." In *Trends Toward Corporatist Intermediation,* ed. Philippe Schmitter and Gerhard Lehmbruch. London: Sage.

Perlman, Selig. 1968. *The Theory of the Labor Movement.* New York: Augustus M. Kelley.

Pinto-Duschinsky, Michael. 1981. *British Political Finance, 1830–1980.* Washington, D.C.: American Enterprise Institute.

Pinto-Duschinsky, Michael. 1989. "Trends in British Party Funding, 1983–1987." *Parliamentary Affairs* 42:197–212.

Plotke, David. 1989. "The Wagner Act Again." In *Studies in American Political Development,* vol. 3, ed. Karen Orren and Stephen Skowronek. New Haven: Yale University Press.

Polanyi, Karl. 1944. *The Great Transformation; The Political and Economic Origins of Our Time.* New York: Rinehart.

Pollock, John. 1977. *Wilberforce.* London: Constable.

Polsby, Nelson W. 1980. *Community Power and Political Theory: A Further Look at Problems of Evidence and Inference.* Berkeley and Los Angeles: University of California Press.

Poulantzas, Nicos. 1969. "The Problem of the Capitalist State." *New Left Review* 58:67–78.

Powell, G. Bingham, Jr., and Guy D. Whitten. 1993. "Cross-National Analysis of Economic Voting: Taking Account of Political Context." *American Journal of Political Science* 37:391–414.

Prestowitz, Clyde. 1988. *Trading Places: How We Allowed Japan to Take the Lead.* New York: Basic Books.

Przeworski, Adam, and Michael Wallerstein. 1988. "Structural Dependence of the State on Capital." *American Political Science Review* 82:11–29.

Punnett, R. M. 1988. *British Government and Politics.* Chicago: Dorsey Press.

Quinn, Dennis P., and Robert Y. Shapiro. 1991. "Business Political Power: The Case of Taxation." *American Political Science Review* 85:851–74.

Quirk, Paul J. 1980. "Food and Drug Administration." In *The Politics of Regulation,* ed. James Q. Wilson. New York: Basic Books.

Quirk, Paul J. 1981. *Industry Influence in Federal Regulatory Agencies.* Princeton: Princeton University Press.

Rawley, James A. 1981. *The Transatlantic Slave Trade: A History.* New York: W. W. Norton.

Register of Members' Interests. 1990. London: HMSO.

Reich, Michael. 1984 "Mobilizing for Environmental Policy in Italy and Japan." *Comparative Politics* 16:379–402.

Rhodes, R. A. W., and David Marsh. 1992. "New Directions in the Study of Policy Networks." *European Journal of Political Research* 21:181–205.

Riker, William H., and Peter C. Ordeshook. 1973. *An Introduction to Positive Political Theory.* Englewood Cliffs, N.J.: Prentice-Hall.

Rioux, Jean-Pierre. 1987. *The Fourth Republic, 1944–1958.* Trans. Godfrey Rogers. Cambridge: Cambridge University Press.

Robertson, John D. 1983. "The Political Economy and the Durability of European Coalition Cabinets: New Variations on a Game-Theoretic Perspective." *Journal of Politics* 45:932–57.

Rogowski, Ronald. 1995. "The Role of Theory and Anomaly in Social-Scientific Inference." *American Political Science Review* 89:467–70.

Romer, Thomas, and James M. Snyder Jr. 1994. "An Empirical Investigation of the Dynamics of PAC Contributions." *American Journal of Political Science* 38:745–69.

Rothstein, Bo. 1990. "Marxism, Institutional Analysis, and Working-Class Power: The Swedish Case." *Politics and Society* 18:317–45.

Sabatier, Paul. 1975. "Social Movements and Regulatory Agencies: Toward a More Adequate—and Less Pessimistic—Theory of 'Clientele Capture.'" *Policy Sciences* 6:301–42.

Safran, William. 1985. *The French Polity.* New York: Longman.

Salisbury, Robert. 1984. "Interest Representation: The Dominance of Institutions." *American Political Science Review* 78:64–76.

Schattschneider, E. E. 1960. *The Semisovereign People: A Realist's View of Democracy in America.* New York: Holt Rinehart and Winston.

Schlesinger, Arthur M., Jr. 1965. *A Thousand Days: John F. Kennedy in the White House.* Boston: Houghton Mifflin.

Schlozman, Kay L., and John T. Tierney. 1986. *Organized Interests and American Democracy.* New York: Harper and Row.

Schmitter, Philippe, and Gerhard Lehmbruch. 1979. *Trends towards Corporatist Intermediation.* London: Sage.

Schneider, Keith. 1991. "For Communities, Knowledge of Polluters Is Power." *New York Times,* March 24.

Schott, Kerry. 1984. *Policy, Power, and Order.* New Haven: Yale University Press.

Shyllon, F. O. 1974. *Black Slaves in Britain.* Oxford: Oxford University Press.

Sked, Alan, and Chris Cook. 1984. *Post-War Britain: A Political History.* London: Penguin Books.

Skocpol, Theda. 1979. *States and Social Revolution: A Comparative Analysis of France, Russia, and China.* Cambridge: Cambridge University Press.

Skocpol, Theda. 1994. *Social Revolutions in the Modern World.* Cambridge: Cambridge University Press.

Skocpol, Theda, and Kenneth Finegold. 1990. "Explaining New Deal Labor Policy." *American Political Science Review* 84:1297–1304.

Skogh, Goran. 1984. "Employers Associations in Sweden." In *Employers Associations and Industrial Relations: A Comparative Study,* ed. John P. Windmuller and Alan Gladstone. Oxford: Clarendon Press.

Smelser, D. P. 1919. *Unemployment and American Trade Unions.* Baltimore, Md.: Johns Hopkins University Press.

Smith, Adam. [1776] 1983. *The Wealth of Nations.* Reprint, Harmondsworth, England: Penguin Books.

Smith, Alison, and Steven Butler. 1991. "Peter Walker to Join Board of British Gas." *Financial Times,* February 9.

Smith, Hedrick. 1988. *The Power Game: How Washington Works.* New York: Random House.

Smith, James Allen. 1991. *The Idea Brokers: Think Tanks and the Rise of the New Policy Elite.* New York: Free Press.

Snyder, James M., Jr. 1992. "Long-Term Investing in Politicians; or, Give Early, Give Often." *Journal of Law and Economics* 35:15–43.

Sobel, Lester A., ed. 1976. *Consumer Protection.* New York: Facts on File.

Sorauf, Frank J. 1992. *Inside Campaign Finance.* New Haven: Yale University Press.

Spotts, Frederic, and Theodor Wieser. 1986. *Italy: A Difficult Democracy.* Cambridge: Cambridge University Press.

Stanley, Harold W., and Richard G. Niemi. 1995. *Vital Statistics on American Politics.* Washington, D.C.: Congressional Quarterly Press.

Steffens, Lincoln. [1904] 1948. *The Shame of the Cities.* Reprint, New York: Peter Smith.

Stigler, George J. 1954. "The Economist Plays with Blocs." *American Economic Review* 44:7–14.

Stigler, George J. 1975. *The Citizen and the State: Essays on Regulation.* Chicago: University of Chicago Press.

Stokey, Edith, and Richard Zeckhauser. 1978. *A Primer for Policy Analysis.* New York: W. W. Norton.

Su, Tie-ting, Alan Neustadtl, Dan Clawson. 1995. "Business and the Conservative Shift: Corporate PAC Contributions, 1976–1986." *Social Science Quarterly* 76:20–40.

Swenson, Peter. 1989. *Fair Shares: Unions, Pay, and Politics in Sweden and West Germany.* Ithaca, N.Y.: Cornell University Press.

Temin, Peter, with Louis Galambos. 1987. *The Fall of the Bell System: A Study in Prices and Politics.* Cambridge: Cambridge University Press.

Thompson, Dennis F. 1993. "Mediated Corruption: The Case of the Keating Five." *American Political Science Review* 87:369–81.

Thorne, R. G. 1986. *The House of Commons, 1790–1820.* Vol 1. London: Secker and Warburg.

Tilly, Charles. 1995. *Popular Contention in Great Britain, 1758–1834.* Cambridge, Mass.: Harvard University Press.

The Tobacco Institute. n.d. *Scope and Activities.* Washington, D.C.: The Tobacco Institute.

Tobin, James. 1988. "Roundtable Discussion: Politics, Economics, and Welfare." In *Power, Inequality, and Democratic Politics,* ed. Ian Shapiro and Grant Reeher. Boulder, Colo.: Westview Press.

Tolchin, Susan J., and Martin Tolchin. 1983. *Dismantling America: The Rush to Deregulate.* Boston: Houghton Mifflin.

Trade Unions and Their Members. 1987. Cm. 95. London: HMSO.

Truman, David. 1951. *The Governmental Process: Political Interests and Public Opinion.* New York: Alfred A. Knopf.

Tsebelis, George. 1990. *Nested Games: Rational Choice in Comparative Politics.* Berkeley and Los Angeles: University of California Press.

TUC. 1982. *Report of the 114th Annual Trades Union Congress.* London: Macdermott and Chant.

Tufte, Edward. 1978. *Political Control of the Economy.* Princeton: Princeton University Press.

U.S. Congress. 1986. "Superfund: Right-to-Know and Hazardous Wastesite Cleanup." Hearing before the House Subcommittee on Commerce, Transportation, and Tourism of the Committee on Energy and Commerce. 99th Cong., 1st sess. Washington, D.C.: U.S. Government Printing Office. 72–99.

U.S. General Accounting Office. 1993. *Competitiveness Issues: The Business Environment in the United States, Japan, and Germany.* GAO/GGD-93–124. Washington, D.C.: U.S. General Accounting Office.

U.S. General Accounting Office. 1991. *Report to Congress, Toxic Chemicals: EPA's Toxic Release Inventory Is Useful but Can Be Improved.* GAO/RCED-91–121. Washington, D.C.: United States General Accounting Office.

U.S. Senate. 1985. "Community Right-to-Know Legislation and Its Regulatory and Paperwork Impact on Small Business." Hearing before the Committee on Small Business. 99th Cong., 1st sess. Washington, D.C.: U.S. Government Printing Office.

Useem, Michael. 1984. *The Inner Circle: Large Corporations and the Rise of Business Political Activity in the U.S. and U.K.* New York: Oxford University Press.

Viscusi, W. Kip, John M. Vernon, and Joseph E. Harrington Jr. 1992. *Economics of Regulation and Antitrust.* Lexington, Mass.: D. C. Heath.

Vogel, David. 1987. "Government-Industry Relations in the United States: an Overview." In *Comparative Government-Industry Relations: Western Europe, the United States, and Japan,* by Stephen Wilkes and Maurice Wright. Oxford: Clarendon Press.

Vogel, David. 1989. *Fluctuating Fortunes.* New York: Basic Books.

Walke, Roger, and David C. Huckerbee. 1989. *PACs Sponsored by Corporations Partly or Wholly Owned by Foreign Investors.* Washington, D.C.: Congressional Research Service, Library of Congress.

Walker, John. 1986. *The Queen Has Been Pleased.* London: Secker and Warburg.

Walker, Peter. 1977. *The Ascent of Britain.* London: Sedgwick and Jackson.

Wallace, Michael, Beth A. Rubin, and Brian T. Smith. 1988. "American Labor Law: Its Impact on Working-Class Militancy, 1901–1980." *Social Science History* 12:1–29.

Wallerstein, Michael. 1989. "Union Organization in Advanced Industrial Democracies." *American Political Science Review* 83:481–501.

Ward, W. E. F. 1970. *The Royal Navy and the Slavers: The Suppression of the Atlantic Slave Trade.* London: Pantheon Books.

Warner, Oliver. 1963. *William Wilberforce and His Times.* New York: Arco.

Warwick, Paul. 1992. "Economic Trends and Government Survival in West European Parliamentary Democracies." *American Political Science Review* 86:875–87.

Washington Representatives. 1992. New York: Columbia Books.

Washington Representatives. 1994. New York: Columbia Books.

Weaver, Paul. 1988. *The Suicidal Corporation.* New York: Simon and Schuster.

Weimer, David L., and Aidan R. Vining. 1989. *Policy Analysis: Concepts and Practice.* Englewood Cliffs, N.J.: Prentice Hall.

Western, Bruce. 1993. "Postwar Unionization in Eighteen Advanced Capitalist Countries." *American Sociological Review* 58:266–82.

White, Michael. 1991. "Walker Tops List of Ex-Cabinet Directorships." *Guardian*, February 9.

Wilkes, Stephen, and Maurice Wright. 1987. *Comparative Government-Industry Relations: Western Europe, the United States, and Japan.* Oxford: Clarendon Press.

Williams, Eric. 1961. *Capitalism and Slavery.* New York: Russell and Russell.

Williams, Gomer. [1897] 1966. *History of the Liverpool Privateers and Letters of Marque with an Account of the Liverpool Slave Trade.* Reprint, New York: Augustus M. Kelley.

Wilson, Frank L. 1983. "French Interest Group Politics: Pluralist or Neocorporatist." *American Political Science Review* 77:895–910.

Wilson, Frank L. 1987. *Interest Group Politics in France.* Cambridge: Cambridge University Press.

Wilson, Graham K. 1985. *Business and Politics.* Chatham, N.J.: Chatham House.

Wilson, Graham K. 1990. "Corporate Political Strategies." *British Journal of Political Science* 20:281–88.

Wilson, Harold. 1971. *The Labour Government, 1964–1970: A Personal Record.* London: Weidenfeld and Nicolson.

Wilson, James Q. 1980. *American Government: Institutions and Policies.* Lexington, Mass.: D. C. Heath.

Wilson, James Q. 1981. "Democracy and the Corporation." In *Does Big Business Rule America?* ed. Robert Hessen. Washington, D.C.: Ethics and Public Policy Center.

Windmuller, John P. 1984. "Employers Associations in Comparative Perspective: Organization, Structure, Administration." In *Employers Associations and Industrial Relations: A Comparative Study,* ed. John P. Windmuller and Alan Gladstone. Oxford: Clarendon Press.

Woodward, E. L. 1938. *The Age of Reform.* Oxford: Clarendon Press.

Working Notes on Community Right-to-Know. June 1991. Washington, D.C.: United States Public Interest Research Group Education Fund.

Wright, John R. 1990. "Contributions, Lobbying, and Committee Voting in the U.S. House of Representatives." *American Political Science Review* 84:417–38.

Zaller, John. 1992. *The Nature and Origins of Mass Opinion.* Cambridge: Cambridge University Press.

Index

Abbott Laboratories, campaign spending by, 81
abolition. *See* slave trade (British), abolition of
access to government: by corporations, 23; by groups, 159–60
Adam Smith Institute (U.K.), 48
advertising, and public support-building, 49
Aims of Industry (U.K. think tank), 48, 88
amakudari. *See* revolving door between government and industry
American Cyanamid Corp.: campaign spending by, 81; lobbying on environmental policy, 193, 194
American Enterprise Institute, 47
American Federation of Labor (AFL), 135; and union rights, 201–2
American Water Quality Improvement Act (1970), 194–95
Amoco, lobbying on environmental policy, 194
antibusiness interests, business losses as opportunities for, 173
antitrust policy, 120, 180; variation in enforcement of, 33. *See also* Sherman Act of 1890
Armed Services Committees, membership and business campaign contributions, 81, 83
associations, types of, 123–24. *See also* business associations, lobbying activities of; trade associations
AT&T monopoly case, 180–82; and antitrust policy, 33

Austria, lobbying activities in, 100
automobile industry: ethical responsibility for products, 176; political activity in Japan, 15

banking industry, and PAC contributions, 95
Becker, Gary, and compensation principle, 31
Bendix Corp., and defense industry corruption, 95
Bhopal disaster, and U.S. policy, 195, 196
Blair, Tony, 87
Boeing Corp., and defense industry corruption, 95
brewers' monopoly case: and industry lobbying, 121, 122–23; and public opinion, 122
brewing industry: success at lobbying government, 119–22; use of political consultants, 107, 110
Britain. *See* United Kingdom
British Clean Air Act (1956), 194
British United Industrialists, and political donations, 88
business associations, lobbying activities of, 99, 123. *See also* Confederation of British Industry
business cohesion: measurements of, 102; and PAC contributions, 129
business confidence, 5; effect of governing party on, 63–66; influence of political stability on, 62–63; and political parties, 78, 171; significance of for policymakers, 67, 180; and

Neil J. Mitchell is Professor of Political Science
at the University of New Mexico